San Diego County Place Names
A to Z

San Diego County Place Names
A to Z

Leland Fetzer

*"Adventures in the Natural History and Cultural Heritage
of the Californias"*

Sunbelt Publications, Inc.
San Diego, California

San Diego County Place Names A to Z
Sunbelt Publications
Copyright ©2005 by the author
All rights reserved. First edition 2005

Edited by Jennifer Redmond
Book design and composition by W.G. Hample & Asssocs.
Cover design by Leah Cooper
Project management by Jennifer Redmond
Printed in the United States of America

No part of this book may be reproduced in any form without permission of
the publisher. Please direct comments and inquiries to:

Sunbelt Publications, Inc.
P.O. Box 191126
San Diego, CA 92159-1126
(619) 258-4911, fax: (619) 258-4916
www.sunbeltbooks.com

"Adventures in the Natural History and Cultural Heritage of the Californias"
A series edited by Lowell Lindsay

08 07 06 05   5 4 3 2 1

Library of Congress Cataloging-in-Publication Data

Fetzer, Leland.
  San Diego County place names, A to Z / Leland Fetzer.— 1st ed.
      p. cm. — (Adventures in the natural history and cultural heritage of the
  Californias)
  Includes bibliographical references.
  ISBN-13: 978-0-932653-73-4
  ISBN-10: 0-932653-73-1
  1. Names, Geographical—California—San Diego County. 2. San Diego
County (Calif.)—Description and travel. 3. San Diego County (Calif.)—
History, Local. I. Title. II. Series.

F868.S15F485 2005
979.4'98'003—dc22
                                                    2005011763

Contents

Preface

When first offered the opportunity to write a guide to San Diego County place names the prospect didn't excite me. The project, I thought, lacked the challenge needed to sustain me through the labor needed to write the book. I also believed that mostly the work had been done. My predecessors had already plowed the field, researchers such as John and Winifred Davidson, H.H. Bawden, and Lena B. Hunzicker. They, altogether, had left thousands of annotated file cards and numerous newspaper articles devoted to place names, dated between 1925 and 1945. Most importantly, there was Lou Stein's well-received *San Diego Place Names*. Phil Townsend Hanna and Evelyn L. Kooperman had also contributed to the cause of San Diego place names. So what was left for me to do? What the publishers needed to complete the undemanding task of compiling a county place-name guide was not me, but a bright high school graduate with an orderly mind and a laptop.

After looking more closely at the situation, however, I decided I was wrong. I discovered that my predecessors had not always done their research. And sometimes their work was out of date, uninformed, and marred by omissions. Particularly, they had not done justice to the county's Indian place names. Yes, a new guide to San Diego place names would repay the effort. The residents of the county deserved a fresh reference work providing documented information about the names of the places where they live, and it would be challenging and satisfying to write it.

A prime reason that a book was necessary was the passing of time. Lou Stein's book is thirty years old. In those three decades new materials have appeared that often superceded what he had to say (A later book, David L. Durham's *Place Names of San Diego* appeared in 2000, but the author's major goal is to provide GPS locations for local places, not systematically explore the origins of place names.) For example, H.E. Salley's *History of California Post Offices, 1849-1976* (1977) is an invaluable tool for identifying early settlements in the county. James W. Hinds' *San Diego's Military Sites,* a typescript dated 1986, provides the names of numerous past and present military posts in the county. The 1998 edition of Erwin G. Gudde's classic *California Place Names* not only has many sound entries on San Diego County places, but also presents new information that casts light on the difficult question of Indian places names. This comes from Margaret Langdon, an authority on the Kumeyaay language, and from William Bright, who has made the study of the Luiseño language much of his life's work. No one who writes about San Diego place names can ignore their research. Also crucial for compiling a new place-name reference work were local histories that saw the light of day towards the end of the century. Those included books large and small about Descanso, Pine Valley, Valley Center, El Cajon, Chula Vista, Spring Valley, Escondido, Del Mar, Blossom Valley, Olivenhain, Coronado, San Marcos, Encinitas, Ocean Beach, Grossmont, Julian, Alpine, La Mesa, Lakeside, Ramona, San Vicente, Carmel Valley, San Pasqual, La Jolla, Oceanside, and Lyons Valley.

Nor did earlier researchers have access to the Internet, a tool that is playing a growing role in place-name research. In this course of writing this book I have utilized the U.S. Bureau of Land Management site on homesteads, the U.S. Board on Geographic Names site on place names, the San Diego Neighborhood site, and others, all to good purpose. (The web addresses are in the Bibliography.)

But the greatest source of new information about San Diego place names comes from recent maps published by the United State Geological Survey (USGS). These maps appeared in three waves: beginning in the 1900s very large-scale 30' quadrangles appeared. Later the survey began to publish maps on a smaller scale, each encompassing an area one fourth of the earlier maps, as 15' quadrangles. Finally, in mid-century the survey began to publish maps that covered one-fourth the area of *these* maps, as 7.5' quadrangles. Each of the maps in these series provided space for yet more place names. Today the survey continues to reissue new versions of the 7.5' maps, revised with the help of aerial photographs. The revisions record new topographic details and names, while the early maps are still valuable as sources for names that have disappeared, for example, names of early farm settlements.

The U.S. Board on Geographic Names, working closely with the survey, now controls the form of all names appearing on the USGS maps; from time to time in the text the reader will note that the board's decisions have altered San Diego place names. (See for example, the entry for Harrison Canyon.) These USGS maps, created with help from the Board on Geographic Names, were mostly unknown or underutilized by my predecessors. Today they serve as the foundation for all serious U.S. place-name studies.

Finally, the thing that convinced me that I should write the book on San Diego place names, was the discovery of errors in earlier books on the subject. Perhaps this is best illustrated by listing some random statements gleaned from my predecessors. The list in the following paragraph is by no means exhaustive, and the reader will note that some of the assertions contradict one another.

The Indian name of Middle Peak in Cuyamaca Rancho State Park was "Igual." This means "the broadest peak." Loveland Reservoir was named for a farmer in the San Luis Rey Valley. Vital Reche named Fallbrook for his hometown in Pennsylvania. Vital Reche named Fallbrook for his hometown in New York. Wire Mountain was named for the nearby Marine Communication School. Olivenhain means "Home of the Olive." Olivenhain was originally called Olivenheim. There is a Guatay Indian Reservation in the county. Guatay means "large rock." Batequitos means "little baptized girls." Batequitos means "flat-bottomed boats."

The reader has no doubt guessed that all of these statements are incorrect. These errors originated in a number of sources. John Davidson, for example, consistently confused Middle and North Peak in the Cuyamacas, and so he muddled the information about them. Some resulted from a cursory dip into a Spanish dictionary, hence the confusion over the name Batequitos. There was a farmer in San Luis Rey named Loveland, but the reservoir was not named for him. Alfred L. Kroeber (41) erroneously wrote that there is a Guatay Indian Reservation in the county, and others have repeated his statement. As a writer of books, I am inclined to deal benignly with these errors. A non-fiction work makes countless assertions as facts, and some of them are bound to be incorrect. As a man who lives in a glass house, I think twice before throwing stones. But still they are errors that require correction.

I am less patient when I observe the same error repeated again and again in different sources. This indicates that writers have simply copied from their predecessors without questioning the accuracy of the statement. For example, virtually all writers say that Carlsbad changed its name to Carl during the First World War, but there is nothing to support the statement. Often repeated is the assertion that Moosa means "old man's beard" in Luiseño, but those who know the language says its meaning is unknown. When an untruth is repeated it is called a canard, a duck. The most famous canard in American history is George Washington's cherry tree, while San Diego's hardiest duck is the claim that Julian nearly became the county seat in the early 1870s. One reason I decided the book was worth writing was the satisfaction of bagging a canard or two during my hunt for place names.

Having made the decision to write the book, I had to decide what would be included and what would be excluded. The rule for inclusion was this: I tried to include all the important contemporary names in the county, as well as those which held special interest because they were picturesque, poetic, or historically significant. This book is a guide to more than 1,600 San Diego place names that I believe to be significant or interesting.

I excluded many historical names because only the specialist remembers them; this includes many Spanish names from the mission era, as well as the names of numerous Indian villages. However, if a place is still occupied, then I strove to include all the names it has had, past and present. I think that a resident of El Cajon would like to know that the Kumeyaay called his valley something like Matari "wide valley" (Davis). The mission fathers called it Santa Mónica, and Spanish-speaking laymen called it Rancho El Cajón, "the box," because it appeared to have no exit. When Americans came they called it Knox's Corners or Knox's Station, for a well-known hotelkeeper. Some late nineteenth century maps identify the settlement as Knoxville. In 1878 representatives from the community returned to the name El Cajon for its post office. The sequence of names, in a few words, gives a resident of the city a summary history of his place.

I have, to the best of my ability, included all the settlements that have ever existed in the county. So the reader will find here Stowe, Black Mountain, Vineyard, Lemon, Howe, El Nido, Siempreviva, Merton, Jessee, and many others, even though he will not find them on today's maps. These were places where once families labored to wrest a living from the land, and nearly always failed, and their settlements should not be forgotten. I also included them to remind the reader that from 1850 to about 1930 San Diego County was ranching and farming country. (Because I have included these names from the past, the book can also serve as a finding list for names not found on contemporary maps. Long ago I read that the heaviest annual rainfall ever recorded in the county was at Nellie, but I couldn't find Nellie on any current maps. This book would have told me that Nellie was the name of the post office for the community on Palomar Mountain from 1883 to 1920.)

I have also included all of the military sites in the county, if they have distinctive names, even if they no longer exist. I included them because they were once unique names on the land, and as a tribute to the role of the military in the county's history. A belated discovery confirmed my decision to include selected military sites. Generals and admirals, understandably, choose to name military posts for other generals and admirals. But there is an exception to this rule: according to U.S. Signal Corps policy, army airfields were to be named for men, usually junior officers, who died in airplane crashes in the line of duty. I am happy to include in my book the names of these young men who died too soon.

I have included all of San Diego City's more than one hundred official neighborhoods. Residents of Birdland, Rolando, Memorial, Allied Gardens, Egger Heights, and all the rest, will find in this book at least a few words about their neighborhoods, and how they got their names. I have also included the names of some 30 prominent gold and gem mines in today's San Diego County. However, because the vast majority of them existed only on paper, I have included none of the thousands of claims registered in *The Julian Mining Records,* such as the Shoo Fly, the Rosebud, and the After Thought.

Two other groups of names I have included in the book: the names of all the Mexican land grants in the county, and all its Indian reservations. The land grants had an extraordinary influence on place naming in the county, and the reservations, no matter how small, often with distinctive Indian names, should not be forgotten.

What have I excluded from the book? Most importantly, I have excluded "about 550" place name entries that appear in Diana Lindsay's comprehensive *Anza-Borrego A to Z* (Lindsay xiv). To include these names, all in the east county, would have been a pointless duplication of effort.

I have not attempted to list the thousands of subdivisions that have been platted in the county's history. A few are here, however, because they thrived and became towns. I have made no attempt to include schools or school districts; while some of their names are distinctive, others were simply borrowed from early American history. Ranches, other than Mexican land grants, I excluded, with exceptions, because their names are fluid, changing as often as their owners. The names of county streets and roads, in their thousands, with few exceptions, you will not find here. I have also excluded most recent forgettable names such as Vacation Isle or Riviera Shores.

After some hesitation, with only a few exceptions, I excluded an intriguing category of place names. Cleary and Stern's *Surfing Guide to Southern California* lists more than 100 surfing sites in the county, many of them with provocative names: Hogan's Unprintable, Zeke's, Peggy's, Old Man's Reef, Guayule, Ann's, Needle's Eye, Sub, Ab—all cry out for explication and elucidation. Alas, for the time being, I must leave them to the surfers. Apostrophes in place names taken from proper names will reflect the commonest usage.

Ideally, every entry includes this information: **Place name**; translation, if in a foreign language; location in general terms (many of the places named are on recent USGS 7.5' topographic maps or in David L. Durham's book cited in the Bibliography); commentary; and references to earlier investigations, in parentheses. Alphabetizing is by word, not letter. I have tried to list names by their most distinctive features, so that the Spanish articles el and la are usually omitted, Rancho Santa Margarita not El Rancho Santa Margarita, but if this was too much of a stretch, I left the article: El Cajon, La Playa.

Abbreviations

BLM	Bureau of Land Management
SDET	*San Diego Evening Tribune*
SDHS	San Diego Historical Society
SDU	*San Diego Union*
SDU-T	*San Diego Union-Tribune*
USGS	United States Geological Survey

Acknowledgments

Many people have contributed to this book. First of all, let me thank Lowell Lindsay for his idea for a book that eventually won me over. The staff of the San Diego Historical Society has been unfailingly helpful. Thank you, John Panter, Dennis Sharpe, Jane Kenealy, Muriel Strickland, keeper of the maps, and others. Individuals include Roger E. Payne, Executive Director of the U.S. Board on Geographic Names, Washington, D.C., (Believe it or not, when I called the board, Mr. Payne answered the telephone. We had a long conversation in which he outlined for me the board's history and present function. May his name live forever!) Thanks also go to Chuck Valverde, Leland E. Bibb, Theresa Murinaka, Ellen Sweet, Christopher Wray, Robin Alter-Haas, Ruth Alter, Albert J. Simonson, Phil Brigandi, Karna Webster, Steve Scott, Philip R. Pryde, Sherillyn Williams Goodwin, and Prof. Thomas E. Case. Thanks to Lynne E. Christenson, San Diego County historian, who helped solve the Old Ironsides problem, and to Harry W. Crosby, who knew all about the Corderos in San Diego in 1770. Randy Hawley, first San Diego city ranger, helped with Mission Trails Regional Park names. James D. Newland generously read the final manuscript and gave me useful comments. Jennifer Redmond played an essential role with Spanish and in seeing the book through the press, as did Diana Lindsay. Richard H. Lawson, a friend of many years, was unfailingly helpful and always a good listener. He read through the entire text, and pounced on more than one foolish error. As always, he made my path strait.

Leland Fetzer
San Diego, California

Introduction

Perhaps the oldest place name in the county based on actual observation is San Miguel (St. Michael the Archangel). Captain Juan Rodríguez Cabrillo, or a priest on board his ship, chose this name in 1542 by consulting an ecclesiastical calendar that told him that September 28, when he first saw the bay, was the archangel's feast day (not the saint's birthday, as is sometimes said.) The name would not hold; Sebastián Vizcaíno in 1602 replaced it with the name San Diego de Alcalá de Henares.

For the next three centuries Spaniards commonly named sites in California, and elsewhere, according to church calendars, an indication of their all-encompassing religious faith. This system provided many durable place names in the county, such as San Diego and Santa Margarita, as well as others further north.

This method for naming has found its critics. Often there were duplications. For example, in San Diego County there was a San Luis at the Padre Dam, and another one in the Julian region, and of course, there was San Luis Rey to the north. No one knows which St. Vincent the San Vicente land grant was named for—there are several. But the chief criticism of such namings is that they violate two modern rules: place names must capture the distinctive nature of the place, whether ethnic, topographical, or biographical, and secondly, the name should be, within reason, unique. There is only one Seattle or Anchorage or Silver Strand, while how many places in the world are named, say, for the twelve apostles? Perhaps the best that can be said for these names, as we know them, is that they record a Spanish presence. This method of naming also has the very practical function of providing the day, but not the year, of discovery, a fact sometimes valuable for the historian, but that means nothing to the public.

Of course, necessity compelled more specific names to identify features on the land, and so navigators, particularly, used what might be called secular names. So there was a Punta de la Loma, "Hill Point." Spaniards called today's Mission Bay Puerto Falso, "False Bay" because it seemed to resemble San Diego Bay to the south, or Puerto Anegado, "Overflowed Bay" because it had flooded shores, especially when the San Diego River broke into it. The Portolá expedition called a feature near the coast Cañada de los Encinos, "Oak Canyon," a name that survives as Encinitas.

The names of Mexican land grants displayed a mix of religious names, natural features, and Indian names. Rancho San Bernardo was religious, Rancho Guejito y Cañada de Palomea was secular (for the meaning of this name see the entry under Guejito), while Rancho Cuyamaca, or Rancho Janal, and many others, were Indian names.

When the first Spaniards came to the county they met a large Indian population with a wealth of place names they employed every day. Some of them the Spaniards understood only poorly. For example the Spaniards found an Indian village near Presidio Hill whose name they recorded as Cosoy (Kosoyi) and another near the mission site upriver they recorded as Nipaguay. To this day no one knows the meaning of these presumably Kumeyaay names. The Europeans recorded the Indian names as they heard them and often these names came into common use. Many of them survive today in the form Spanish speakers recorded them 200 years ago.

The Indians in San Diego County speak two totally unrelated languages. While one is related to distant Ute and Aztec languages, the second is close to other California Indian languages. Those living north of a line from the southern limits of the San Luis Rey valley (not the river) speak a language of the Takic family of the Uto-Aztecan stock. This is the Luiseño-Juaneño language, with three dialects in the county, Luiseño, Cupeño, and Mountain Cahuilla. South of that line in San Diego County Indians speak the Kumeyaay (formerly called Diegueño, see Lindsay 213-215) language of the Yuman family of the Hokan stock. In this book the word Kumeyaay is used inclusively to incorporate the dialects of Iipai, Tipai, and Kumeyaay. Spelling is based on Margaret Langdon in Gudde (*California Place Names*), and Couro and Hutcheson (*Dictionary of Mesa Grande Diegueño).* (Modified from William F. Shipley, "Native Languages of California," in Heizer, 80-90).

Spanish speakers recorded Indian place names as best they could from two languages that differed widely in pronunciation and structure from their own language. One example drawn from each language will suffice to illustrate the problems that arose. Near the San Luis Rey River was a place that Luiseño speakers called *waxáawu-may* "little frog." Spanish speakers wrote this down as Guajome, a name that survives today (Gudde 155.) In Kumeyaay country many place names began with the element *'ehaa* "water" (the letter ' indicates a glottal stop "like a catch in the throat." Couro and Hutchison 101). Spanish speakers recorded this as ja- and so today we have the place names Jacupin "hot water," Jamul "foamy water," and Janal "rippling water." By contrast, the Luiseño word for water is *páala,* hence the place name Pala (Gudde 276). Early Spanish documents record hundreds of Indian place names, the vast majority no longer in use. Still, a glance at this book's text will show that many have survived, often colored by the rules of Spanish spelling.

A crucial event in the history of San Diego place names was the coming of the Americans to the county after the Mexican-American war, beginning a new era with some new principles for naming sites and settlements. It also brought a great increase in the density of place names as the American settled everywhere in the county in much larger numbers than had existed during the Spanish period. What had been a thin network of enormous, sparsely-populated ranches became scatterings of small ranches, farms, and settlements, with new names for the towns and the topography around them.

In some cases the Americans retained the Indian and Spanish names unchanged as they found them. This explains the abundance of Spanish names still common in the county, from Campo to San Onofre and from San Diego to Santa Ysabel, as well many Indian names in Spanish spellings. However, many times an English name replaced the original Indian or Spanish; see Mission Bay, for example.

Often the newly-arrived Americans named places for some feature they observed. These might be called, in a general way, descriptive names. Hence the many places named for oak, pine, grapevine, and boulder. An animal observed gave us Quail Canyon, Bear Valley, and Wolf Canyon. Distinctive features gave us Long Potrero and Round Potrero. Sometimes an incident triggered the naming process. An unusual event occurred and the namer, inspired, drew from it to name the place. See, for example, Bucksnort Mountain, Deerhorn Valley, and Centipede Mountain.

Even more common were personal names that now peppered the landscape, a kind of naming that is absent in the Spanish period. This gave us names like Murphy Canyon, Harbison Canyon, Merriam Mountains, Muth Valley, and many, many more. Most of these dated officially from the USGS topographic maps when surveyors questioned local people, asking, "What do you call that mountain?" The answer might be, "We call it Jones Mountain because Jones runs his cattle there." And so Jones Mountain appeared on the map. Such names often present problems for the investigator because long ago rancher Jones returned to his childhood home in Texas, leaving little more than memories behind him. The researcher must search through census reports or homestead records to identify, if he can, the elusive Mr. Jones. Sometimes the surveyors made errors when they recorded personal names. For examples, see Channing Meadow and Mariette Creek.

Sometimes settlers brought with them the names of their hometowns or places they remembered from the past. These imports are traditionally called transfer names. Europe gave the county Sorrento, Glencoe, Kensington, and Jesmond Dene. From the United States came Wynola, Fallbrook, Oneonta, Minneapolis Beach, and others.

The coming of the railroad in 1885 brought many names to the county. Railroad names were whatever the railroad officials wanted them to be, since they were not under government control, as were the names of post offices. The railroads tried to find short unusual names that could not be confused with other points on the line. Classic railroad names in the county are Agra and Don. (For the description of an occasion when the Santa Fe Railroad disagreed with a local community on the choice of a name, see the entry under Carlsbad.) Because the owners of the National City & Otay Railroad wanted to sell land along its line, they did not favor short and snappy names, but those with sentimental appeal. See Sunnyside and Bonnie Brae for examples.

The great boom year of 1887 gave the county many community names—some short-lived subdivisions, but others tough survivors. New was the use of Spanish community names, probably the result of the enthusiasm evoked by the enormous success of Helen Hunt Jackson's *Ramona,* published in 1884 just before the boom, with most of its action set in San Diego County. Good examples are Chula Vista and Escondido, and of course, Ramona.

Rarely namers borrowed from the Bible for place names, and so the county has Mounts Ararat and Nebo and Carmel Valley. Very rarely they fixed honorific names on the landscape, to honor their heroes. For some reason, as the reader will see, Spanish-War Admiral George Dewey did well among county place names.

The end of the nineteenth and early twentieth centuries saw the appearance of perhaps the most sophisticated place names of all, acronyms, neologisms formed by combining parts from several words to make one, a kind of word-play. See, for example, Gravilla, Camp Wolahi, Pomerado, and others. (Not that acronyms are a modern invention. In 1635 the Connecticut town of Say-brook was named to memorialize British Lord Say and Sele, and Lord Brooke. See Stewart 52.) Finally, perhaps the ultimate in naming, reverse spelling, makes its only occurrence in the county. I won't give the name away, but it all began with National City.

Most of the interest in place names focuses on the *specific,* the Solana in Solana Beach, the Birch in Birch Hill, the Coleman in Coleman Grade, but often the *generic,* as in Beach, Hill, and Grade in these names, provide us with valuable information about a region and its namings. They can enlighten us about the play of languages the region has seen, and tell us something about the kind of people who settled the region, and some of the turnings in its history.

One of the most striking aspects of San Diego generic names is the coexistence of Spanish and English twins, both used freely, surely evidence (as though it was needed) that the county is situated in a linguistic borderland. There is the English meadow or pasture, but often the observer will see that potrero is used in its place. Cerro sometimes appears on the map, but so does hill. Valley or canyon (yes, ultimately the Spanish *cañon)* seems to be interchangeable with cañada.

On the other hand, sometimes one form seems to have crowded out the other. One would expect the twins, mountain and sierra, but sierra does not appear on county maps, although it is on many early Spanish documents. The Spanish *ciénega* as the English cienega for a wet meadow seems to have displaced the English swamp or bog or marsh, the last appearing only in the recent Sweetwater Marsh and San Sebastian Marsh. The Spanish term mesa has also triumphed, for there are at least seven of them in the county. It has captured the field probably because there is no good English equivalent—table mountain or flat-topped mountain are clumsy.

The desert has many distinctive terms not found nearer to the coast. The term wash occurs frequently, for example, Mud Hills Wash or Quartz Vein Wash, but near the sea it appears rarely. The desert has tanks or tinajas (sometimes spelled tenajas,) natural pools collected in desert canyons. It has sinks and badlands, and bajadas, alluvial fans. (As is the case with the county in general, note the mixture of Spanish and English names.) In the desert occur oases, sometimes with palms. The desert has several wells, such as Harpers Well and Coyote Wells, a name for water emerging on flat land; otherwise the term spring is used. Near the coast there is only one such feature, Russian Well, near Imperial Beach. The generic name is appropriate, because the water emerged on flat land near the beach.

For most American speakers the most unexpected term in the desert is the name cove, such as Mammoth Cove, Kenyon Cove, and Stag Cove all in the Borrego region (The specific name stag is very literary; for an earthier local term, see Bucksnort Mountain). Most of us think of a cove as a small inlet, for example, La Jolla Cove. However, in the southern U.S. the term describes the entrance to a deep valley, and that is what we have in San Diego's desert. This suggests that a southerner named these features.

The coastal strip has its unique terms as well. The most conspicuous of these is lagoon, a term used to describe a body of fresh water with a connection to the sea. West county has as least seven of them. My dictionary tells me that the word is not derived from the Spanish *laguna,* "lake," but from the French *lagune* or Italian *laguna.* The coastal region also has at least three sloughs with distinctive names: Cudahy, Famosa, and Gumbo.

The county's short rivers have few "forks" like northern California's famous "north fork of the west fork of the south fork." The tributaries leading to the main stream tend to have distinctive names. See for example Boulder Creek, Cedar Creek, Ritchie Creek, Dye Creek, etc., all feeding into the San Diego River. And because our short rivers rapidly rise and fall with the winter rains, bridges and ferries are unknown among the county's place names.

Some of the generic names in the county have a literary cast. Such, for example, is the term glen, a Gaelic term that Sir Walter Scott made popular in his novels. Some namers knew that properly the qualifier should follow the generic, but some did not. So we have Glen Lonely (correct) not far from Hidden Glen (incorrect). In the county there are a few dells, a word that makes me, for one, think of fairies. A rare anomaly among the names in the county is stream, as in the Cuyamacas' Cold Stream. My guess is that an eastern surveyor came up with this name. Perhaps he was from Maine where this generic term is very common (Stewart 250). Locals certainly called it Cold Creek, creek being the preferred name for a small stream everywhere. In the county there are no rills, branches, becks, or runs, and no brooks with the exception of Fallbrook, a name brought from the Atlantic slope, and the modern Fernbrook.

New names will certainly appear on county maps. For example, at a time when population is still growing in the county, developers will give us at least a few names that will take root. One of these is EastLake, a large development in Chula Vista. The word is needed, it is short, there are lakes not too far away, and the development lies east of the older, established communities, and so it will probably persist.

Some names have been overlooked; they should be on maps but they are not. Residents of Alpine use the name Sacratero Valley (see entry under Sacaton) to describe a location in Japatul Valley, but it is not on any maps, including the USGS 7.5' Alpine Quadrangle. Perhaps it will appear on the next revision. A Ramona author, Ruth B. Meyer (i, 39), several times refers to a Rubber Hill within the town's limits. It is on no map I have seen, but it should be.

In the last few years at least three names have appeared on revised USGS topographic maps that did not appear on earlier versions. These are Elena Mountain, Silverdome Peak, and Elanus Valley (for details consult the entries for these names). This suggests that there is hope for yet more noteworthy local place names, printed on revised maps with the approval of an august government agency. Summing it all up, I am pleased to say that the story of place names in San Diego County has not ended, and the quintessentially human task of fitting names to the landscape, to make a nameless place a known place, will surely continue so long as we exist.

San Diego Place Names A-Z

- A -

Admiral Baker Navy Recreation Center. On the north bank of the San Diego River above the San Diego Mission. This was originally part of the 400-acre **Jacques Farm** founded by Burkill Jacques in 1895. In 1941 the farm became part of Camp Elliot. In 1955 the center was named for Vice Admiral Wilder D. Baker, commandant of the 11ᵗʰ Naval District. (*SDU,* August 7, 1952; *SDU,* November 2, 1968)

Adobe. (Span. "sun-baked brick") Probably referred either to muddy water or raw, exposed earth. It might also refer to a place where an adobe house once stood. **Adobe Falls** is in Alvarado Canyon just north of Interstate 8. **Adobe Flats** is six miles northwest of Mesa Grande. **Adobe Springs** is eight miles northwest of Warner Springs. (Durham 1)

Agra. Santa Fe Railroad loading station on Rancho Santa Margarita, now Camp Pendleton. Either from the Latin *agra,* "field" or the Indian city of Agra. If it is named for the Indian city, then this is the only Asian transfer name in the county. (Hanna 3; Stein 1)

Agricultural Park. At the northwest corner of Mission Bay between Pacific Beach and the road to Los Angeles. A racetrack that opened in May 1869. Where early San Diegans went to bet on the ponies. (SDHS Subject File "Place Names")

Agua. (Span. "water, stream, spring") A common name for almost any appearance of water in the county. Early American mapmakers with no Spanish and a little Latin sometimes cited this as Aqua, "water", for example, as in Aqua Caliente. **Agua Caliente.** (Span. "hot spring") The best known hot springs in the county were in the desert (see Lindsay 30-31), in the Lagunas, and at Warner Springs. For a discussion of the name see Warner Springs. **Agua Dulce.** See **Sweetwater. Agua Hedionda** (Span. "stinking spring") is south of Carlsbad

1

on the coast. It is the name of a Mexican land grant, **Rancho Agua Hedionda**, 13,311 acres, granted to Juan María Marrón in 1842. An alternate name for the grant was Rancho San Francisco. The Portolá expedition noted the lagoon on July 17, 1769, naming the stream for **San Simon Lipnica** (correctly Blessed, not a Saint), a Pole who died in 1482. In spite of what many people may think, "stinking" had nothing to do with the lagoon, but refers to a sulfur spring nearby. The name has been a bit of an embarrassment. Perhaps understandingly, Juan Marrón preferred the name Rancho San Francisco for his grant. When SDG&E built a power plant here, it rejected the name Hedionda Power Plant (Stinking Power Plant?) for Encina Power Plant. (Cowan 12, Pourade, *Explorers* 135; Stein 2). **Agua Tibia Creek, Mountain, Wilderness Area.** (Span. "warm spring") A large spring three miles east of Pala gave its name to other places in the area. Site also of a historic ranch (still existing today) that George Marston once owned. Site of Manuelita Cota's famous "fort." Nellie van de Grift Sanchez (Sanchez 36) said she heard this place referred to as "Shinbone Spring," from Latin *tibia*, but I have never seen this name in print. Was someone pulling her leg? **Agua Zarca.** See **Cocktail Spring.** (Stein 3)

Aguaje de San Jorge. See **Spring Valley.**

Aguanga Mountain. The town is in Riverside County but the nearby mountain is in San Diego County. (Luiseño "dog place" from *awáal* "dog" plus the common locative *–nga*) For another suffix of this sort see Pechanga in Riverside County. (Gudde 5)

Airplane Ridge. In Cuyamaca Rancho State Park above Green Valley Campground. This may be the only airplane crash site permanently marked on a county map. In December 1922 a de Havilland biplane with two flyers disappeared after leaving Rockwell Field on North Island. The wreck with human remains was found in May. A monument marks the site. This place name appeared for the first time on the 1960 Cuyamaca Peak 7.5' quadrangle.

Alder Canyon. Eleven miles northeast of Warner Springs near the Riverside County line. Named, no doubt, for the common water-loving native white alder. Durham (1) points out that this place has been labeled on topographic maps as Elder Canyon in 1903 and Adler Canyon in 1960. Men who make maps sometimes make mistakes. (Stein 129-130)

Aliso Canyon. (Mexican Span. "alder or sycamore") Near the coast a mile north of Las Flores. Mexican Spanish made no distinction in name between two different trees, white alder and western sycamore, both of which grow near water from the coast to about four thousand feet altitude. (Gudde 8)

Alligator. Alligator-shaped features inspired two coastline names. **Alligator Rock** is south of Ocean Beach near Santa Cruz Avenue. **Alligator Point** or **Head** is at La Jolla Cove. (Durham 2; Schaelchlin 8)

Allied Gardens S.D. Eastern Neighborhood. Louis L. Kelton and Walter Bollenbacher developed this large subdivision, opening it for sales in 1955. To build their subdivision they bought a thousand acres from the Waring estate. They first called themselves Allied Contractors; hence the name. (*SDU,* July 2, 1973)

Allison Springs, Station. See **La Mesa.**

Almond. Nine miles north of Ramona in Pamo Valley. Had its own post office from 1896 to 1914. A typical early farm settlement; perhaps farmers here specialized in growing almonds. The *San Diego City-County Directory* for 1897 listed 18 adult residents at this place. (Salley 5)

Aloha. (Hawaiian "hello" and "good-bye") Station on the National City & Otay Railroad less than a mile from Sweetwater Reservoir. Here U.S. Grant, Jr. had a country cottage which survives today. The 1916 Hatfield flood devastated this station, like all features on this railroad. (Durham 2; Webster 27-28)

Alpine Berry Fields. See **The Willows.**

Alpine. Thirty miles east of San Diego off Interstate 8. Was originally called **Viejas Stage Stop,** because it was on the road to the Viejas Valley, then **Alpine Center.** Some have written that ivory importer B.F. Arnold founded this town in 1883. He was a town benefactor but the first settler was in fact Edward Alanson Foss, his family, and others who arrived much earlier, in 1876. They were farmers and bee-keepers. The settlement got its own Alpine School in 1878. An apocryphal story states that the place got its name because it resembled Switzerland. It is also 2,000 feet higher in elevation than San Diego—does that make it alpine? The town got its post office in 1885. A mile or so south of the town is **Alpine Heights.** (La Force 57-74; Salley 5; San Diego County School Records Inventory; Stein 4)

Alta. (Span. "high") A station on the San Diego, Cuyamaca & Eastern Railroad, named for the Alta Ranch near today's Grossmont Summit. In 1892 Hervey Parke (of the pharmaceutical firm Parke, Davis) bought 600 acres here to raise citrus, naming it the Alta Ranch. It had a railroad siding, many structures, and a farm pond that Parke called **Lotus Pond** (See that entry). After Ed Fletcher and William B. Gross developed the Alta and Villa Caro Ranches the Alta Station was renamed Grossmont in 1913. (Durham 30; Guy 43-49)

Alta Vista S.D. Southeastern Neighborhood. (Span. "high view") Named for the Alta Vista Suburb and Alta Vista Suburb Tract, dating from 1906 and 1907. It was later subdivided in the 1960s. (Security Title 2)

Alvarado Canyon. Extends from Grossmont west to Mission Valley. Interstate 8 runs through it. Named for either Francisco María Alvarado, or less likely, Juan Bautista Alvarado, early Spanish San Diegans. For **Alvarado Estates** see **Hidden Mesa.** (J. Davidson, "Alvarados Among First Settlers," *SDET,* September 14, 1935)

Amago. Sometimes called **La Jolla Amago,** because it is located on the La Jolla Indian Reservation. It had a post office from 1900 to 1902. Named for Pio B. Amago, the first postmaster. (Salley 6)

Ames Valley. Five miles north of La Posta. Named for Julian Ames (b. 1803 in Plainfield Connecticut) and his three sons, proprietors of Coches Rancho. They were prominent early ranchers in the district east of El Cajon. (Durham 2)

Anahuac. See **Iñaja.**

Anderson Valley. Four miles southeast of El Cajon Mountain. Named for the Alpine rancher Nicholas Anderson. (La Force 495; *San Diego City-County Directory, 1899-1900*)

Anegado, Puerto. See **Mission Bay.**

Angel Mountain. In the Mesa Grande District, just south of Highway 76. Named not for the divine, but for Mesa Grande rancher, J.N. Angel. (Quinn 10; Stein 5)

Antone Canyon. Just north of La Posta. Probably named for Teely (?) Antone, 50-year old Campo "cattle herder" who appears in the 1880 census. (Durham 2.)

Apex. See **Escondido.**

Ararat, Mount. East of Bonsall and west of Interstate 15. A member of the local Frazee family gave this peak its Biblical name. This is a common name for an isolated mountain, the kind of place where Noah landed his ark. (J. Davidson, "San Diego County's Mt. Ararat," *SDET,* October 13, 1939; Gudde 16; Stein 84-85)

Arkansas Canyon. Opens into San Felipe Valley six miles northeast of Julian. Named for George Ushrey, a woodcutter native of Arkansas who settled here in 1872. In 1883 Tom Daley was murdered in the canyon; writers often confuse the two men. (Jasper, *Julian* 13; *SDU,* March 28, 1883; Stein 6)

Arrowmaker Ridge. On east slopes of Cuyamaca Peak, west of Highway 79. Kumeyaay village area. The name obviously refers to local Indians and their handiwork (Durham 2)

Arroyo Poco. Two miles northwest of Escondido. The U.S. Board on Geographic Names approved this name in 1990. A case of an English speaker misunderstanding Spanish. Probably it was intended to be a translation of "little creek," but poco means "a little bit," not "small in size." Should have been Arroyo Chico. Note that the board does not pass linguistic judgment on the names submitted to it. (Durham 34; Gudde 296)

Arroyo Seco. (Span. "dry creek") In Cuyamaca Rancho State Park near Green Valley Campground, and also six miles north of Boucher Hill on Palomar Mountain. The original meaning of arroyo in Spanish was "stream," but English speakers usually interpret it as "valley." A common name for a short-lived watercourse, or a valley containing a short-lived stream. (Durham 2)

Arsenic Spring. Two miles north of Jacumba. It's not unusual for springs to contain elements such as sulfur or arsenic, but how did the people who named the spring know it held arsenic? The name raises the question, but doesn't answer it. However, the name may simply refer to "bad water," that is, unpalatable water. (Durham 3)

Atkinson Settlement, Grade. Lemuel Atkinson and his brother Henry developed a five-mile-long toll road between Foster and Shady Dell (between Lakeside and Ramona) in 1873. At the upper end of the road was the toll station. Roughly the route followed today's Highway 67. It was very steep and so the more easterly and gentler Mussey Grade supplanted it. From 1878 to 1880 there was a post office at Atkinson, with Lemuel Atkinson the first postmaster. (LeMenager, *Ramona,* 65, 67; Salley 11)

Avondale. A station on the National City and Otay Railroad between Sunnyside and Aloha. In 1892 J.H. Clough developed a lemon ranch here. The name is typical of the genteel names on the railroad. Possibly it was named for Avondale, Ohio, suburb of both Cincinnati and Dayton. On the San Diego 1915 15' Quadrangle, as are the other towns on the line. (J. Davidson, "San Diego County Gazeteer," *SDET,* April 5, 1940)

Aztec City. According to Blackburn's 1931 Map of San Diego County, this place was on the Pacific at the Mexican border. Like many, it was probably a subdivision that died aborning. However, the sheer incongruity in the two elements of its name should guarantee it some kind of immortality, at least in print.

- B -

Bailey Creek. Two miles southeast of Santa Ysabel. It flows into Jim Green Creek. Probably named for L.N. Bailey, no relation to Julian's founder, Drury Bailey. L.N. Bailey settled near Wynola in 1877. Charles Bailey, his brother, farmed with him. (Jasper. *Trail-Breakers...* 77-79)

Bailey's Vale, Meadow, Resort, Lodge. Theodore O. Bailey settled near Crestline on Palomar Mountain in 1887 where he ran a resort. A religious man, he held services at nearby Sunday School Flat. He also called his place Palomar Lodge. (J. Davidson, "Bailey's Founder Lured by Palomar's Greenness," *SDET,* September 3, 1937)

Balboa Park. Originally called **City Park**, it was set aside by city trustees in 1869-1870. When time came to celebrate San Diego's 1915 Panama-California Exposition a contest was held to find what the authorities thought was a more distinctive name. The winner, announced in October 1910, was suited to the spirit of the exhibition, but lacked local color. Vasco Núñez de Balboa, 1513 discoverer of the Pacific, never approached San Diego. Other names proffered in 1910 were Horton, Silvergate, Pacific, and Darien. The surrounding area is called **Balboa Park S.D. Central Neighborhood.** (Christman 39)

Baldhead Spring. See **Sweetwater Spring.**

Ballast Point. Just inside Point Loma in protected water. Also the site of the Spanish fort **Castillo de Punta Guijarros** ("Fort of Cobblestone Point") and the American **Fort Guijarros**. In 1734 José González named it Punta de los Guijarros, "Point of the Cobblestones." Others had noted that the small rounded rhyolite boulders common in the San Diego coastal area and especially numerous here made excellent ballast. The English name apparently arose when American ships began to anchor here early in the nineteenth century, using the beach rocks for ballast. Often it's said that these small boulders were used to pave streets in Boston, having been taken there as ballast, but I can find no documentation that this was, in fact, done. Sometimes called **Cobblestone Point** in the American era. (Engelhardt, *San Diego,* 176; Gudde 25; Stein 7)

Ballena Settlement, Valley. (Span. "whale") Eight miles northeast of Ramona on Highway 78. Got its name because a nearby ridge, now called Whale Peak resembled a whale. This area, outside Mexican land grants, was popular with early American farmers and ranchers. It had its own post office 1870-1894 and 1896-1902. The *San Diego City-County Direction, 1889-1890,* listed 56 farmers and small businessmen living there with their families, probably more than at the present. (Gudde 25; Salley 13; Stein 7)

Bancroft. A number of features centered on Bancroft Drive in Spring Valley. A slight hill with a once impressive view, **Bancroft Point** is to the west. On October 9, 1885, Rufus K. Porter sold his Helix Farms for $8,000 to the illustrious California historian H.H. Bancroft (1832-1918). Thereafter Bancroft used the **Bancroft House** as a winter home. In the *San Diego City-County Directory, 1887-1888,* Bancroft listed himself as "Bancroft, H.H. Postmaster and blacksmith shop." (Adema 63-69)

Bandy Canyon, Falls. One mile southeast of San Pasqual. Named for John D. Bandy who filed for 80 acres of land in the mouth of the canyon on Dec. 12, 1882. The falls above the homestead are on Santa Maria Creek. (*SDU,* December 13, 1882)

Banker's Hill. West of Balboa Park between First and Fourth Avenues and south of Hillcrest. Once, in part, called Florence Heights, 1903-1904. Never an official neighborhood; architects Irving Gill, William Hebbard, Richard Requa, and Frank Mead designed houses in this affluent district. People had the impression that many bankers lived here, hence the name. For an excellent walking tour of Banker's Hill see Schad 96-97. (Kooperman 271-272)

Bankhead Springs. Four miles northwest of Jacumba. Highway 80 from Richmond Virginia to San Diego was named for Senator John H. Bankhead of Alabama in 1916. The springs, a resort, dates from 1915 and took its name from the highway. (Stein 8)

Banner. Eight miles east of Julian on Highway 78. In August 1870 assayer Louis Redman discovered the **Redman Mine.** This mine (called the Redmond Mine on the 1997 Julian 7.5' Quadrangle) is located about a quarter of a mile up Chariot Canyon south of Highway 78. Producing between $25,000 and $50,000 in gold, it was the first important mine "over the hill" from Julian. Supposedly Redman planted a banner at the site and so it became known as the **Banner Mine**, giving a name to features in the district. **Banner City** arose on a constricted flat nearby. Like many other mining towns in the county it was graced with the title of city, such as Julian City, Coleman City, Emily City, etc. The town had its own post office from 1873 to 1877, then again from 1883 to 1906. Stein says the town had a population of 1,000, but this is probably about three times too high. **Banner Grade**, completed in 1871, connected the new town with Julian. **Banner Mine Road**, built in the early 1890s, led directly from Julian down to Banner past many producing mines. It was sometimes called **Foster Grade**, for Joe Foster, county supervisor and road building advocate. Surviving today, it is badly eroded; it is also very steep. (Fetzer, *Good Camp,* 33-57; Stein 9)

Barber Mountain. Four miles north of Dulzura. Possibly named for the early settler, Reuben W. Barber, or the gold miner George W. Barber. (Stein 9, Schmid 31)

Barber Station. In the 1870s this was a stage stop on the Tijuana River on the road to Yuma. It was at the ranch of C.W. Barber, who sold out in 1874 for $1,500. (*SDU,* January 4, 1874)

Barham. This was a settlement with a store, etc., in today's San Marcos, northwest of the intersection of San Marcos Blvd. and Rancho Santa Fe Road. John H Barham named it for himself. It got a post office with Barham as postmaster in 1883, but it was discontinued in 1888. A school was there in those years also. In 1887 Barham founded **Glen Barham** southeast of the intersection. This was advertised as a resort. (Carroll 23; J. Davidson, "Swiss Beauty Surpassed by Glen-Barham, Claim," *SDET,* February 12, 1937; Salley 14; San Diego County School Records Inventory)

Barker Valley. On the West Fork of the San Luis Rey River on eastern slopes of Palomar Mountain. Possibly named for Alejandro (Alexander) Barker, a leader of the Cupeño band and later a rancher. (*SDU,* July 18, 1893)

Baron Long Ranch. See **Viejas.**

Barona. East of Lakeside and south of Ramona. The name comes from the title of a Mexican land grant, **Cañada de San Vicente y Mesa del Padre Barona**, 13,316 acres). Padre José Barona was a friar at San Diego (1798-1811) and San Juan Capistrano (1811-1831). He was a humble and obscure missionary, but a great favorite of the Yorba family, one of whom owned the grant, and so they attached his name to a mesa and the title of the grant. The **Barona Indian Reservation**, 5,181 acres), named for the padre, was established in 1931, along with the **Viejas Indian Reservation**, 1,609 acres) to provide a home for the Indians displaced by El Capitan Reservoir. There is also a **Barona Valley** and **Creek**. Also see **San Vicente.** (Cowan 89; Gudde 275-276)

Barrett. About six miles southeast of Dulzura. The original name of the settlement was **Cottonwood**, but a post office under the name of **Barrett** existed from 1915 to 1936. The name honors George W. Barrett and his sister who settled in the area in 1879. In 1919 construction began on the **Barrett Dam** to make **Barrett Lake** on Cottonwood Creek in 1922. **Barrett Junction** is on Highway 94. (Salley 14; Gudde 27)

Batequitos Lagoon. (Span. from northwestern Mexico *batequi,* "a hole dug in a riverbed to find water." *Batequitos* is the diminutive plural of *batequi.* The source is Yaqui *bate'ekim*. Bright 21, Gudde 28) North of Leucadia. Padre Pedro Font first recorded this name in 1776. (Gudde 28) The source of its water is San Marcos Creek. Because the origin of this name is so obscure, there has been much controversy over its meaning and its spelling; frequently it is spelled Batiquitos. Hanna (26) said it meant "flat-bottomed boats," presumably from Spanish *batea* "flat-bottomed boat." Winifred Davidson said it meant "little baptized girls." This probably because she confused the 1769 Portolá expedition camping place here with one further north at Cristianitos Canyon, where Father Crespí did in fact baptize two Indian girls. (Davidson Place Name File) Gudde's explanation, above, seems very convincing. (Stein 10)

Bathtub Rock. See **Flat Rock.**

Battle Mountain. See **Mule Hill.**

Bay Ho S.D. Northern Neighborhood. The bay is Mission Bay, and the Ho probably comes from the title of the English novel, *Westward Ho!* (1855) by Charles Kingsley. In England there is a town Westward Ho!, the exclamation mark required, the name taken from the novel. My dictionary tells me that the word "Ho!" registers surprise or delight or derision.

Bay Park S.D. Northern Neighborhood. Bay Park's original name may have been **Bayside Village**, shown on early maps between Overlook and Moreno and dating back to the boom year of 1887. Bay Park was probably named for subdivisions such as Bay Park Village, 1936, or Bay Park Vista Subdivisions, 1950-1952. (Security Title 4)

Bay Point. See **Crown Point.**

Bay Terraces S.D. Southeastern Neighborhood. Probably named for South Bay Terrace, a large subdivision annexed by the city of San Diego in 1969. (*SDU,* September. 4, 1969)

Bayside Village. See **Bay Park.**

Beacon Hill. A station just east of Encanto on the San Diego Cuyamaca and Eastern Railroad. Probably a transfer name from Boston's Beacon Hill. (Christian Brown Interview)

Bear. When the first Europeans arrived they found grizzly bears everywhere in the county, but no black bears. Black bears came only in the twentieth century as escaped pets or animals drifting down from the San Jacinto Mountains whose ancestors were brought to southern California in the 1920s. Bear place names seem especially common in the north central area. In the county see **Bear Canyon,** near Warner Springs; **Bear Creek,** near Mesa Grande; **Bear Ridge,** near Escondido; **Bear Spring, Bear Spring Flats, Bear Valley** near Rodriguez Mountain; and **Bear Valley,** south of Descanso. **Bear Valley Reservoir.** See **Lake Wohlford.** (see Abbot; Durham 4-5)

Beaver Hollow. A small valley between Jamul and Lawson Valley. Opens into the Sweetwater Valley. An oddity, because native beavers were unknown in the county. The generic place name, hollow, is unusual for the county. (Durham 5)

Bee Canyon. Two of these are in the county. One is two miles southeast of Dulzura, and the other opens into the San Luis Rey Valley below Boucher Hill. It's assumed that they were named for European bees, introduced into the county after the Civil War, giving rise to a major industry. Their owners scattered bee colonies all over the county to utilize native flowers. For a description of the bee tree location in the canyon near Dulzura, see the *SDU* for January 30, 1869. (Durham 5)

Beeler Canyon, Creek. Two miles south and west of Poway. Named before 1900 for a German bee keeper, Julius Buehler. A good example of an English speaker writing down a German word as he heard it. (Stein 11)

Bell Bluff. Near Japatul Valley east of Alpine. The *SDU* for November 25, 1879, mentions an M.R.J. Bell fighting brush fires on his leased ranch on the Sweetwater River. His name was probably the source of this place name. The generic place name, bluff, is rare in the county except along the ocean. (Durham 5)

Bell Valley. Three miles east of Potrero. The *Great Register of Voters* for 1890 lists a James Scott Bell, native of Tennessee, living at Cottonwood (Barrett). He is a possible source for this place name. (Durham 5)

Belmont Park. See **Mission Beach.**

Bennington U.S. Cemetery. An early name for Ft. Rosecrans National Cemetery. Named for the victims of the explosion of the U.S.S. Bennington in San Diego harbor on July 21, 1905, resulting in 65 fatalities. (Davidson Place Name File)

Bernardo Settlement, Mountain. See **San Bernardo.**

Beverly. A station on the San Diego Cuyamaca and Eastern Railroad. Located just west of Encanto. (Christian Brown Interview)

Big Potrero. See **Potrero.**

Birch Hill. Near Crestline on Palomar Mountain. Nothing to do with trees. This place was named for two English brothers, Henry (Harry) and Arthur Birch. As the greenest of greenhorns, they came to live on Palomar Mountain in the 1890s. Returning to England, according to Stein (12), Arthur was killed in the Boer War (I have never been able to verify this), and Harry became Lord Birch. In fact, Henry William Birch did not have a title but he did have the bluest blood. According to the British *Who Was Who 1916-1928* Henry William Birch (1854-1927) "...m. 1897 Kate Hazeltine, d. of R. Anson Yates of San Francisco. Inherited Loudwater under will of maternal grandfather and The Grove, Old Windsor, under will of Miss Thackeray, 1879." This has all the ingredients of a novel. Who was Kate Hazeltine? Did she become the mistress of Loudwater and The Grove, Old Windsor? Who was dear Miss Thackeray? What really happened to Arthur? All of this was a long way from Birch Hill on Palomar Mountain. (Wood 67-68)

Bird Rock. On coast near La Jolla Hermosa Park. Named for rock that had the shape of a bird. There was a Bird Rock Coastal Defense and Anti-Aircraft Training Center here 1942-1945. (Gudde 36, Schaelchlin 194)

Birdland S.D. Eastern Neighborhood. Located east of Linda Vista on Kearny Mesa and not to be confused with the cluster of streets named for birds near Hillcrest. Called this for its many streets named for birds—from Bobolink Street to Tern Street.

Bishop Rock. Southernmost portion of Cortes Bank far off the Coronado Islands. Fifteen feet below the surface. Named for the Philadelphia clipper *Bishop* that foundered here in the fog in 1855. (Gudde 36; *U.S. Coast Pilot,* 42)

Bishop Stevens Campground. East of Julian on Highway 78. Named for Rt. Rev. W. Bertrand Stevens, Bishop of Los Angeles (Episcopal) who died August 22, 1947.

Black Horse Mountain. See **Mount Gower.**

Black. A name for a wooded or brushy place, but so general that it is not a very memorable place name. There are two **Black Mountains** in the county. One is just west of Mesa Grande. Plainly visible from Interstate 15, the second is west of Poway. This mountain was once called **Cordero Mountain.** See **Cordero.** In 1963 the U.S. Board on Geographic Names rejected an attempt to change the name of this peak to Santa Maria Mountain, probably because there were already too many other places in California with this name. In addition, Cowles

Mountain was sometimes called **Black Mountain**. There was a settlement called **Black Mountain** located one mile south of the summit of western Black Mountain. It had a post office from 1888 to 1903. It is on Blackburn's county map of 1931 and the La Jolla 15' Quadrangle of 1903. The *San Diego City-County Directory, 1901* listed only seven adult males living in Black Mountain. In the area just west of Mesa Grande are **Black Canyon** and **Black Butte**, the latter a rare county generic name. (Durham 6; Salley 21; Stein 13)

Blacks Beach. Between Scripps Institution of Oceanography and Torrey Pines State Beach and State Reserve. San Diego's only clothing optional beach—clothing optional is the politically correct term for a nude beach. In 1992 the U.S. Board on Geographic Names formally changed the name of South Torrey Pines State Beach to Blacks Beach. Named for William H. Black who developed the ultra-exclusive La Jolla Farms subdivision, complete with a "Black Gold Stable," above the beach in about 1950. He was a Texas oil millionaire who died in 1967 at the La Jolla Beach and Tennis Club golf course—with his clothes on. (Durham 6; *La Jolla Light,* July 3, 1986)

Bloomdale Creek. Flows into Sutherland Reservoir from the north. There was a Bloomdale School, 1893-1916, on the Santa Ysabel Ranch between Mesa Grande and Mesa Chiquita. Possibly named for the school. (San Diego County School Records Inventory)

Blossom Valley. North of Interstate 8 five miles east of El Cajon. Not a developer's name, but from Elmer G. Blossom who bought 100 acres of land here in 1912. On his ranch he grew fruit, especially peaches. Some of his olive trees survive at the site today. (see Blossom)

Boal. Station on the San Diego & Arizona Railroad. Between Chula Vista Junction and **Otay**. Named for John E. Boal, manager of the San Diego Land and Town Co. (1860-1934.) (Biographical files)

Bob Owens Canyon. Flows into Cottonwood Creek below Barrett Dam. The origin of the name is obvious, but I have not been able to identify Mr. Owens. (Durham 7)

Boden Canyon. Opens into Santa Ysabel Creek three miles east of San Pasqual. Named for William Boden. He appears on the BLM website as a homesteader in 1900; his homestead was near Warner Springs. Peet (195) refers to a San Pasqual settler as "Billie Boden." On some maps mistakenly given as Roden Canyon. (Durham 7; Stein 13)

Bohemia, Bohemian Grove. See Descanso.

Boiling Spring Ravine. One mile west of Mount Laguna settlement. Correctly the water bubbles, not boils, because it is a cold spring. (Davidson Place Name File; Durham 7; Schad 202)

Bone Canyon. At the north end of Ingraham St. in Pacific Beach. Named for Sam W. Bone who had an unsuccessful development here in 1890. (J. Davidson, "San Diego County Gazeteer," *SDET,* June 14, 1940)

Boneyard Canyon. Opens into Barrett Lake. Assumed to be animal bones, source unknown. Ranchers sometimes dragged all their dead livestock to one place to spare themselves unpleasantness; this may be the origin of this name. (Durham 7; Stein 14).

Bonita. (Span. "pretty") Community on the lower Sweetwater River founded in 1884. Originally it was a station on the National City & Otay Railroad. Got its post office only in 1898. The Kimball brothers of National City ran sheep in the Sweetwater Valley, and Frank Kimball had a pond constructed there that he called Laguna Bonita. The generic name was lost, but the specific name survives. (Phillips, *National City,* 104; Salley 23; Webster 25)

Bonnie Brae. (Scots, "pretty bank of a stream or lake") On Sweetwater branch of the National City & Otay Railroad between Bonita and Sunnyside H. M. Higgins, a music publisher of Scottish extraction, developed a lemon ranch at this site in 1871. The name probably came from the song "Loch Lomond." "By yon bonnie banks and by yon bonnie braes…" (Anonymous, "Bonnie Brae"; Webster 25)

Bonsall. On the San Luis Rey River midway between Oceanside and Pala. Originally the town was called **Mount Fairview**, for a nearby hill, then **Osgood**. Under this name it had a post office 1881-1884 and again in 1888-1891. Joseph O. Osgood was the chief engineer of the California Southern Railroad in 1880, and it's said that local residents chose the name to induce Mr. Osgood to build the railroad through the San Luis Rey Valley; unmoved, he chose the Santa Margarita River Valley instead. Supposedly, wanting a new name for their post office, local people submitted the names of three citizens, Reed, Favorite, and Bonsall, to the government. It chose **Bonsall** in 1890. James A. Bonsall was a local minister and a nurseryman. Note there was some overlap with Osgood, and there were probably two post offices with these names located not far apart for a time. (J. Davidson, "Mt. Fairview First Name for Bonsall," *SDET,* July 6, 1934; Salley 23; 158; Stein 14)

Boomer Beach. Just south of Point La Jolla. Inspired name for a surfing beach. The boomers must be mighty waves coming ashore. (Cleary and Stern 194)

Bootleger (sic) Field. See **Rosedale Landing Field.**

Boring Creek. Flows into Jim Green Creek two miles east of Santa Ysabel. Probably named for J. M. Boring, Julian farmer, who appears in the 1890 *San Diego City-County Directory*.

Bossun Shoal. See **Zuñiga Shoal.**

Bostonia. A district three miles northeast of El Cajon. Isaac Lankershim originally grew wheat on this land. In 1886 two Bostonians, Charles Crosby (there is still a Crosby Street in the district) and William S. Souther bought 585 acres here where they planted grapes and citrus. They called their spread **Boston Ranch**; sometimes it was called **New Boston.** O.W. Cotton subdivided the ranch in 1887, giving it the name of **Bostonia Acres**, then **Bostonia**; it also had a small commercial center. The town did not have its own post office until 1894, suggesting the development struggled in its early years. (Davidson Place Name File; Gudde 43; Salley 24)

Bottle Peak, Bottle Peak Spring. South of Lake Wohlford. Stein (16) says it was named for the shape of the peak, but Ryan (138) says it got its name because the fire lookout on its summit resembled "a bottle sitting on the rock."

Boucher Hill. At the western end of Palomar Mountain in Palomar Mountain State Park. Named for William E. Bougher (sic), prominent early settler, and his family. The spelling of the hill's name probably reflects the pronunciation of the family name. (USGS mapmakers seem to have obtained their place name information from interviews, not from printed sources.) Mr. Bougher was a resident of Nellie on Palomar Mountain in 1899-1900, according to the *San Diego City-County Directory.*

Boulder. The surface rock in most of the county is white granitic stone left from the Peninsular Batholith of long ago. Breaking easily along planes, its lines become softened as it exfoliates to make conspicuous boulders of all sizes and shapes. These boulders have given us several place names. Two **Boulder Creeks** are in the county. The first flows out of Cuyamaca Lake to join the San Diego River. Dammed in 1887 it has long been a source of water for the flatlands to the west. The other is in the desert near Imperial County. Two places known as **Boulder Oaks** can be found in the county. One is near La Posta on old Highway 80 in Cleveland National Forest, while the other is about six miles north of Lakeside. (Durham 8)

Boulevard. Fifteen miles east of Campo where Highway 80 and 94 merge. A settlement that had its own post office in 1919. Named for the highway, very important in the town's development, especially as it brought visitors from steamy Imperial County. (Salley 24; Stein 16)

Boundary Creek, Peak. The peak is east of Campo and the creek is near Jacumba. Both features are named for their proximity to the Mexican border. (Stein 16)

Box Canyon. The best known feature with this name is on Highway S-2 near Mason Valley (see Lindsay 87-88), but this name is also given to a canyon on San Marcos Creek east of Carlsbad. Here teenagers delight in diving from high rocks into pools, to the horror of their elders. Box canyons seemingly have no exit, but in fact the name appears here to simply designate narrow rocky canyons.

Branson City. About one mile east of Julian. Lawyer Lewis C. Branson unsuccessfully sought to develop a town site here after the gold discoveries. The town may have had a store, saloon, and dance-hall, but certainly had a post office from August 19, 1870, to October 13, 1870. (Jasper, *Trail-Breakers,* 10; Salley 24)

Bratton Valley. South of Lyons Valley and Peak. The Bratton family, headed by Napoleon Bratton, settled here in the 1870s. (Schmid 23-28; Stein 17)

Brown Field Naval Auxiliary Air Station. East of Imperial Beach and Interstate 5. Named for Commander Melville S. Brown. He died when trying to make a dead-stick landing near Descanso on November 2, 1936. (*SDU,* August 8, 1962)

Bubble-up Creek. Due south of Pala in the San Luis Rey Valley. The U.S. Board on Geographic Names approved this distinctive name in 1991. (Durham 9, 54)

Buckman Springs. Four miles south of Pine Valley. Also known as **Soda Springs.** Long a small settlement on the road east from San Diego. It was the site of a commercial enterprise to bottle and sell the water under the name of "Buckman Springs Lithia Water," but the water was never successful because it was discolored (Vezina). Named for early settler Amos Buckman, 1820-1898. (Gudde 49)

Bucksnort Mountain. North of Warner Springs near the Riverside county line. Probably based on an incident: a mapmaker heard a buck snort and thought it would be a good name for the mountain. This is an inspired local name that belongs in a western novel. (Durham 9)

Buena Vista Creek, Hills, Lagoon. (Span. "good view") Between Guajome and San Marcos ranches. Portolá visited this district in 1769. Originally a Mexican land grant of 1,184 acres, **Rancho Buena Vista** was granted to an Indian, Felipe, in 1845, but it came into the hands of Jesus Machado. In 1890 the San Diego Central ran its line from Oceanside to Escondido with a center station they called **Buena Vista.** According to Stein (19) when it needed a new station in 1908, it called the old one **Buena** and the new one **Vista.** However, there was a Buena post office in 1883 and a Vista post office in 1882. Another name for lower Buena Vista Valley near El Salto was **Milpitas** (Mex. Span. "cornfields"). In 1858 Louis Rose had a copper mine here (Harrison 192). Near Warner Springs there is also a **Buena Vista Creek,** with no connection to the coastal place name. (Cowan 20; Durham 10; Gudde 51; Salley 27)

Bull Pasture. Four miles east of Boucher Hill on Palomar Mountain, and also near Highway 79 in northern part of Cuyamaca Rancho State Park. Nature requires that bulls be fenced away from cows, hence the name. (Durham 10)

Bunton Flat, Valley. Five miles south of Santa Ysabel in Pine Hills district. Named for William Bunton who ranched in this vicinity in 1870. The previous owner, John Ivy, was murdered. (J. Davidson, "Bunton Valley Originally Ivy Ranch," *SDET,* April 21, 1939; Durham 10)

Burlingame. Between 30th and 32nd Streets, and Kalmia to Nutmeg Streets. One of San Diego's most attractive subdivisions. Developed from 1912 to 1929. See Covington for perhaps the most engaging book about a San Diego residential district. Probably named for Burlingame, California, which was named for Anson Burlingame, diplomat (1822-1870.) (Gudde 52)

Burnt Mountain. South of Valley Center. Known by this name as early as 1911. Wild fires are common in the county, but this seems the only place name that records their presence. (Durham 10)

Burnt Rancheria Campground. On Sunrise Highway not far from Mt. Laguna Settlement. A rancheria in early county history was an Indian village. I have never been able to find much about this place, but the name is too distinctive to omit. Sometimes when a rancheria was abandoned, it was burned to destroy vermin, etc., and this may be the source of the name. (Durham 10)

Butterfly Farm. On Palomar Mountain. Members of the W.F. Hewlett family, especially daughter Esther, collected and sold butterflies and moths from their ranch to collectors all over the country for about five years after 1913, so they called their place Butterfly Farm. They also ran a resort here they called **Planwydd,** except for Cardiff possibly the only Welsh place name in the county. (Wood 85-86)

- C -

C.J. Miller, Camp. At the Del Mar race track during the Second World War. A Marine Corps athletic training base. (Hinds 30)

Cabrillo Canyon, Bridge. In Balboa Park. Highway 163 runs through it. Named for Juan Rodríguez Cabrillo who discovered San Diego Bay in 1542. The name dates from the 1915 Panama-California Exposition. (Cabrillo Bridge over the canyon was opened April 12, 1914.) Before that date it was called **Pound Canyon.** This was where stray animals were impounded, particularly livestock, after the 1873 no-fence law. Also it was the site of municipal wells. (Christman 90; Pourade, *Glory,* 108)

Cabrillo National Monument. President Woodrow Wilson established it by proclamation in 1913. Juan Rodríguez Cabrillo made his first California landing here in 1542. This site on Point Loma, with its fine views and easy accessibility, is one of the most popular national monuments in the country.

Cactus Park. One mile east of Lakeside. Established by Hugo Thum of Pasadena who made a fortune selling sticky flypaper. Deeded to the county in 1928. Over a hundred acres with natural and planted cactus, it was an experimental plot for growing spineless cactus as cattle feed. Now the site of El Capitan High School. (Davidson Place Name File; J. Davidson, "San Diego County Gazeteer," *SDET,* July 26, 1940; Lakeside 121-122)

Cajon Gap. See **Mission Gorge.**

Calavera Peak, Lake, Canyon. (Span. "skull") Six miles east of Oceanside on the old Hedionda Ranch. Why this cluster of place names occurs here is unknown.

Calavo Gardens. Subdivision on the south and east sides of Mt. Helix. In 1926 F.F. Eberts of Escondido won a contest to invent a brand name for the California Avocado Growers Association—he contributed "Calavo." As the winner he got a box of avocados as a prize. (McGrew, *Hidden Valley,* 44)

Callan, Camp. Occupied the coast from La Jolla Shores to south of Del Mar. From 1941 through 1945 it was an army base with emphasis on coast artillery training. Named for Army General Robert E. Callan (1874-1936). (Gudde 61; Hinds 90)

Camajal y el Palomar Rancho. Mexican land grant given to Jonathan Trumbull Warner in 1846. The American authorities rejected his claim. Camajal referred to two Indian villages that Hill (110) believes were at Mesa Grande. Palomar means "pigeon roost" in Spanish, probably referring to the abundant band-tailed pigeons in the area or the mountain. (Cowan 22; Gudde 61)

Cameron Corners, Station, Valley. Two miles north of Campo. Early records identify this place under its Kumeyaay name **Matacawat** or **Mataquequat** probably from *'emat* "place, earth" plus *'ehwatt* "red" (Couro and Hutcheson 3). The 1873 J. Blanco map shows Cameron Corners as **Clay** (Alvarez 126-127). This is a rare example of English speakers translating a Kumeyaay name into English. Cameron Corners was named for a Scottish-born settler, Thomas Cameron, who was here in 1870. Although the Cameron family was here early, the name Cameron Corners is not old; it does not appear on the reliable 1931 Blackburn map, but Cameron Valley does. (Gudde 62; *SDU,* October 27, 1870; Stein 21)

Camp. See under specific names, for example, **Hearn, Camp.**

Campo Settlement, Station, Valley. (Span. "field" or in some cases "camp") When this place got its first post office from 1868 to 1875 it had a Kumeyaay name, **Milquatay**, from *'emill* "meadow" (Couro and Hutcheson 4), and *'etaay* "big" (Langdon, in Gudde 155). Founded by L.H. and S.E. Gaskill who came here in the late 1860s. There was a Milquatay School in 1867. Because so many settlers came here from Texas, it was sometimes called **New Texas** or **Little Texas. Campo Indian Reservation** dates from 1893 and has 15,010 acres of land. (Gudde 63; Pryde 136; Salley 33, San Diego County School Records Inventory; Stein 22)

Camps Grove. See **Dulzura.**

Cañada de Clemente. See **San Clemente Canyon.**

Cañada de las Lleguas. See **Rose Canyon.**

Cañada de los Bautismos. See **Cristianitos Canyon.**

Cañada de los Encinos. See **Encinitas.**

Cañada de Osuna. See **Murray Canyon.**

Cañada de San Diego. See **Mission Valley.**

Cañada de Santa Praxedis de los Rosales. See **Las Flores.**

Canary Cottage. See **Stingaree.**

Cannon Ball Road. See **Imperial Highway.**

Canyon City. Between Campo Creek Bridge and Potrero. On the Arizona & Eastern Railroad and Highway 94 near the Mexican border. Unofficially this place is known as **Dogpatch**; it is so designated on the 1996 AAA San Diego County map. The name comes from Al Capp's comic strip, Li'l Abner, very popular in the 1940s and 1950s. A neglected hamlet, this is where sweethearts Li'l Abner and Daisy Mae find a backward backcountry home. (Durham 12; Stein 23)

Cape Horn. The southern extremity of South America. A nineteenth century name for an obstacle that must be overcome. There was a **Cape Horn Tunnel** on the San Diego Flume that pierced a ridge called Cape Horn. (Cuyamaca 1903 30' Quadrangle; Gudde 65)

Capitan Grande. See **El Capitán Grande.**

Cardiff-by-the-Sea. On the coast between Solana Beach and Encinitas. Cardiff is the capital of Wales. The place's original name was **San Elijo.** (See the entry under this name) J. Frank Cullen (d. 1934), who came to San Diego from Boston, developed the town in 1911; it got its post office in 1912. According to Kooperman (27), his wife, Esther N. Cullen, was from Wales, hence the transfer name. The developer gave it street names from the British Isles and Ireland. The original settler here was Hector Mackinnon who lived with his family north of San Elijo Lagoon at a place called **Mackinnon's Landing.** Mackinnon Ranch Road is near the site today. (BLM website; Hartley 73; Salley 35; *SDU,* June 16, 1889; Stein 24)

Carl Spring. Three miles south of Descanso Junction. Named for Carl O. Brenner, forest ranger at Descanso from 1912 to 1916. (Friends, *Descanso,* 54)

Carlsbad. Three miles south of Oceanside. The original German name was Karlsbad, "Karl's Spa," but the German spelling was never used. The Carl was Charles IV, (1316-1378), notable for his conquests in Bohemia, today's Czech Republic, where the original spa still exists as Karlovy Vary. Before the town was founded the place was called **Frazier's Station**, for John A. Frazier, a farmer who found mineral springs on his land similar to those at the European Karlsbad. The Carlsbad Land and Mineral Water Company developed the town in 1886, with the post office established that year. Several writers assert that Carlsbad changed its name to Carl during World War I because of anti-German feeling, but a search through the *San Diego City-County Directory* for 1915-1920 shows no name change. If the town was serious about changing its name it could have taken a new name for its post office, as did Potsdam in Missouri,

Brandenburg in Texas, Kiel in Oklahoma, and Thalheim in California (Stewart 373), but it did not. Perhaps informally the town's citizens preferred the name Carl, but that is another question. The Santa Fe Railroad disliked the name Carlsbad because it conflicted with Carlsbad, N.M., also on its lines, so apparently an early name of the station was Carl, as photographs of the station show. (Gudde 66; Salley 35; Stein 35)

Carlton Hills. See **Fanita Ranch.**

Carmel Mountain, Valley, Carmel Mountain S.D. Northern Neighborhood, Carmel Valley S.D. Neighborhood. (Hebrew, *karmel,* "vineyard, orchard") Southeast of Del Mar. Many residents no doubt identify the name with Carmel, California; a few children undoubtedly believe it has something to do with candy. In 1905 the Catholic Sisters of Mercy established Mercy Hospital Farm in lower McGonigle Canyon, calling a nearby hill Mount Carmel for the Biblical hill near Jerusalem (I Kings xvii). The farm appeared on the 1943 Del Mar 7.5' Quadrangle. In the 1940s rancher Robert Stevens bought the farm and changed its name to Mount Carmel Ranch. In time this name became attached to the valley, originally only the lower portion of McGonigle Canyon. (Gudde 66; Northrop 16; Stein 25)

Carnation City. See **Oceanside.**

Carney Canyon. Five miles southwest of Mesa Grande. Named for an early rancher, William Carney. (Stein 25)

Carroll Canyon. Heads near Miramar and enters into Soledad Valley. Named for Thomas Carroll who had a ranch here. (*SDU,* September. 21, 1891)

Carroll Dam, Reservoir. See **Lake Hodges.**

Caruso Hill. A knoll just east of Grossmont. According to one account, Enrico Caruso bought land here. There is absolutely no evidence for the purchase; if tenor Enrico Caruso had bought land in Grossmont its developer Ed Fletcher would have told the world about it. (J. Davidson, "San Diego County Gazeteer," *SDET,* January 1, 1940)

Casa de Oro. (Span. "house of gold") Southeast of Mt. Helix near Highway 94. Originally called **Casa de Oro Avocado Estates.** Sale of 10-acre plots began in April 1929. During the 1920s avocado boom, the fruit was called "green gold." Grow avocados and you could make a lot of money, or so the salesmen said, hence the name of the subdivision. (Adema 138)

Case Springs, Lake. Two miles west of Margarita Peak. Named for Alden B. Case, a farmer in the San Luis Rey district in 1894. (Stein 26)

Castillo de Punta Guijarros. See **Ballast Point.**

Castle. Three older and larger houses in the county seem to merit this name, at least in the public mind. **Del Mar Castle** is in north Del Mar. Bostonian Marston Harding built this impressive house in 1927 at a cost of $150,000 (many millions today) on 43 acres of land near the Snakewall Property (See **Snakewall**). The San Diego firm of Requa-Jackson designed it in emulation of palatial houses in Spain (Ewing 178-180). **Old Castle** or **Moosa Castle** is off Interstate 15 north of Escondido. Isaac Jenkinson Frazee built it in 1893. Constructed of native stone, three stories tall, it has notable towers. Frazee was an artistic Scottish immigrant with nine children. This castle has been much remodeled (Freeman). Amy Strong built **Strong Castle** northeast of Woodson Mountain and northwest of Ramona with the help of professional architects in 1916-1921. It has 27 rooms, 12,000 square feet of living space, and a windmill. A dressmaker for San Diego's wealthiest women, Miss Strong often traveled to Europe in search of the latest fashions, and as a consequence the house clearly shows European architectural influences. (Meyers 58-60)

Castle Park. A district in south Chula Vista. Probably got its name from the subdivision dating from 1923. Everything a place name should *not* be—there's no castle here, and no park. (Security Title 7)

Castro Canyon. Near Pala. Named for either Ramon or Zacarias Castro. (Stein 26)

Cedar. Western cedars, sometimes called incense cedars, grow well in the county at higher, moister locations, and can be an important timber tree. There are two **Cedar Creeks** in the county. One is a tributary of the San Diego River, rising near William Heise County Park and flowing into the San Diego River, while another enters the San Luis Rey River south of Boucher Hill. **Cedar Creek Falls** is on Cedar Creek just before it joins the San Diego River. **Cedar Canyon** and **Little Cedar Canyon** open to Dulzura Creek. However, the cedars here are the Tecate Cypress (*Cupresses forbesii)* a small tree growing in arid places. (Durham 14)

Centipede Mountain. Southeast of Lake Wohlford, elevation 2,127 feet. On Blackburn's 1931 Map of San Diego County. Did someone see a centipede here and name the mountain for it? (Davidson Place Name File)

Cerro de la Calavera. See **Calavera Peak.**

Cerro de la Hechicera. (Span. "hill of the witch") Two miles southeast of San Felipe. (Durham 14)

Cerro de las Posas. (Span. "hill of the pools or wells") Range of hills south of the San Marcos Valley. Probably refers to pools along watercourses. (Davidson Place Name File; Durham 14)

Channing Meadow. Three miles northeast of Buckman Springs near Kitchen Valley in Cleveland National Forest. Named, very probably, for W. Harry Chowning (sic), prominent Laguna rancher. In *San Diego City-County Directory 1887-1888* he is listed as a "stock raiser." Almost certainly this was a mapmaker's error that reflects the name's pronunciation. (Durham 14)

Chappo. On the Santa Fe Railroad between Ysidora and Ranch House on what was once the Santa Margarita Ranch. Gudde (74) suggests that the name comes from Spanish *chapo,* "a short person" from Aztec *tzapa* "dwarf."

Chariot Canyon, Road. Just south of Banner and Highway 78. Named for the **Golden Chariot Mine**, discovered by George V. King in February 1871, second in production only to the Stonewall Mine in the district. South about five miles from Banner, it yielded about $700,000 in gold. It is on the 1997 Julian 7.5' Quadrangle. The road from the mine to Banner was built with Indian labor under Joseph Swycaffer's direction. (Fetzer, *Good Camp,* 49-50)

Cherry Canyon, Flat. The canyon is six miles northeast of San Felipe, and the flat is on the north shoulder of Cuyamaca Peak. Since these are remote locations, the cherry in question is probably the native choke cherry, not the cultivated variety. (Durham 14)

Chet Harritt Dam. A dam, built in 1962, to make Lake Jennings east of Lakeside in Quail Canyon. Chester (Chet) Harritt was the general manager of the Helix Irrigation District from 1926 to his death in 1948. (Miller)

Chicarita Creek. Three miles south of Poway. According to Gudde possibly an error for the Spanish *chiquita,* "little." (Gudde 76; Stein 27)

Chico Ravine. One mile west of Burnt Rancheria in the Lagunas. This is a classic example of a hybrid place name in a locality where two languages are spoken. Spanish "little" combined with the English generic "ravine." (Durham 14)

Chief Mountain. Two miles northeast of Pala. Named for the **Pala Chief** Mine; it is 500 feet west of the peak. In 1903 John Giddens, Frank A. Salmons, Pedro

Feiletch, and Bernard Heriot (Hiriart) discovered the Pala Chief Mine, named for the nearby Indian Reservation. It produced tourmalines, beryls, and kunzite (named for the gemologist Dr. George F. Kunz), a highly desirable rose-colored gemstone. It is on the 1997 Pechanga 7.5' Quadrangle. (Durham 14; Foord 163)

Chihuahua Creek, Valley, Mining District. East of Oak Grove and Highway 79. According to Gudde (76), "José Melandras, a goatherd who loved solitude, settled first near Warner Hot Springs. When too many people came to the valley, he moved farther inland to a place near Dead Man's Hole, and finally to the valley that became known as Chihuahua, for his native state in Mexico."

Children's Pool. South of Point La Jolla. This is an inlet traditionally called "The Swimming Hole" because it offered protected water. However, at high tide dangerous waves sometimes troubled the inlet. In 1931 Ellen Scripps (1836-1932) financed construction of a breakwater to shelter the inlet, and it was renamed Children's Pool. (Schaelchlin 10-11)

Chimney. Aside from two features in the desert (see Lindsay 118, 131), there are **Chimney Creek** near Doane Creek on Palomar Mountain, **Chimney Flats,** east of Boucher Hill also on Palomar Mountain, and **Chimney Lake,** an intermittent lake two miles west of Warner Springs. These may have been named for natural features or for chimneys that marked abandoned cabin sites. (Durham 15)

China Point. On San Diego Bay east of Point Loma at La Playa. Chinese fisherman once fished and lived here. On an 1895 map of the bay. (J. Davidson, "Chinese Settle on Point in San Diego Bay," *SDET,* November 8, 1935)

Chiquito Peak. (Span. "little") Two miles west of Descanso. Another classic hybrid place name. Sometimes called **Descanso Peak.** (Durham 15)

Chocolate Creek, Canyon. They are south of El Capitan Reservoir, and open to it. Perhaps from the color of the water, or less convincingly, these features got their name from an incident when padres served hot chocolate to Indians here. John Davidson quotes a mission document as saying that water for the mission "comes from a grove called El Chocolate which lies below the sierra of Cuyamat [Cuyamaca]." This suggests that the place might have had a Kumeyaay name, reconstituted as "chocolate." (J. Davidson, "El Cajon Named by Mission Padres," *SDET,* June 15, 1934)

Chollas Creek, Valley. (Mex. and Calif. Span. "a kind of cactus of the genus Opuntia"). About five miles south and east of the business district in San

Diego. The place appears on the 1782 Pantoja map as an Indian village called Ranchería de las Choyas near Indian Point. Station on the San Diego Cuyamaca & Eastern Railroad, it has given its name to the **Chollas View S.D. Southeastern Neighborhood.** Also the location of the **Chollas Heights Navy Radio Station,** established in 1916 and closed in the 1990s. **Chollas Reservoir** was originally part of the system that brought water to San Diego from Otay Lake. (Gudde 78; Hinds 64)

Christianitos Canyon. See **Cristianitos Canyon.**

Chula Vista, Chula Vista Junction. (Span. "pretty view") With Escondido, the most successful of the 1887 boom towns. An enterprise of Colonel William G. Dickinson, who laid out a suburb of fruit farms under the auspices of the San Diego Land and Town Company. Got its post office in 1890 and incorporated in 1911. **Chula Vista Junction** was on the National City & Otay Railroad. (Gudde 79; Salley 41; Webster 7)

Cienega Flats. One mile east of Rodriguez Mountain. (Stein 29; Durham 15)

City Heights. In eastern San Diego centered on University Ave. The district has had a bewildering series of names that reflect subdivision titles. This area was first called **Teralta,** possibly from the Spanish for "high ground." The name is suspect—either Terralta or Tierra Alta would be expected. Perhaps an English-speaking person's idea of a Spanish place name. Subdivided in the boom year 1887. It was subdivided again in 1906 as **Teralta** and **Teralta Heights.** In 1911-1912 the local post office was called **Teralta. City Heights** was subdivided in the same area in 1906-1907. From 1912 to 1986 the post office was called **East San Diego.** Then it became **City Heights.** The district was annexed to the city of San Diego in 1923. Today there are two San Diego Mid-City Neighborhoods, **City Heights East** and **City Heights West.** (Durham 23; Salley 61, 212; Security Title 9, 14, 46)

City Park. See **Balboa Park.**

Clairemont. One of San Diego's most populous northern districts. In 1950 Carlos Tavares and Associates began to develop 14,000 houses here on 4,000 acres. Tavares named the subdivision for his wife, Claire Tavares. It now includes these San Diego Northern Neighborhoods: **Clairemont Mesa West, Clairemont Mesa East,** and **North Clairemont.** (Claire Tavares Interview)

Clam, The. A small high knoll at La Jolla Caves that juts out like a clamshell. This is a popular spot for divers to (illegally) jump off the cliff into the ocean. (Schaelchlin 4)

Cleveland National Forest. President Theodore Roosevelt created it by executive order on July 1, 1908. Named in memory of President Grover Cleveland who died about a week earlier, June 24, 1908.

Clevenger Canyon. From Ramona descends to San Pasqual Valley. Named for the Clevenger family, father Archibald, son John, wife, and children. They were among the first San Pasqual settlers, in 1872. (Peet 65)

Clover Flat. Area five miles northeast of Campo, and a station on the San Diego, Arizona & Eastern Railroad. Enough people lived here to justify a Clover School as early as 1891. (Durham 16; San Diego County School Records Inventory)

Cobbleback Mountain. See **Woodson Mountain.**

Cobblestone Point. See **Ballast Point.**

Coches. (Mexican Span. "pigs") Five miles east of El Cajon on Interstate 8. Very small (28 acres) land grant, **Cañada de los Coches,** was given to Apolinaria Lorenzana in 1843. This became the ranch of Jesse Wilbur Ames, baptized a Catholic as Juliano Ames, April 17, 1838. He had a farm, a mill, and a winery here. Treasure seekers destroyed all the early buildings. Also **Coches Valley** and **Creek.** (Cowan 28; J. Davidson, "San Diego County Gazeteer," *SDET,* November 23, 1942)

Cockatoo Grove. In Telegraph Canyon on Proctor Valley Road on Otay Mesa. One of the more unusual county names. A contemporary, Alf Lansley (19), states that a man named Seiss had 160 acres of land at this location. As a hobby he raised white crested Australian cockatoos. Lansley recalled seeing the birds in a large cage located close to the road. The trees in the grove were eucalyptus. According to Davidson, the man was Charles Seiss and he was an Austrian citizen naturalized August 19, 1889, in San Diego. On Cuyamaca 30' 1903 Quadrangle. (J. Davidson, "San Diego County Gazeteer," *SDET,* January 24, 1941; Gudde 84)

Cockleburr Canyon. Opens into the sea south of San Onofre. One of the few places in the county named for a weed. (Durham 16)

Cocktail Springs. First stage station north of San Diego, on the divide between Sorrento Valley and San Dieguito Valley. Also called **Agua Zarca,** (Span. "light blue, azure"). This probably referred to the milky color of the water. It was also called **McKellar Stage Station.** A Scot named Ellery McKellar, reputedly with a fondness for the bottle, maintained this station, hence the name.

Mentioned in the *SDU,* August 7, 1875. (J. Davidson, "Writer Tells of Cocktail Springs," *SDET,* February 23, 1934; Ewing 38-40)

Colb Valley. Just east of the Hale Observatory on Palomar Mountain. Named for William J. Kolb (sic) or possibly Isaac Kolb, (see 1880 U.S. Census, 263), both settlers on the mountain. A mapmaker probably misspelled the name. (Durham 16; Stein 30)

Cold Beef Mine. Just south of the Golden Chariot Mine in Chariot Canyon, five miles south of Banner. Originally this was the Gold Reef Mine, but its owners bowed to public opinion and changed its name to the Cold Beef Mine, which is what everyone called it. Never a major producer, it had the most distinctive name in the district. On the 1997 Julian 7.5' Quadrangle. (Merriam 26)

Cold Spring, Stream. On the east side of Cuyamaca Peak, draining into the Sweetwater River. As noted in the Introduction, the generic, stream, is unexpected.

Cole Grade. On Rincon Indian Reservation. The road from Valley Center to the San Luis Rey Valley. Possibly named for John W. Cole who was a county official active in road building in the 1930s. (Index to the *SDU,* John W. Cole)

Coleman. Frederick Coleman was born in Kentucky in 1829 and was probably a former slave. The 1880 U.S. Census stated that he was a "Mu[latto]." Farming in the county in 1863, he married an Indian woman, took up land west of Wynola, and in January 1870 discovered placer gold in a stream named for him, **Coleman Creek,** not far from the San Diego River, beginning the Julian gold rush. A tent city on its banks was called **Coleman City.** Recruiting local Indian men as laborers, he built **Coleman Grade** between Santa Ysabel and Julian. Also see **Coleman Flat** five miles south of Santa Ysabel. (Durham 16; Fetzer, *Good Camp,* 8-11)

College Area S.D. Mid-City Neighborhood. Centered around San Diego State University which moved to this site in February 1931.

Combs Peak, Camp. The peak, at 6,191 feet elevation, is at the eastern end of Chihuahua Valley north of Warner Springs, and the camp, a locality, is six miles north of Warner Springs. John Combs was a well-known store owner active in both Descanso and upper San Luis Rey Valley. (Durham 16-17; Friends, *When Descanso,* 28-35; *SDU,* October 25, 1891)

Conejos Creek, Valley. (Span. "rabbits") Just south of El Capitan Reservoir. King Creek formerly joined the stream and the two combined were called **South**

Fork of the San Diego River. The name is a partial translation of Kumeyaay "rabbit house" *Hellyaaw Nyewaa,* the name of an Indian village at this location. (Couro and Hutcheson 21; Durham 17)

Coogan Ranch. One mile south of Buckman Springs on Buckman Springs Road close to Interstate 8. Hollywood movie star Jackie Coogan bought the ranch in the late 1920s for $159,000. In 1936 he was a passenger in a car with his father as driver when the car was involved in an accident resulting in his father's death and three other fatalities. Coogan sold the ranch for $40,000 and fled. (*SDU,* May 8, 1938)

Cordero. A cluster of former names in the Sorrento area. The name Cordero comes from the Spanish word for "lamb" and hence "the Savior." The San Diego place names, however, came from one or more men named Cordero who lived in this district in the 1770s and later: Joaquin Ignacio, soldier; Francisco; and Mariano Antonio, soldier. Sheepherders, one or more of them had a ranch house east of El Camino Real and south of Carmel Valley Road. According to Gudde (222) "the Cordero brothers" participated in the 1769 Portolá expedition. They were probably the soldiers Joaquin Ignacio and Juan Mariano. **Cordero** was a station on the California Southern Railroad midway between Del Mar and Selwyn. The name survives only as a street in Del Mar. See **Black Mountain, McGonigle Canyon, Loop's Beach,** and **Peñasquitos Slough.** (Bancroft I 735; J. Davidson, "Cordero Rich in History Telling," *SDT,* October 25, 1935; Ewing 10-14; Gudde 222; Northrop 9)

Core-Columbia S.D. Central Neighborhood. South of Little Italy. Named for the city's central business and administrative center and Columbia St., which runs north of Broadway between State and India Streets.

Coronado. (Span. *coronado* "crowned" from *corona* "crown") The name was suggested by an event dating from the Vizcaíno maritime expedition of 1602. Clergy on board Vizcaíno's ship saw four offshore islands on November 8, 1602, and called them Las Islas de los Coronados, referring to Los Cuatro Martíres Coronados, "the four crowned martyrs" who died for the faith during the reign of the Roman emperor Diocletian. In 1886 Elisha S. Babcock, H.L. Story, and others, organized the Coronado Beach Company to develop what was called the **San Diego Peninsula** because it had been a 4,185-acre land grant dating from 1846 held by Pedro C. Carillo called the **Rancho Peninsula de San Diego**. In January 1886 the company announced a naming contest with a $50 prize for the new community. More than 100 names, of widely varying origins and few of them Spanish, were submitted, including Cork, Serraland, Coronado Beach, Ingleside Beach, Monitor City, Villamar, La Frontera, Welcome City, Brooklyn, Estrella, Yalta [Yalta!], Bella Marine, Corona,

Belvedere, Hesperides, Ultima Thule, Lands End, Finnisterre, Beulah [a Biblical name], Shining Shore, Campobello, Hiawatha, The Lido [Ital. "fashionable beach"], Ojo del Puerto [Span. "eye of the port"], and El Cosoy [see **Cosoy**]. However, the name chosen was—Miramar, for Emperor Maximilian's palace on the Adriatic. (This was before E.W. Scripps came to San Diego to live. See **Miramar**.) "One of the owners" (very probably H.L. Story) wrote a letter to the *SDU* on January 27 protesting that the name Miramar was difficult to pronounce and recommending Coronado Beach instead, because it was a local name referring to the nearby islands. His opinion was accepted and Coronado Beach, or Coronado, it would be. (*SDU,* January 24, 27, 28, 1886) For other naming contests see **Marbello** and **Serra Mesa**. **Coronado Heights,** on lower San Diego Bay at the beach side, was a development dating from 1887 put on the market by the Coronado Beach Company. It was also a station on the Coronado Railway, Bay Belt Line. Ships waiting to enter San Diego Bay often lie out to sea off Coronado at a location called **Coronado Roads.** Compare with Hampton Roads off Hampton Virginia. **Coronado Tent City.** See **Tent City.** (Durham 17; Gudde 91)

Corral Canyon Spring, Mountain. The spring is west of Lake Morena, while the mountain is just north of Lake Sutherland. Stein says the mountain was given this name because of a large clearing on the mountain resembling a corral. (Durham 17; Stein 32)

Corte Madera Lake, Mountain, Valley. (Span. "wood yard") Five miles southwest of Pine Valley. In the 1870s rancher James E. Flinn was the first to settle in this area. In 1925 the tract was bought by a group of wealthy San Diegans for private ranches; in many cases their families still own them. Old money for San Diego, they are sometimes called "the Corte Madera Set." (Bawden 41; Gudde 92)

Cortes Bank. A hundred miles off the Coronado Islands. Captain Cropper first noted this underwater feature from his ship *Cortes* in 1853. Often misspelled as Cortez. Truly dedicated surfers make the long trip from the mainland to ride the huge waves here. See **Bishop Rock.** (Cleary and Stern 237; Gudde 92; *U.S. Coast Pilot,* 42)

Cortez S.D. Central Neighborhood. Named for the El Cortez Hotel located in the center of the neighborhood.

Cosmit Indian Reservation, Peak. Located off Engineers Road on North Peak in the Cuyamacas. Only 80 acres, dating from 1875. Engelhardt in his *San Diego Mission* (255) gives the name as Cusmich. It is a Kumeyaay name, but the meaning is unknown. (Kroeber 40; Pryde 64)

Cosoy. Also spelled Kosoyi. In 1769 the Spaniards found this Indian village near what would become Presidio Hill. Recorded in many early documents, and assumed to be a Kumeyaay name, its meaning is unknown. In 1897 residents of what became Gravilla applied for Cosoy as the name of their post office, but the authorities rejected it. (Engelhardt, *San Diego Mission,* 349; Salley 85)

Costa Brava. See **Silver Strand.**

Cota. Located eight miles southeast of Pala on today's Highway 76 on the Rincon Indian Reservation. Cota is a popular Luiseño family name, but perhaps the name came from Manuelita Cota, well-known Luiseño leader. Had its own post office from 1886 to 1890. The first post master was Philip S. Sparkman, a remarkable English immigrant who published early studies of Luiseño culture and language still valued today. Sparkman also maintained a store at the place where he was murdered (shot and his throat cut) for his money on May 19, 1907. No one was ever prosecuted for the crime. (Salley 49; *SDU,* May 21-22, 1907)

Cottonwood Creek, Canyon, Valley. Cottonwood is a common, water-loving, western tree. The creek rises in the southern Laguna Mountains and flows southwest to the Mexican border. Here it suffers a name-change, becoming the Tijuana River. The U.S. Board on Geographic Names in the late 1940s refused to change the stream's name to Tia Juana River. An earlier name was **Jesús María Creek.** There are also **Cottonwood Creeks** near Encinitas, Fallbrook, and Palomar Mountain. **Cottonwood Settlement.** See **Barrett.** (Durham 17; Gudde 93-94; Stein 33)

Couser Canyon. From the south opens into the San Luis Rey Valley three miles west of Pala. Named for R.V. Couser who settled in this district in about 1900. (Stein 34)

Cowles Mountain. Off Mission Gorge Road, three miles southwest of Santee. Highest point in the city of San Diego, at 1,591 feet elevation. Named for George A. Cowles (pronounced Coals, but the common pronunciation today is Cow-lz) who settled in the El Cajon Valley in 1879. It has been called **Black Mountain** (J. Davidson, "Restoring Old Names Urged," *SDET,* October 11, 1935)**, Mission Mountain** for the San Diego Mission, and **Long Range Mountain** (Blackburn 1931 map of San Diego County), perhaps because it can be seen from far away. (J. Davidson, "San Diego County Gazeteer," *SDET,* March 20, 1943). It also has been called **S Mountain,** because of the large S formerly painted high on the mountain by San Diego State University students. **Cowles Spring.** See **Dog Spring.** (Gudde 97 [He calls it Crowles Mountain.]; Stein 34)

Cowlestown, Cowlesville. See **Santee.**

Cranes Peak. On the south side of San Pasqual Valley, 1,054 feet elevation. Named for the nineteenth century Crane family. Peet (139) lists L.D. Crane and Myrle Crane as 1894 members of the San Pasqual Literary Society. (Durham 18)

Cravath Mine. See **Escondido Mine.**

Crescent Valley. See **Lake Hodges.**

Crest. About five miles east of El Cajon on La Cresta Road. Originally there were two communities at this location, **La Cresta** (north), largely developed by Barney Cornelius, and **Suncrest** (south)**,** but both names were merged as **Crest** in the 1960s. The name no doubt comes from the fact that the community is on the crest of a hill. In the 1920s promoters sold very small lots here for less than fifty dollars. In the 1930s the *San Diego Sun* offered lots here for $35 if you subscribed to the newspaper. The lots were intended only for seasonal use, but the automobile made it possible to live permanently in the area. (J. Davidson, "Suncrest Once Favorite Camp Site of Primitive Indians, Belief," *SDET,* November. 11, 1938; J. Davidson, "San Diego County Gazeteer," *SDET,* June 5, 1942; Lay 66-67)

Crestline. Road along the summit of Palomar Mountain. A good name that tells all.

Cristianitos Canyon. (Span. "the Christians" [diminutive]) Sometimes spelled Christianitos. Originates in Orange County and joins San Mateo Canyon near the Pacific. The Portolá expedition camped here on July 22, 1769, and Crespí named it **San Apolinario**, whose feast day is July 23. Soldiers called it **Los Cristianos** "the Christians" (the diminutive form came later.) Crespí also called it **Cañada de los Bautismos** "Valley of the Baptisms." These secondary names came from the fact that Crespí baptized two little Indian girls here. (Durham 18; Gudde 96, Stein 28)

Crosley Saddle. Five miles northwest of Boucher Hill in the Palomar District. The Vail Lake 1953 7.5' Quadrangle shows a nearby Crosley homestead. The generic, saddle, is unusual. (Durham 18)

Crouch Valley. Two of them. One is between Oceanside and Carlsbad. The other is in the Lagunas on the Sunrise Highway. These are two locations where Herbert Crouch, well-known English immigrant (d. 1927), owned land and ran his sheep. See his *Memoirs* at the SDHS. (Durham 18; Davidson Place Name File)

Crown Point. In Mission Bay. Originally the colorless but honest Bay Point. When developers got hold of it in the 1930s for their own reasons they called it Crown Point. Where in Mission Bay does royalty live?

Crystal Pier. At Pacific Beach. When the pier was built in 1927 it had a short-lived dance hall at the end of the pier called the Crystal Ballroom, complete with a suspended glittering crystal sphere. The ballroom is gone but the name survives. (Kooperman 56)

Cuca Land Grant. Immediately east of Pauma Rancho on the San Luis Rey River. This grant was claimed in 1845 by María Juana de los Angeles, 2,174 acres. Later known as **Mendenhall Ranch** for a prominent ranching family. The name Cuca has been a puzzle. Bright (in Gudde 98) thinks it may be a Kumeyaay name for a root or fruit, although it is in Luiseño territory. Stein (68) asserts that it is a Spanish word meaning "a root used as a coffee substitute." Sometimes spelled Kuka. (Cowan 31)

Cudahy Slough. In today's Moreno District not far from the San Diego River. Early in the twentieth century the Cudahy Meat Packing Company purchased the local Hardy slaughterhouse at this site, giving the slough its name. Only Cudahy Place survives today to mark the spot. On the La Jolla 1953 7.5' Quadrangle. (Durham 18; Friends, *When Descanso,* 72)

Cueros de Venado Land Grant. (Span. "deer hides") Granted to Juan María Marrón in 1834. It did not come before the U.S. Land Commission under this name, but possibly as the Agua Hedionda Grant. (Cowan 32)

Cupa. See **Warner Springs.**

Custom House Peak. See **El Cajon Mountain.**

Cutca Valley. On the northwest side of Palomar Mountain. Another puzzling, probably Indian, name. According to Bright (in Gudde 99) its meaning is unknown, but it is in Luiseño territory. Also known as **Hut Cut Valley.** (Stein 35)

Cuyamaca. Kumeyaay *'ekwii* plus *'emak*, "cloud" plus "behind," but the element *'emak* refers to the *preceding* element, so that an adequate translation would be "behind the clouds." Couro and Hutcheson (3) give it as *'Ekwiiyemak,* "Cuyamaca. (literally, behind the clouds)." Originally this was an Indian village just north of Stonewall Peak, but the name was applied to the surrounding **Cuyamaca Mountains,** 30 miles east of San Diego. Settlers called its highest peak, the second highest in the county at 6,512 feet elevation, **Cuyamaca Peak** or **South Peak** because it is the southernmost of the three Cuyamaca peaks or **Sawmill Peak** because as early as 1870 it had a sawmill on its wooded eastern slopes. **Rancho Cuyamaca** was a land grant of 35,501 acres given to Agustín Olvera in 1845. A post office on the rancho, now in the state park, was called **Stonewall** from 1873 to 1876, then **Stratton** for local rancher James Stratton from 1887 to 1888, then **Cuyamaca** (never Cuyamaca City) 1888 to 1907. The post office was at the **Stonewall (Jackson) Mine**, largest gold mine ever in today's San Diego County. (Presumably a Southerner named the mine Stonewall Jackson for the Confederate general; it's usually said that Jackson was dropped from the name because local citizens resented honoring a Confederate officer.) By far the mine's most productive years were 1887-1890 when a new owner, California governor Robert W. Waterman used his money to sink a 600-foot shaft at the mine and hit a bonanza. After spending a bundle, Waterman found gold worth a million dollars. The mine closed when it ran out of gold ore, not when it was flooded, as is often said. The mine produced $2 million in gold from 1870 to 1891 when gold was worth $20.67 an ounce. (Fetzer *Good Camp* 59-76) As of 1932 most of the rancho became **Cuyamaca Rancho State Park.** Built at the site of a former CCC camp, a school camp, **Camp Cuyamaca,** has been in the park since 1945. A reservoir, **Cuyamaca Lake,** was created behind **Cuyamaca Dam** on Boulder Creek near the park in 1887. From 1924 to about 1950 developer Ed Fletcher operated **Cuyamaca Lodge** at a site uphill from Highway 79 near Cuyamaca Lake; after it closed it became state park property and was razed. Stein (35) says that he once heard the name Cuyamaca as **Queermack.** An English speaker, overwhelmed by the exotic name, reshaped it as Queer Mack, an example of original folk etymology. In 1933 the U.S. Board on Geographic Names, fortunately, rejected the name Cloud Peak for Cuyamaca Peak. (Cowan 32; Durham 19; Langdon in Gudde 99; Pryde 24; Salley 52)

Cuyapaipe Indian Reservation, Peak. (Kumeyaay, *'ewii-yaapaayp* "leaning rock." Langdon in Gudde (99), and Couro and Hutcheson (5) give the same spelling and meaning.) It is in the southern Laguna Mountains. This is a striking rock formation on the reservation, dating from 1893, which has 4,102 acres. The peak, at 6, 378 feet elevation, is the third highest in the county. (Pryde 64)

- D -

Daley Flat. Three miles south of Santa Ysabel. Named for Thomas Daley, Julian resident, Irish immigrant, bachelor, stockraiser, and butcher. (Durham 19; Jasper, *Trail-Breakers,* 108-109)

Daly Creek, Flat. Four miles northwest of El Cajon Mountain on the Barona Indian Reservation. Named for Thomas J. Daley (sic), attorney and promoter. About 1890 copper was discovered here which was mined until about 1920. (Durham 19; LeMenager, *Ramona,* 117-119; LeMenager, *Off* 121-126)

Dameron Valley. On Palomar Mountain northeast of Boucher Hill. Named for rancher Mit Damron (sic) who came here in the 1860s. (Durham 19, Stein 37)

Dan Price Creek. Two miles north of Julian. Named for a rancher who came to Julian in 1884 with his family. (Jasper, *Trail-Breakers,* 178)

Daney Canyon. Eight miles north of Lakeside, opening into San Vicente Valley. Probably named for members of the Daney family, several of them lawyers, who had interests in the Ramona area. (Biographical File)

Darnall S.D. Mid-City Neighborhood. Takes its name from Darnall Elementary School which in turn was named for Orton Darnall. He was on the San Diego City Board of Education, 1927-1949. An earlier name for this district was **Redwood Villages,** definitely not a San Diego name. (*SDU,* December 27, 1951)

Davidson, Camp. YMCA camp in Pine Hills. Named for banker G. Aubrey Davidson (d. 1957). He was chairman of the California Pacific International Exposition of 1935-1936 in San Diego. (Biographical File)

Davis Spring. See **Iron Spring.**

Daviston. See **Jamacha.**

De Luz, De Luz Creek. Eight miles northwest of Fallbrook. At least three theories have been advanced to account for this name, none of them completely convincing or documented. Early records show this place as **Corral de Luz.** It's been said that the original name was Corral de Luce, for an Englishman who brought a herd of horses here. Spanish speakers then reshaped the strange English word Luce (by Spanish folk etymology) into a familiar Spanish word *luz,* "light." Unfortunately, I have never been able find a Luce who lived in the north county. Another theory asserts that it was named for a Basque sheepherder named Luz. There is also the possibility it was somehow related to the meaning of "light." The place got a post office in 1882 as Deluz. **De Luz Station** is on the junction of the De Luz railroad spur. **De Luz Heights** is about five miles east of De Luz. (Anonymous, *History* 73; J. Davidson, "Briton Gives Name to Beauty Spot," *SDET,* October 2, 1936; Philip S. Rush, "El Corralito de Luz," *Southern California Rancher,* July 1951, 3; Stein 38)

Deadman. Finding a corpse is memorable, and several county place names are based on that experience. **Deadman Flat** is five miles south of Santa Ysabel. The exact source of the name is unknown. **Deadman Hole** is in a canyon five miles south of Oak Grove. In 1858 a Butterfield driver found a corpse at a spring here. From there the story grew: Jasper thought three (or was it five?) bodies had been found there, all victims of foul play. (Durham 19; Jasper *Trail-Breaker,* 350-353). **Deadman's Point. (Punta de los Muertos** on the 1782 Pantoja Map). Now inland at Market Street and Harbor Drive. The dead men were sailors who died at sea from scurvy. Debate rumbles about where the dead men came from. The most convincing theory is Harlow's (8), who said they came from two ships, the *San Carlos* under Vicente Vila that anchored at Point Guijarros on May 1, 1769, and Perez's *San Antonio* which arrived on April 11, 1769. Others don't agree. See Pourade, *Silver,* 160. (Durham 19; Gudde 103, 304; Kooperman 278)

Deer. A popular specific place name. Deer are common all over the county. **Deer Canyon,** near Del Mar; **Deer Lake,** an ephemeral lake a mile southeast from Julian; **Deer Park,** five miles northeast of Pine Valley, the site of some gold mining; and **Deer Spring,** on Cuyamaca Peak. (Durham 20)

Deerhorn Flat, Spring, Canyon. Five miles northeast of Dulzura. This is a classic example of a name originating from a specific incident. John and Albert Walker, early settlers, here found two dead bucks, their horns locked. The double horns, thrown into a tree, marked the place. (Schmid 30)

Dehesa (Span. "pasture ground") At the head of Harbison Canyon, a mile from Sycuan Indian Reservation. First post office in 1885 under the name **Sweetwater,** from the nearby river, then as Dehesa in 1888. (Gudde 105; Salley 54)

Dehr Creek. Six miles south of Santa Ysabel in Pine Hills. Named for John Dehr, an early settler. (J. Davidson, "San Diego County Gazeteer," *SDET,* March 1, 1940)

Del Cerro S.D. Eastern Neighborhood. (Span. "of the hill") The neighborhood is located on a prominent hill with outstanding views. This was the name of the original subdivision dating from April 1955. Perhaps it was modeled on the name of Del Mar. (Security Title 13)

Del Dios. (Span. "of God, God's place") Five miles west of Escondido. A development of small homes now annexed to Escondido. (Stein 37)

Del Mar. (Span. "of the sea") The town, probably, like Ramona, got its name from the title of a literary work, Bayard Taylor's one-page poem "The Fight of Paso Del Mar." In the poem "Pablo of San Diego" and "Bernal, the herdsman of Chino" meet on a narrow path above the sea and duel with knives, plunging to mutual deaths on the rocks below. The setting resembles Point Loma, but Taylor published the poem in 1849 before he had visited California, and so that is unlikely (*Poetical Works,* 1883, 108-109. The poem's text is also in Innis 15-17). Possibly Juliana Osuna of Rancho Peñasquitos or the wife of Theodore M. Loop, an early promoter of the town, came up with the name. Developed in 1884. Post office established in 1885. **Del Mar Heights S.D. Northern Neighborhood** is in the city of San Diego just east of Del Mar and west of Interstate 5. **Del Mar Racetrack**, under the auspices of the Del Mar Turf Club, Bing Crosby president, had its first season in 1937. For more about the poem see **Russian Well.** For Del Mar Castle see **Castle.** (Davidson Place Name File; Gudde 105; Salley 54; Stein 38)

Derby, Camp. Temporary army camp in 1935 in Balboa Park for the California-Pacific International Exposition. Named for Lieutenant George H. Derby, army officer and humorist stationed in early San Diego. (Hinds 52)

Derby Dike. In 1853 the same Lieutenant George H. Derby supervised the building of a dike to divert the San Diego River from the bay, where it was depositing unwanted silt, into False Bay, now Mission Bay. His dike washed out in 1855, and was replaced in 1876. The river now flows directly into the ocean. (Gudde 107)

Descanso. (Span. "resting place") Originally called **Guatay**. Thirty-five miles east of San Diego on the Sweetwater River. According to Margaret Langdon, Guatay was a Spanish pronunciation of Kumeyaay *wataay* "big house," that is, "ceremonial house" from *'ewaa* "house" plus *'etaay* "big" (Gudde 155). Before the construction of Highway 80 about 1920, the approach to the settlement from the west came directly from Viejas. The route required a hot, dry thousand-foot climb over the Puertezuelo, the historic "little pass," with a sharp drop to the Sweetwater River and cool shade under spreading oak trees. Descanso was indeed a place to rest. The post office, **Descanso,** was established in 1877. Sometimes it's said the name is related to a specific incident when Ysadora Ellis welcomed a party of surveyors to "Descanso." (Friends, *Descanso,* 4). **Descanso Junction.** Two miles south of Descanso on Highway 80. In 1912 E.D. and Marie McDonald platted a subdivision here they called **Bohemia,** and Billy Ryan tried to develop a resort here called **Bohemian Grove,** no doubt emulating the famous rich man's playground on the Russian River. **Descanso Peak,** see **Chiquito Peak.** (Salley 35; Stein 38)

Devil. According to Gudde (107) devil names are very common in California. **Devil's Canyon** opens into San Mateo Canyon in the extreme northwestern part of the county. **Devil's Jumpoff** (a steep bluff) is seven miles southwest of Santa Ysabel above the San Diego River. **Devil's Punchbowl,** a swirling waterfall, is in the lower stretches of Boulder Creek above the San Diego River. (Durham 21; Stein 39)

Dewey Corners. Near Campo. This is an example of an honorific name. Charles F. Emery named this place, where he had a store, in honor of Admiral George Dewey and his recent triumph at the Battle of Manila in 1898. There was also a Dewey Mine in the Grapevine District named for the admiral. (J. Davidson, "Two Places in S.D. County Named for Dewey after Manila Victory," *SDET,* n.d.)

Dexter Peak. One mile southwest of Descanso. This is another honorific name. The U.S. Board on Geographic Names named this peak for John Porter Dexter (d. 1960), a resident of the area, in 1961. (Durham 21; Gudde 108)

Dexter Valley. This is an early name for Moreno Valley leading north from Lakeside. E. Dexter, surveyor and Civil Engineer, had a home here with a stop on the San Diego and Cuyamaca Railroad called **Dexter Station.** (Lakeside 8, 27)

Dick Spring. East of Oak Grove on Highway 79. Stein (39) says it was named for a dog, Dick, that once fell into the spring.

Dictionary Hill. Ridge north of Sweetwater Reservoir. Was originally called **Lookout Mountain** because of the fine views from its summit. In 1910 the Interstate Realty and Improvement Co. bought 480 acres here that it subdivided as East San Diego Villa Heights. When a person bought a $109 set of encyclopedias he got a lot free. This site became known as **Encyclopedia Heights,** but somehow this was transmogrified into **Dictionary Hill,** a name that, at least, was two syllables shorter. Most lot owners lost their land for non-payment of property taxes. (Adema 117-119; Gudde 109; Stein 39)

Distoma. See Linda Vista.

Divide. Named for Tecate Divide between La Posta and Boulevard. See **Tecate Divide.** Had its own post office 1889-1890. It's difficult to understand why a post office was needed at this remote location; possibly it was a stage stop. (Durham 11, Salley A2)

Division. Five miles west of Campo on the Mexican border. A typical official railroad name. On the San Diego Arizona & Eastern Railroad. (Stein 40)

Dixon Lake. Three miles northeast of Escondido. Named for James B. Dixon (d. 1978) an official of the Escondido Mutual Water Co. (McGrew, *Hidden Valley,* 40)

Doane Lake, Valley, Creek. In Palomar Mountain State Park. Named for brothers George and John Doane who homesteaded in the area in the 1860s. They sold out in 1905. (Gudde 110, Stein 40)

Dodge Valley. Just east of Oak Grove. Named for F.E. Dodge who came here for his health in 1887. (Durham 22; Stein 40)

Dog Spring. On the west side of Cowles Mountain. Formerly known as **Cowles Spring.** (Stein 34)

Doghouse Junction. Near the summit of Otay Mountain on unpaved roads. Was it named for a doghouse that is no longer there? (Brandais 121-122; Durham 22)

Dogpatch. See **Canyon City.**

Don. (Span. "gentleman") Eleven miles north of Oceanside on Santa Fe railroad. Ideal succinct railroad name. (Durham 22; Hanna 88)

Donohoe Mountain, Spring. Near Dulzura. Named for Stephen A. Donohoe, an early settler and mine operator. (Durham 22; Stein 40)

Dos Picos County Park. Five miles southwest of Ramona. Named for two nearby hills of nearly identical height. (*SDU,* August 28, 1971)

Double Peak. Six miles northeast of Rancho Santa Fe. No doubt named for its double summit. (Durham 22; Stein 40)

Doyleville, Doyleville Creek. At Agua Hedionda Ranch. Place of residence and nearby stream named for James Doyle, a Scottish stone mason and farmer. (J. Davidson, "Doyleville's Namesake Teamster," *SDET,* July 21, 1939)

Dry Lake. See **Laguna Seca.**

Dubbers. Station on San Diego Arizona & Eastern Railroad between Titus and Carrizo Gorge. Probably named for a railroad civil engineer Adolph Dubber. Louise B. Dubber was his widow. Obituary *SDU,* January 3, 1937. (Durham 22; Stein 41)

Duckville. A collection of shacks on the east side of Mission Bay, some with names such as Hotel de Mallard, Greenwing Teal, and Sprig. A favorite male hunting and fishing getaway, from 1885 to about 1930. On the 1903 La Jolla 15' Quadrangle. (Durham 22; Kooperman II 574)

Dulzura, Creek, Summit, Valley, Camp. (Span. "sweetness") Forty miles east of San Diego on Highway 94. Supposedly named by Isadora Hagenbuck, an early settler's wife. Once a great center for bee culture, hence the name. John S. Harbison, the honey king, stationed hives here. Got its own post office in 1886. **Dulzura Camp.** In 1911 the U.S. Army established a camp from where cavalry could patrol the nearby Mexican border. The post was at a place called **Camps Grove** for its owners Charles and Lillian Camp. (Hinds 30; Salley 60; Schmid 48; Stein 41)

DuPont, Fort. See Fort Stockton.

Durasnitos Spring. (Span. *duraznitos* "little peaches") Four miles west of Ramona. (Gudde 116; Stein 41)

Dutch Flats. Dutch is the early American name for German, from *Deutsch* "German." This was 500 acres of mud flats on the north end of San Diego Bay that was dredged out to create military bases on solid ground yet further north. On the 1859 U.S. map of San Diego Bay this feature is called **Grass Flats.** (J. Davidson, "No Clue to 'Dutch Flats', Navy, Marine Base Site," *SDET,* December 3, 1937; Durham 22)

Dutchman Canyon. Near Dulzura. Named for a German sheepherder who died before 1880. Dorothy Clark Schmid, Dulzura historian, won approval of this name from the U.S. Board on Geographic Names in 1974. (Schmid 153; Stein 21)

Dyar Spring. In Cuyamaca Rancho State Park four miles southeast of Cuyamaca Peak. Named for the Dyar family from Michigan via Beverly Hills who owned Rancho Cuyamaca from 1923 to 1933. (Durham 23)

Dyche Valley. On the eastern slope of Palomar Mountain. Named for George V. Dyche who bought the farm of Joseph Smith, first settler on the mountain, after Smith's murder in 1868. (Stein 41)

Dye Canyon, Mountain. Nine miles east of Ramona. Named for John S. Dye, from Kentucky. He settled here in 1865 after marrying a local girl, Mary Ann Warnock. (Jasper, *Trail-Breakers,* 256-257)

- E -

Eagle. Golden eagles were, and are, common in the county; they played an important part in Indian ceremonies. **Eagle Crag** is located four miles northwest of Boucher Hill on Palomar Mountain, elevation 5,077 feet. The generic crag is unusual for the county, and hints that the namer had literary interests. **Eagles Nest** is located in the northeast corner of the county within Los Coyotes Indian Reservation. Originally Hiram Keyes and his wife settled here in the 1880s. According to Stein (42) Keyes translated the Cahuilla name for this place into English as Eagles Nest. Ed Fletcher later purchased it for recreation for his large family. Here they had horses for riding, a pond, etc. For an early sketch of the place see Douglas Gunn's *Picturesque San Diego* illustration no. 44. **Eagle Peak** is ten miles southeast of Ramona, elevation 3,226 feet. Constructed in 1889, **Eagle Peak Road** led from Lakeside to Pine Hills. The completion of El Capitan Reservoir in 1933 flooded its central portion. (Durham 23) **Eagle-High Peak Mine.** Located about a quarter-mile east of Julian off "C" Street. William Moran registered the Eagle Mine in April 1870. Eventually it connected with the adjoining High Peak Mine that was registered a month earlier. The two mines produced between $50,000 and $100,000 in gold. On the 1997 Julian 7.5' Quadrangle. Now a popular walking tour leads through the privately-owned mines, from one side of the hill to the other. (Fetzer, *Good Camp,* 18-20)

Earthquake Bay. The 1855 *Geological Map of the Country Between San Diego and the Colorado River,* drawn by W.P. Blake, gives this name to the coast between San Juan Capistrano and San Diego, following the assumed route of the Rose Canyon Fault. The name never stuck, but perhaps as a salutary warning, it should have.

East Field. On Otay Mesa. Established April 7, 1918. Named for Major Whitten J. East, probably a fatality in an airplane crash. Deactivated after World War I. (Hinds, 99-100)

East Grade. This is a popular name for east-west County Road S-7 from Palomar Mountain to Lake Henshaw.

East San Diego. See **City Heights.**

East Village S.D. Central Neighborhood. East of the Gaslamp District. Once was **South College Neighborhood,** for San Diego City College. It includes Petco Park, a baseball stadium completed in 2004. The late architect Wayne Buss named the neighborhood in emulation of Manhattan's East (Greenwich)

Village (*SDU-T,* December 12, 2004, J1-5). A West Village will no doubt appear in the future.

Eastwood Creek, Hill. Joseph Stancliff planned a townsite a mile west of Julian he called **Eastwood.** Gone, but the name survives in the creek and hill. (Durham 23, 37, Jasper, *Trail-Breakers,* 30)

Eatonville. See Encinitas.

Echo Dell, Valley. Where Boulder Creek crosses over Boulder Creek Road west of Cuyamaca Peak. (Durham 23)

Echoes. Seven miles southwest of Temecula, four miles northeast of Howe. Supposedly named for a dry well that yielded only echoes. Had a post office 1886-1887. (Salley 62; Durham 26)

Eckener Pass. Three miles east of Boulevard. After leaving Los Angeles, on August 27, 1929, a German airship, the *Graf Zeppelin,* flew over this area on its famous west-east world flight. The captain was Dr. Hugo Eckener (sometimes spelled Eckner.) Named by a local developer, M.D. Johnson; Eckener Pass was the site of a small community. (*SDU,* August 27, 1929; J. Davidson. "San Diego County Gazeteer," *SDET,* July 4, 1941)

Egger Highlands S.D. Southern Neighborhood. Named for Robert J. Egger (1901-1978), a Swiss immigrant, farmer, dairyman, and developer. In 1962 the Robert Egger no. 1 oil well was drilled in this area. It was dry. (Obituary *SDU,* January 21, 1978; Pryde 106)

Eisenecke Valley, Creek. (German "iron corner") Midway between Dulzura and Potrero. Name used by Mr. and Mrs. Billie Bloch (a very German name) for their ranch, possibly because of surrounding cliffs. On the Cuyamaca 1903 30' Quadrangle. (Gudde 119)

El Cajon. The Kumeyaay name for this valley was Matari meaning "wide valley" according to Edward H. Davis (*Diegueño,* n.p.). The padres called it **Rancho Santa Mónica** (for the mother of St. Augustine), but the Mexican land grant was called **Rancho Cajón de San Diego.** Including 48,799 acres, it was granted to María Antonio Estudilla de Pedrorena in 1845. This name, "the box" was given to the valley because it appeared to be completely enclosed; in fact it drains to the north and the San Diego River. After the American conquest it was called **Knox's Corners** or **Knox's Station** for Amaziah Knox, a hotel-keeper. On T.D. Beasley's Map of San Diego County the settlement was called **Knoxville.** This might have become the name of the post office, and possibly the town, but this name was already in use in northern California. In 1878 the town's first post office was established as **El Cajon. El Cajon Mountain.** Elevation 3,684 feet. Often erroneously called El Capitan Mountain probably because of its proximity to the dam and reservoir of this name. Benjamin Hayes (290-291) called it **Custom House Peak,** probably because with its massive cliffs it resembled a large building. (Cowan 21; Gudde 119; Salley 63)

El Camino Real. (Span. "royal road") Originally this meant a public road connecting settlements or missions, but now it has come to mean the north-south road connecting the California missions. (Gudde 62)

El Campo, Camp. See **Camp Lockett.**

El Capitán Grande. On the San Diego River five miles east of Lakeside. The Spanish term *capitán* referred to the leader of an Indian band; the English equivalent was Captain. This title, El Capitán Grande, may have referred to an outstanding early Kumeyaay leader, Francisco. The Kumeyaay name for the large Indian village that existed here for many years was **Kwellyemak** (Couro and Hutcheson, 29), meaning "behind the mountain." (For a discussion of the element *emak* see the entry under **Cuyamaca.**) The name El Capitán Grande, referring to the Indian village, was used as early as 1853. The Indian reservation **Capitan Grande Indian Reservation** (without the Spanish article) dates from 1875 and includes 15,753 acres. When **El Capitan Dam** and **Reservoir** (with the article and without the word Grande) were established in 1933, following years of litigation, the reservoir flooded most of the reservation. The residents moved either to the Barona Indian Reservation or the Viejas Indian Reservation. In the nineteenth century many white settlers lived on or near the reservation; it had its own post office from 1886 to 1887 and from 1891 to 1895. For an article on the place's name and role in the Indian uprising of 1775 see Rensch, "Cullamác." (Pryde 136; Salley 63)

El Cerrito S.D. Mid-City Neighborhood. (Span. "little hill") The most important subdivision in this area was called **El Cerrito Heights,** 1926-1928, 1951. Probably named for the slight rise in the terrain at about 56th St. and El Cajon Blvd. Because the neighborhood has been developed over a long period of time it has a great diversity of architectural styles. (Security Title 14)

El Desembarcadero. See **Spanish Landing.**

El Granito Springs. Just east of Grossmont. First exploited in 1876. Early in the twentieth century its water was sold commercially on a large scale as "soda pop." The spring is now paved over. There's still an El Granito Ave. near this location. (Guy 84-89; Kooperman II 38)

El Monte County Park. Its name has nothing to do with a mountain. Gudde (245) says Spanish *monte* means "woods, or a mountain densely covered with trees." El Monte got its name because of the dense growth of oaks and other trees in the San Diego River Valley at this place. See El Monte in Los Angeles County. (Gudde 122)

El Moro. See **Morro Hill.**

El Nido. (Span. "nest") Settlement on San Ysidro Creek between Janal Rancho and Jamul Rancho. Lost when Lower Otay dam was built in 1897. The *San Diego City-County Directory, 1895,* lists 29 adult males, probably most with families, living here. The place had its own post office from 1888 to 1900. (Durham 35; Salley 64)

El Prado Meadow. Two miles west of Monument Peak in the Lagunas. This is a classic tautology: Spanish *el prado* means "meadow," so this place is named Meadow Meadow.

El Salto. (Span. "jump, leap") A waterfall two miles from Oceanside on Buena Vista Creek. (Durham 24)

Elanus Canyon. Formerly this was a nameless canyon opening into Murphy Canyon in San Diego. In 1977 the U.S. Board on Geographic Names officially named it Elanus Canyon for *Elanus leucurus,* scientific name for the white-tailed kite. If you see a large white bird hovering over grassy fields in this area, you've seen an *Elanus Leucurus.* (Durham 23-24; Unitt 43)

Elena Mountain. This feature, elevation 3,257 feet, appeared for the first time on the Barrett Lake 1960 7.5' Quadrangle. Surveyors and cartographers are notorious for their custom of placing the names of girlfriends or wives on USGS maps, and my guess is that now we have at least one example of this kind of naming in San Diego County. But this begs the question: who is Elena?

Elfin Forest. West of Lake Hodges. In 1959 three promoters bought 20 acres here and developed it into a large private camp (*SDU,* March 1, 1972). Elfin Forest is another name for chaparral. Note the book title by W. S. Head, *The California Chaparral: An Elfin Forest.*

Elliott, Camp. Its original name was **Camp Holcomb**, probably for Major General Thomas Holcomb, Commandant of the U.S. Marines in 1937. Established in 1941 on 26,000 acres north of San Diego as far as Poway. It was both a Marine Corps and Naval base. At times the California National Guard also was based here. The last of the base was liquidated in 1960. The camp's name honors General George S. Elliott, USMC, 10th Marine Corps Commandant, 1903-1910. (Durham 11; Hinds 71-80)

Ellis Spring. On Old Highway 80 west of Descanso. In 1970 dedicated as "Ellis Wayside Vista Point" for Charles Ellis (1834-1919), Norwegian immigrant and major landowner in the region. (Friends, *Descanso,* 16)

'Ellykwanan. See **Santa Ysabel.**

Elvira. On the Santa Fe Railroad ten miles north of San Diego. Unknown Spanish woman's name. This was a railroad maintenance center that closed in 1958. On La Jolla 1996 7.5' Quadrangle. (Davidson Place Name File)

Emerald Hills S.D. Southeastern Neighborhood. Named for the subdivision called Emerald Hills Country dating from 1950. (Security Title 15)

Emeralite Mine. See **Mountain Lily Mine.**

Emery. Eight miles east of Descanso between Pine Valley and Buckman Springs. The original name of this place was one of the more colorful in the county: **Un Gallo Flat.** (Span. "one rooster") Three early settlers tried to raise chickens here, but predators took all of them except one rooster. They protected it by bringing it in the house every night. Hence the name, still on the Mt. Laguna 1960 7.5' Quadrangle. Emery was named for William S. Emery, early settler. It had its own post office from 1882 to 1887. Emery's wife came up with an earlier name, **Glen Cliff.** Stein (143) says postal authorities rejected it because this name was already in use in California, but there was never a Glen Cliff in California. The name survives as Glencliff Camp on Cuyapaipe 1942 15' Quadrangle. (J. Davidson, "One Rooster Gives Valley Name," *SDET,* March 9, 1934; Durham 24; Salley 66; Stein 143)

Emily City. Small tent town along Coleman Creek west of Julian early in the 1870 gold boom. Note the term "City" typical of many mining settlements. Emily's identity is unknown. (Durham 83)

Emory, Fort. In 1942 the U.S. Army built this base at the south end of Silver Strand, at a place sometimes called Coronado Heights. Gun emplacements here were equipped with heavy artillery. Named for Brigadier General William H. Emory (1811-1887), who was topographical engineer for Kearny's army of

1846-1847, and who fought in the Civil War. The U.S. Navy took over the base in 1948. (Durham 70-71, Gudde 123, Hinds 24)

Encanto. (Span. "enchantment") Also **Encanto Southeastern S.D. Neighborhood.** Its original name was **Klauber Park.** Abraham Klauber subdivided it in 1891. His daughter Alice supposedly chose the area and renamed it for its charming climate and sea views. The district got its own post office in 1909. Annexed to the City of San Diego in 1916. (Gudde 123; Salley 67; Stein 44)

Encinitas, Encinitas Valley, Creek. On the coast between Cardiff and Leucadia. The Portolá expedition called it **Cañada de los Encinos** (Span. "canyon of the oaks"). Site of a Mexican land grant named **Rancho Encinitos** or **Cañada de San Alejo**, granted to Andrés Ibarra, 4,431 acres, 1842. See **San Elijo.** Nathan Eaton, hermit and bee keeper, supposedly the brother of Civil War General C. Eaton, built the first house here in 1881, hence the early name **Eatonville** (*SDU,* July 9, 1884.) In 1881 the first station at the site on the California Southern Railroad was called **Encinitos.** The townsite was laid out in 1883 with its own post office, **Encinitas,** with a change in spelling, a year earlier. (Cowan 33-34; Gudde 123; Salley 67; Stein 45)

Encyclopedia Heights. See **Dictionary Hill.**

Engineer. Engineer Creek and **Springs** are located about a mile east of Dulzura. This was near a surveyors' camp for the never-to-be-built Texas and Pacific Railroad. (Surveyors were then often called engineers.) Before this, the place was called **Harbison's Field,** because John Harbison stationed beehives here. **Engineers Road.** Leaves Cuyamaca Lake and proceeds five miles northwest to Boulder Creek Road. Developer Ed Fletcher sponsored this road because it connected the lake with his development at Pine Hills. In 1917-1918 army engineers from Camp Kearny worked on the road to gain practical experience, hence the name. Not completed until the 1930s. (Davidson Place Name File; Fetzer *Year,* 46-48; Schmid 139)

Escondido, Escondido Creek. (Span. "hidden") The Spanish word designated a hidden water source as *agua escondida,* and this appears to be the origin of the place name here. However, as early as 1861 Dr. George McKinstry called the place Escondido in his diary, now at the SDHS. The masculine form Escondido may have come from the nearby Escondido Mine, dating from the late 1850s (see below). Originally the site was on the Rincón del Diablo land grant. In 1885 a Los Angeles syndicate, the Stockton Company, began to develop a town site here. The first post office, 1881-1883, located at Deer

Springs Road on the road to Los Angeles was called **Apex** (Latin "summit")
because it was at a high point on the road. In 1883 the post office moved to the
town site and took the name Escondido. The **Escondido Canal** is not in the
town, but brings water from the San Luis Rey River to Lake Wohlford. It dates
from the early twentieth century when irrigation water was brought to Escondido.
Escondido Mine. At a very early date prospectors discovered a one-mile out-
cropping of gold ore parallel and west of today's Bear Valley Parkway, and
mostly south of Highway 78, about two miles from the center of Escondido.
The earliest discovery at the south end of the lode was called the Escondido
Mine. Dr. George McKinstry recorded miners at work here in 1859 in his diary
at SDHS. After 1897 it was called the **Cleveland-Pacific Mine** because Ohio
investors bought it. As late as 1925 it had eight employees. Total production
was an estimated $250,000, but this may be too high. To the north of the
Escondido Mine was the **Oro Fino Mine** (Span. "fine gold"), owned by O.J.
Stough of San Diego. On the north side of Highway 78 was the **Cravath Mine**,
named for farmer and miner August K. Cravath. All the mines were eventually
razed and the land sold for farm and home sites. All that remains from the
mining days are the street names El Dorado Dr. and Zlatibor Ranch Rd., which
in the Czech language means "Golden Grove Ranch Road." (Weber 120, 123,
142) **Lake Escondido** see **Lake Wohlford.** (Gudde 124; McGrew *Hidden Valley,* 19, 23 et seq.; Salley 8)

Esmeralda Mine. (Span. "emerald") This is a gem mine located four miles
northwest of Mesa Grande. It is on the 1996 AAA San Diego County Map. This
was a popular name for a mine—there were at least five of them in California.
There is also an Esmeralda County in Nevada. All were probably named for
Esmeralda, the Spanish gypsy heroine of Victor Hugo's novel, *The Hunchback
of Notre Dame,* 1831. (Gudde 124-125; *Mining*; Weber 89-91)

Eucalyptus. These hardy drouth-resistant trees brought from Australia in the
nineteenth century have thrived in the county and given birth to numerous place
names. According to one source, San Diego merchant E.W. Morse planted eucalyptus seeds in his garden as early as 1869 (Davidson Place Name File).
Eucalyptus Pass see **Grossmont Summit. Eucalyptus Canyon** led from Spring
Valley west of Mount Helix. In 1880 Charles S. Crosby planted these trees here
in what became **Eucalyptus Park** (Adema 141). **Eucalyptus Hills** is a residential district northwest of Lakeside dating from about 1920. Its trees were
planted in 1914 (Lakeside iv). **Eucalyptus Reservoir** was the terminus of the
San Diego Flume; long since dry, it is now the site of Briercrest Park in the
Grossmont District. (Durham 25; Stein 46)

- F -

Fairbanks Ranch, Lake. One mile south of Rancho Santa Fe. In 1926 the Hollywood actor Douglas Fairbanks Sr. bought about 800 acres here from the Lusardi family. He called it **Zorro Ranch** for his best-known movie *The Mark of Zorro*. Promoters developed the property for residential housing in the 1990s. (Stein 46)

Fairfield. A shipping station at the salt works at the southern end of San Diego Bay. (J. Davidson, "San Diego County Gazeteer," *SDET,* September 12, 1941)

Fairview, Mount. See Bonsall.

Falda. (Span. "skirt") Railroad station six miles east of Oceanside on Santa Fe Escondido line. Given this name because it was on the lower skirts of a hill named Loma Alta. (Gudde 128)

Fallbrook. Just east of Camp Pendleton. Debates over the source of this transfer name have been confusing, but everyone agrees that Vital Reche named the town. The place where he settled was first called **Reche's Grove,** now today's Live Oak County Park. Often repeated are Phil Townsend Hanna's words that "Vital Reche settled here from Fallbrook N.Y. in 1869. Becoming a bee keeper, he gave to his honey the brand name of his former New York home. Eventually, the brand name became the name of the community." Reche is recorded in the 1860 census (he spelled his name Ritchie), so Hanna's date is incorrect, and to the best of my knowledge there has never been a town in New York called Fallbrook. Reche also told the census taker that he was born in Canada. And why not simply say that the honey was named for Fallbrook and not the other way around? In his brief biography of Reche, Guinn (1099) says Reche was from Fallbrook, Pennsylvania, and Stein (47) repeats his words. Investigators at Fallbrook unraveled this tangle by looking into the family history of Reche's wife, Amelia Magee Reche. According to a published history of Tioga County, Pennsylvania, her family, railroad builders, established a company town called Fall Brook in that county. Reche, then, transferred that town's name, important in the history of his wife's family, from Tioga County Pennsylvania to San Diego County. However, Reche himself may have lived at some time in this Pennsylvania town. ("Pioneer Families: Reche and Magee," *Oceanside Enterprise,* August 22, 1985.) The town has moved its center several times; its present location was once called **West Fall Brook. Fall Brook Junction** is on the railroad line. The post office has also moved several times. During its history the town has been spelled Fall Brook, Fallbrook, Fall Brook, Fallbrook. (Gudde 128; Salley 70; Stein 47)

Falls, The. A waterfall on Morena Creek four miles northwest of Morena Village. (Durham 76)

False Bay. See **Mission Bay.**

False Point. Half way between Medanos Point and La Jolla, just north of Pacific Beach. Probably got its name because from a certain angle in foggy weather it might resemble Point Loma. (Durham 26; Gudde 232)

Famosa Slough. (Span. "famous") South of San Diego River east of Ocean Beach. The origins of the name are unknown, but it might have been named for nearby Famosa Blvd.

Fanita Ranch. In the 1880s developer Hosmer McKoon bought a large tract of land west of Santee with the intention of subdividing it. To honor his wife, Fannie M. McKoon, with a little judicious editing, he named the development Fanita Ranch. In 1907 members of the Scripps family, in particular Josephine Scripps, bought the 4,300-acre ranch. In 1956 the Scripps family sold out to a development company called Carlton Industries, hence **Carlton Hills,** etc. The old name survives in four local streets named Fanita. (Gudde 350; *SDU,* December 9, 1956)

Farley Flat. See **Guatay (2).**

Farr. Station near Encinitas on the Santa Fe Railroad. The source of the name is unknown, but a good guess would be that Mr. Farr was a railroad official at the intermediate level. An early name for the place was **Stewart Station.** (Not to be confused with **Stuart**, north of Oceanside.) (Durham 26; Ryan 33)

Felicita County Park. South Escondido. There was indeed a real Felicita La Chappa, a Kumeyaay resident of San Pasqual and daughter of Captain Ponto. Dr. Ben F. Sherman, an Escondido optometrist, composed a spectacle in her name with a 100-person cast and 50 on-stage horses that was performed first on September 9, Grape Day, 1927, and the succeeding three years. The performances were in a natural outdoor bowl, now in the park. He based the play on a collection by Elizabeth Judson Roberts, *Indian Stories of the Southwest.* In the play Felicita, an Indian maiden, aids an American soldier wounded in the Battle of San Pasqual. (Peet 14, 88-95)

Ferguson Flat. Three miles northeast of Julian. The 1870 U.S. census shows a Charles Ferguson, gold miner, 29, native of Arkansas, living in Julian. Perhaps he lingered long enough in the district to give his name to the place. (Durham 26; Stein 47)

Fern. Yes, there are a number of ferns native to the county, some of them quite attractive. **Fern Creek** flows into De Luz Creek west of De Luz, while **Fern Flat** is on Cuyamaca Peak. **Fernbrook** is a settlement south of Shady Dell on Old Mussey Grade. (Stein 47; Durham 26)

Filaree Flat. Three miles northwest of Monument Peak in the Laguna Mountains. Filaree is a common introduced weed, *Erodium,* sometimes valued as livestock feed. (Durham 26; Stein 47)

Finger Canyon. Opens into Dillon Canyon six miles east of Imperial Beach. A distinctive name that perhaps describes the canyon's drainage pattern. (Durham 26)

Fire Mountain. Four miles southeast of Oceanside. Reddish rock outcroppings on the mountain may have given it its name. (Durham 26; Stein 47)

Fisherman's Point. A point projecting into San Diego Bay at a place once called Roseville, now Shelter Island. This was a center for early Portuguese fishermen. On the 1859 U.S. Coast Survey of San Diego Bay it is called **Fitch's Point,** for prominent San Diego resident Henry Delano Fitch (1799-1849). (Davidson Place Name File; Durham 26)

Five Points. Formerly near where Washington St. ended and four other streets joined it. The construction of Interstate 5 annihilated it. (Durham 26)

Flat Rock. On the beach at Torrey Pines State Beach. Sometimes called **Bathtub Rock** because someone has carved a bathtub-shaped excavation on its upper flat surface. Many fantastic stories have been told about the origins of the bathtub: Indians dug it to provide fresh fish for the padres; it was an Indian bathtub; prospectors dug it in search of oil or coal (but no prospector would dig a test hole at the tide line). The excavation has apparently been there at least since 1890. (Breder; J. Davidson, "Cordero Beach Rich in History," *SDET* October 25, 1935; Schad cover, 31)

Flathead Flats. One mile west of Monument Peak in the Laguna Mountains. Possibly refers to a rock formation. (Durham 26)

Fleetridge. See **Rose.**

Fletcher. Although Ed Fletcher (1872-1955) was the most prominent developer in the county's history, he was diffident about naming his projects for himself—a trait not common among promoters. (See, for example, **San Carlos.**) Fletcher developed **Fletcher Hills** between El Cajon and La Mesa in 1927 and

1928, but then the Depression hit. Revived after World War II. **Camp Fletcher,** on Engineers Road a half mile above Cuyamaca Lake, was a Boy Scout camp from the late 1920s into the 1930s. Fletcher donated the land for the camp; further support came from the Sciots (not Scouts), a Masonic organization. The camp always suffered for lack of water, and closed in 1938. Its main building was called **Olmsted Lodge** for Frederick Law Olmsted Jr. (1870-1957), one of the planners of the original California State Park System, often confused with his stepfather with the same name who lived from 1822 to 1903. When Fletcher developed Solana Beach in 1923 he donated land for **Fletcher Cove Beach Park.** (Fletcher 259)

Flinn Springs. Off Interstate 8, eight miles east of El Cajon. Named for early settler James Ebenezer Flinn, born in Missouri in 1841, who married a neighborhood girl, Mary Ames, in 1874 after taking up land here. His father was Dr. William E. Flinn who is sometimes credited with founding the home place. Also known as **La Viñita** (Span. "little vineyard") because the Flinns made and sold wine at their farm. (J. Davidson, "Names of 2 Pioneers Perpetuated at Picturesque S.D. Spot," *SDET,* February 24, 1939; Gudde 132; Stein 48)

Florentine. Between Imperial Beach and the Mexican border. Adjective formed from the name of the city of Florence, Italy. A distinguished but not distinctive name. This place was important enough to have its own post office from 1890 to 1892. Associated with the larger settlement of Oneonta. (Durham 53; Salley 73)

Forester Creek. Four miles northwest of El Cajon along La Cresta Road. Probably named for a fraternal order, the Foresters. The *San Diego City-County Directory 1899-1900* notes that the Ancient Order of Foresters met in El Cajon on Saturday nights. The meeting hall may have been near Forester Creek. (Durham 27)

Forster City. Located at the mouth of San Onofre Creek. It had a post office from 1879 to 1883. Planned in 1879, Forster City was to have been a community for English immigrants. It was named for John O. Forster, an English-born rancher in southern California after 1833. He owned the Santa Margarita Ranch at the time. (Durham 67; Salley 75; Subject File "Place Names")

Fort. See under specific names, for example **Rosecrans, Fort.**

Fort Robinson Station. Station on the San Diego Cuyamaca & Eastern Railroad north of Grossmont. May take its name from William Robinson, son of Judge J.W. Robinson. Possibly it was called Fort because military maneuvers took place here at one time. (J. Davidson, "San Diego County Gazeteer," *SDET,* October 17, 1941, Hanft map inside front cover; Subject File, "Forts")

Fortuna Mountain. East of Tierrasanta in Mission Trails Park. Elevation 1,292 feet. Named for the Fortuna Ranch in this area west of the Fanita Ranch in the 1920s. (Subject File "Springs, Wahita")

Foss Lake. Five miles northeast of Oceanside. Named for David R. Foss, native of New Hampshire, who was a storekeeper in San Luis Rey in 1871. See the 1880 U.S. Census. (Stein 50)

Foster Canyon, Settlement. Five miles north of Lakeside. Named for Joseph (Joe) Foster (1857-1933), rancher, stagecoach operator, and long time county supervisor in the early twentieth century. Foster was the terminus of the San Diego Cuyamaca & Eastern Railroad. Had its own post office 1893 to 1916. **Foster Grade** see **Banner.** (Durham 27; Salley 76)

Four Corners. Two are in the county, both on back roads. One is located four miles north of El Cajon Mountain where three truck trails meet. A second is five miles north of Morena Reservoirs. (Durham 27; Stein 50)

Frazier Point. On Palomar Mountain, south of Crestline Camp. Named for James Frazier who settled there with his wife. (J. Davidson. "San Diego County Gazeteer," *SDET,* October 31, 1941)

Frazier's Station. See Carlsbad.

French. Most of the place names of this sort memorialize Frenchmen who came to the county to raise sheep in the period 1870-1900. Some of them were apparently Basques, a people long associated with sheep culture. They centered their activities on Palomar Mountain, as well as in Ramona and elsewhere. **French Canyon.** Opens to the sea near San Onofre Mountain. **French Creek** and **Mountain** are on Palomar Mountain. **Upper** and **Lower French Valley** are also on Palomar Mountain, the site of a sheep ranch run by French immigrants. The California Institute of Technology bought the land to construct the Palomar Observatory (J. Davidson, "San Diego County Gazeteer," *SDET,* October 31, 1941.) **French Mountain.** Six miles southwest of Rodriguez Mountain. (Durham 28; Stein 50)

Frey Creek. Flows into the San Luis Rey River east of Pala. Named for George and John Frey, cattle-raisers and bee keepers, who homesteaded before 1900. (Durham 28; Stein 50)

Fruit. From 1870 to 1920 fruit, sent north to Los Angeles and other parts, especially after the coming of the railroad in 1885, composed an important segment of the county's economy. "The growing of fruit and the manufacture of fruit products were the county's largest source of income [in 1910]." (Pourade, *Gold,* 139). **Fruit Vale.** A settlement on the Santa Fe Railroad not far from Olivenhain. (*SDU* September 17, 1885.) Another center of fruit growing was at the south end of San Diego Bay. **Fruitland** was six miles south of National City. Captain A.H. Wilcox, son-in-law of Santiago E. Argüello, named the place. It had its own post office from 1882 to 1885, and became a station on the National City and Otay Railroad. **Fruitdale** was in the same district. It appears on the San Diego 1904 15' Quadrangle. According to Pourade *Glory* (161), Fruitdale was the home ranch of Zachary Montgomery, father of the flight pioneer John. J. Montgomery. (Durham 28; Salley 78)

Fry Creek. At the headwaters of the West Fork of the San Luis Rey River on the east slopes of Palomar Mountain. Named for homesteader Andrew Fry who took up land on the mountain in 1884. (BLM website; Durham 28)

Fuente de San Jorge. See **Spring Valley.**

- G -

Galloway Valley. Two miles west of Alpine. Named for the Galloway family who settled here in 1909. Head of the family was Neil Galloway (d. 1962). (Durham 28; La Force 329-331)

Gammon Shoal. South of Zuñiga Shoal off North Island. Named for Captain Abner S. Gammon, master of the *Mary Glover.* He sailed out of San Diego Bay in the 1880s. (MacMullen, "Who")

Gapich. Mentioned in President Grant's proclamation of December 27, 1875, creating nine county Indian reservations: "Potrero—including Rincon, Gapich, and La Joyo." John Davidson says that this refers to Yapichi near the Cuca ranch, and that the name is Luiseño, meaning, oddly enough, "stomach rumbling." (J. Davidson, "Gapich Former Indian Village," *SDET,* May 6, 1938; McHenry 22)

Garlic Flats. Three miles south of Rodriguez Mountain south of the La Jolla Indian Reservation. Some of the native alliums do smell like onions, maybe garlic. (Durham 28; Stein 50)

Garnet Peak, Mountain. These two are less than two miles apart in the northern Lagunas. In the county semi-precious stones occur in a broad belt from Pala to Jacumba, so it is not at all surprising that garnets occur here. (Durham 28; Stein 51)

Gaskill Peak. Just east of Lawson Valley, eight miles north of Barrett Junction. Elevation 3,836 feet. Named for English immigrant Christopher Gaskill, not a member of the Gaskill family from Campo. He owned 420 acres of land here. Surveyors named it for him about 1910. (Davidson Place Name File; Durham 28; Stein 41)

Gaslamp S.D. Central Neighborhood. A name coined in the 1970s to encapsulate the district on 4th, 5th, and 6th Streets from Broadway to Pacific Highway. This redevelopment has been a roaring success. The name Gaslamp (sometimes Gaslamp Quarter) nicely captures the nostalgic spirit of a past era. (see Bugbee and Flanigan; Kooperman II, 17-18)

Gateway S.D. Mid-City Neighborhood. Located just north of Mount Hope Cemetery. Probably named for the Gateway Center, a large commercial and shopping district.

Gem Hill. Two miles northwest of Mesa Grande. Elevation 4,058 feet. Center of a gem-mining district, with especially valuable tourmalines. See **Himalaya Mine** and **San Diego Mine**. (Durham 28; Stein 51)

George Washington Mine. See **Washington Mine.**

Gibbs Airport. See **Montgomery.**

Gillespie Camp, Field. When the Marines established an airfield north of El Cajon for parachute training early in World War II they turned to the past to find its name. Marine Major Archibald H. Gillespie (1810-1873) participated significantly in California in the Mexican-American War. It became a county airfield in 1954. (Hinds 31-32)

Gird Canyon, Mountain. Both near Bonsall. Named for Henry H. Gird (1827-1913), a farmer and rancher who bought 4,590 acres of land here in 1876 and settled in 1880. This was on the Monserrate land grant. Because he experimented with local viticulture, the native grape of southern California was named for him, *Vitis Girdiana*. (Guinn I, 568)

Gleason Point. Now Bahia Point, named for the hotel, in Mission Bay. Probably named for Major Henry J. Gleason, (d. 1902), prominent citizen of Pacific

Beach. Gleason Point was still on the 1953 La Jolla 7.5' Quadrangle. The name survives as Gleason Road at this location. (*SDU,* July 13, 1902)

Glen Barham. See **Barham.**

Glen Cliff. See **Emery.**

Glen Lonely. Eight miles southwest of Descanso. Near Japatul School. Oddly enough, the first settlers in this area were Germans; it's doubtful that they named the place. One of the county's more appealing place names. (J. Davidson, "San Diego County Gazeteer," *SDET,* November 28, 1941; Durham 28)

Glen Oaks. See **Oak.**

Glencoe. Located in Cameron Valley. Thomas Cameron, immigrant, named it Glencoe for a place where he attended school in Argylshire, Scotland. San Diego County's Glencoe School was established in 1887. (J. Davidson, "San Diego County Gazeteer," *SDET,* November 28, 1941; San Diego County School Records Inventory)

Glenview. At Los Coches Road and old Highway 80. Formerly known as **Lakeview,** suggesting a view towards Lindo Lake at Lakeside. The name change occurred in 1936. (*SDU,* December 28, 1936)

Glorietta Bay. Sometimes called **Glorietta Bight.** Southeast of Coronado, fronting Tent City, in San Diego Bay. The name was in use in 1888. Gudde (145) suggests that it was chosen for its association with "glory" but in Mexico *glorieta* refers to a small plaza. (J. Davidson, "San Diego County Gazeteer," *SDET,* November 28, 1941)

Goat. Not native to the county, of course, but they are valuable animals that can survive in difficult arid conditions. **Goat Canyon** is near Imperial Beach in Border Field State Park. **Goat Island** is in Morena Reservoir. **Goat Mountain** is near Manzanita, while **Goat Peak** is north of Lakeside. (Durham 28-29)

Gobblers Knob. Seven miles southwest of Jamul. This is a common western name for an isolated peak. There are ten of them in Colorado, and three in Washington State, but this is the only Gobblers Knob in California (U.S. Board on Geographic Names website). When Europeans arrived here they found no native turkeys in the county, but the birds have been introduced from time to time; at the present they're doing quite well, thank you. The generic, knob, is rare in the county; it is a very early American name for a solitary peak (Stewart 132). It would be interesting to know who introduced the name here. There is also a **High Knob Mountain** in the county. (Durham 29)

Gold King Mine, Gold Queen Mine. See **K-Q Ranch.**

Gold Reef Mine. See **Cold Beef Mine.**

Golden Chariot Mine. See **Chariot.**

Golden Hill S.D. Central Neighborhood. Daniel Schuyler (d. 1921) developed this area in 1887. It was a 40-acre development with generous 100-foot by 140-foot lots between 16th and 25th, and A and Market Streets. The neighborhood was named "Golden Hill" by resolution of the city trustees in February 1887. "With the mountains' proud peaks so lofty and still,/ Tis a picture worth seeing from Golden Hill," someone wrote in the *Golden Era* in March of that year. Hubert Guy (93-94) said that the neighborhood got its name because Kate Sessions planted many yellow-blooming acacias here, but this requires confirmation. (J. Davidson, "San Diego County Gazeteer," *SDET*, December 5, 1941)

Golden Lotus Temple of All Religions. See **Swami's.**

Golden Triangle. Between Freeways 8, 52, and 805. It occupies virtually the same area as **University City S.D. Northern Neighborhood.** This is a busy commercial and apartment/condominium district with a memorable name, much more memorable than University City.

Goldfish Point. A rocky promontory east of La Jolla Cove. What were once called ocean gold fish are now called garibaldi. (J. Davidson, "San Diego County Gazeteer," *SDET*, December 5, 1941)

Goodan Ranch. See **Stowe.**

Goose Valley. In Pamo Valley two miles northeast of Ramona. A classic example of folk etymology—English speakers reshaping a Spanish word to fit their own language pattern. Ramona has had a Quaker (Friends) community from the mid-1880s. A place where a number of them lived was called in Spanish *El Valle de los Amigos* "Valley of the Friends." English speakers subsequently altered *amigos*, emphasizing the last syllable to make it into "goose," so Goose Valley. Both terms, Valle de los Amigos and Goose Valley, co-exist side by side on the Ramona 1988 7.5 Quadrangle. Sometimes it is said that the place was at Spencer Valley, but this is not correct. (Davidson Place Name File; Stein 52)

Gopher Canyon. Opens into the San Luis Rey Valley south of Bonsall. Cave J. Couts Jr. said John Combs named this place in the early 1870s because of its numerous gophers. This is where Charles Hatfield grew up and conducted his first rain-making "experiments." (Durham 29; Subject File "Bonsall")

Gordon Point. Two miles north of Boucher Hill on Palomar Mountain. Commemorates Donald H. Gordon (1883-1968), pioneer aviator. Born in Massachusetts, he grew up in Bostonia. Becoming deaf, he lived on Palomar Mountain the last 25 years of his life. (Durham 29; U.S. Board on Geographic Names 1971)

Gower, Mount. Five miles east of Ramona. Named for one of the discoverers of the Washington Mine near Julian, surveyor John T. Gower who owned land near here. Also known as **Black Horse Mountain** for a half-mythological black stallion. (J. Davidson, "Wild Stallion Said Responsible for Name of Black Horse Mountain," *SDET,* March 17, 1939; Stein 85)

Grant Hill Central S.D. Neighborhood. Grant Hill is between K and Island, and 26th and 27th Streets. Presumably named for President U.S. Grant whose widow and son moved to San Diego in the 1890s. Now the location of Grant Hill Park, dating only from the 1940s. (Subject File "Grant Hill")

Grantville. North of Interstate 8 and east of Interstate 15 along the San Diego River. Presumably named for President U.S. Grant. Promoters hoped to attract a post-Civil War "Soldiers Home" to this area in August 1887, but they were never successful. The name Grantville could not be used for a post office because there was already a Graniteville in Nevada County. When the post office was first established here it was called **Holabird,** from March 24, 1888, to July 10, 1888. This was to honor W.H. Holabird, Manager of the San Diego Development Company (There's still a Holabird St. in Grantville). From 1890 to 1896 the post office's name, for reasons unknown, was changed to **Orcutt,** usually said to honor Charles R. Orcutt, a local scientist, but Salley says it was to honor Herman C. Orcutt, its first postmaster (157). Then in 1897 the post office was moved to Gravilla where it remained until 1905 (see the entry under **Gravilla**). The *Golden Era* (January 1888) said this about Grantville: "...the finest climate the sun ever shone on. Neither hot nor cold; no malaria. Life becomes a pleasure, and grief vanishes." The name Grantville today describes the bustling commercial community in the area; it got a post office only in 1960. Now **Grantville S.D. Eastern Neighborhood.** (J. Davidson, "San Diego County Gazeteer," *SDET,* August 31, 1943, December 12, 1941; Durham 29; Salley 95, 157)

Grape Day Park. In central Escondido. By 1900 Escondido had evolved as a grape-growing district specializing in Muscat of Alexandria grapes made into sun-dried raisins. To celebrate the region's most important crop, the first Grape

Day was held in 1908; it survived until 1950. One inducement to attend was free grapes for all. The park was established to host the celebration. (McGrew, *Hidden Valley,* 72-76, 294)

Grapevine. The southern California native grapevine, *Vitis Girdiana,* thrives in moist places from the sea to about the 3,000-foot elevation. Father Serra said about grapes near Presidio Hill: "There are pretty and large vines; in some places they are loaded down with grapes." Most of the grapevine places are in the desert, but there is a **Grapevine Creek** near Potrero. For **Grapevine Mining District** see Lindsay (181). Also see **Gird Canyon.** (J. Davidson "Name of Grapevine," *SDET,* March 18, 1938)

Grass Flats. See **Dutch Flats.**

Gravilla. Very close to Grantville, but the La Jolla 1903 15' Quadrangle distinguishes the two places. This may be the first acronym in county history: it combines (incongruously) the words gravel, from nearby gravel pits, and villa. The post office of this name survived from 1897 to 1905 when it was the post office for the Grantville district. The community had applied for the name Cosoy, the Indian village near Presidio Hill, but the postal authorities rejected it. (Durham 29; Salley 85)

Gravity Hill. In the county the best-known example of the "gravity phenomenon," found elsewhere in many locations in the U.S., is on the west side of Dictionary Hill in La Presa. The driver of a car climbs a steep street that levels off. He stops his car on the level, but it rolls backward! (Of course the car is not on the level at all.) The street has attracted, like, crowds of teenagers and even curiosity seekers from as far away as Los Angeles.

Green Dragon Colony. In 1894, friend of many artists and governess for the U.S. Grant Jr. family in San Diego, Berlin-born Anna Held (not to be confused with the actress with the same name) bought land on Prospect St. in La Jolla to establish an artist's colony. Its eleven houses were home to many artistic visitors over the years. She found the name for her establishment in the title of a short story "At the Green Dragon" that was in a collection written by her friend, the British writer Beatrice Harraden. The collection was called *In Varying Moods* and Blackwood published it in England in 1894 and Putnam's in the U.S. the same year. In the story there is a Green Dragon Inn that Anna Held apparently admired. (Kooperman 269-270; Ridgely)

Green Valley. There are three of these in the county. One is two miles east of Leucadia and is sometimes called **New Encinitas** (Hartley 179). Another is seven miles southeast of Escondido, and the third is in Cuyamaca Rancho State

Park. The last is identified with the history of the Lassitor and Mulkins family. Site of the Dyar home in upper Green Valley. (Durham 30; Stein 53)

Green's Farm Camp. This was an outlying camp for Camp Elliott on Old Escondido Road east of today's Interstate 15. Now part of Miramar MCAS. (Hinds 79-80)

Gregory Springs. Located where Imperial Ave. crosses Chollas Creek. It was used for drinking and bathing in the 1880s and the 1890s. Named for Captain F.A. Gregory, an early owner. (Anonymous, "Many")

Griffin. North of Vista on Buena Vista Creek. Named for James M. Griffin, the first settler here. He was also a county supervisor. Griffin got its own school in 1895 but never had a post office. (*SDU,* December 8, 1886; San Diego County School Records Inventory)

Grizzly Camp. A U.S. Army camp that existed briefly in 1918 at Oceanside. (Hinds 51)

Grossmont. Between La Mesa and El Cajon. Ed Fletcher developed Grossmont in 1906, 1908, and 1910 together with theatrical promoter, William B. Gross, for whom the development was named. (They tried the name Mount Gross, but that seemed too pretentious, maybe too Gross.) The two men met by accident in Yellowstone Park. In 1902 Fletcher bought Villa Caro Rancho and part of the Alta Ranch in the area. After meeting Gross, he conceived the idea of developing an artist's colony using Gross's name. Not above reducing lot prices to induce purchases from selected buyers, Fletcher attracted Ernestina Schumann-Heink, a famous German contralto and one of Fletcher's warmest admirers; Carrie Jacobs Bond, author of "The End of a Perfect Day," and "Just A-Weary-ing for You" (somehow it seems right that she named her Grossmont house "Nest-O-Rest"); Owen Wister (briefly); and many other talented residents. The terrain was difficult, and Fletcher was derided for his audacity. (His detractors called Grossmont "Fletcher's Folly.") Grossmont got its own post office in 1910. The former Alta Station on the San Diego Cuyamaca & Eastern Railroad changed its name to **Grossmont Station** in 1913. **Grossmont Shopping Center,** located a mile or so northwest of Fletcher's Grossmont, was built early in the 1960s, coinciding with the completion of Interstate 8 which bypassed La Mesa. **Grossmont Summit.** This is the high point on the road between San Diego and El Cajon; it overlooks El Cajon Valley. Before Fletcher's Grossmont development it was called **Eucalyptus Pass.** Carrie Jacobs Bond wrote in a Grossmont poem, "The wild birds chant their carols,/ The flowers bloom ga-lore./ Out in God's lovely garden/ How could I ask for more?" (see Guy; Salley 87; Stein 53-54)

Grove, The. See **Lemon Grove.**

Guajome Land Grant, Lake. East of San Luis Rey Mission. Grant to Andrés and José Manuel, two Indians, 2219 acres in 1845. The name comes from *waxáawu-may,* Luiseño "little frog." In 1851 Abel Stearns bought the ranch to give to his sister-in-law Ysidora Bandini Couts as a wedding present. (Cowan 38; Gudde 155; Stein 54-55)

Guatay. For the original Guatay see **Descanso.**

Guatay (2). Five miles east of Descanso on old Highway 80. Originally called **Farley Flat** for Andrew Farley and his family who settled here in 1869. However, after the place that had been called Guatay officially became Descanso in 1877, the name Guatay was available. In 1917 Farley Flat chose Guatay as the name of its post office. For the etymology of the Kumeyaay word Guatay see **Descanso.** (Durham 30; Friends, *Descanso,* 18; Salley 87)

Guejito y Cañada de Palomea Land Grant, Creek. Between San Pasqual and Mesa Grande Indian Reservations. According to Gudde (155), "Guejito is perhaps a diminutive of *guijo* Span. 'pebble'; or it may be for *güeja,* which in northwest Mexico refers to a gourd vessel…" Palomea may be a misprint for Paloma (Span. "dove"). The grant, 13,299 acres, was given to José María Orozco in 1845. (Cowan 38-39; Stein 56)

Guijarros, Fort. See **Ballast Point.**

Gum Tree Cove. On the shore of Sweetwater Reservoir. This is the only reference I have found in the county to gum tree as a synonym for eucalyptus. (Durham 30)

Gumbo Slough. In San Diego Bay at the mouth of Switzer Creek. Gumbo is a thick New Orleans soup featuring okra. A descriptive term for what must have been very sticky mud on the bay's shoreline. (Pourade, *Glory,* 242)

Gunn Canyon. Three miles northwest of Warner Springs. Here in the 1880s and 1890s an English immigrant named Bob Gunn ran a popular saloon he called Bob's Place. The canyon commemorates his name. (Durham 30; Jasper, *Trail-Breakers,* 372-380)

Gunpowder Point. On San Diego Bay west of Chula Vista. From 1916 to 1918 the Hercules Powder Company operated a plant here to extract potash and acetone from kelp. The nearby Coronado Belt Railroad served the factory, which was notable for its rank air. Now part of the Sweetwater Marsh National Wildlife Refuge. (Kooperman II 586)

- H -

Hakupin. See **Warner Springs.**

Hale Observatory. On Palomar Mountain. It is named for George Hale (1868-1938), astronomer and sponsor of the Mt. Palomar Observatory. He obtained six million dollars from the Rockefeller Foundation to complete the observatory. The Hale Observatory was dedicated June 3, 1948.

Hansen's Ponds. In 1926 Spring Valley developer Fred J. Hansen acquired Sweetwater Springs (see that entry). He built dams to capture spring water at the site, and the reservoirs took his name. (Adema 107-108)

Harbison Canyon. It is named for John S. Harbison who settled here in 1869, having brought 110 beehives to the county on the steamship *Orizaba*. He became the largest shipper of honey in the county, and the founder of an industry. By 1874 he was shipping out hundreds of thousands of pounds of honey every year; San Diego County produced more honey that year than any other county in the U.S. Harbison had hives all over in such places as Honey Springs and Engineer Springs. (J. Davidson, "Harbison Canyon Famed for Honey," *SDET,* August 28, 1936; Stein 57)

Harbison's Field. See **Engineer Springs.**

Harbor Island. See **Shelter Island.**

Harborview Central S.D. Neighborhood. Located on San Diego Bay. Probably an unknown official coined this name. Never a subdivision.

Harmony Grove. Six miles northeast of Rancho Santa Fe. On the stage road between Escondido and Cardiff. A place always associated with spiritualism. In 1896 the Harmony Grove Spiritualist Camp Meeting Association was incorporated. It has held annual meetings here on a 13-acre plot owned by the association for many years. The association got a new church in 1970-1971. Its detractors sometimes call Harmony Grove **Spook Canyon.** (McGrew, *Hidden Valley,* 283-284; Stein 57)

Harper Creek, Valley. East of Cuyamaca Rancho State Park. Named for the Harper family, Eli A. Harper and his sons Julius and Eli Akim, who settled here in the 1870s. For information about them see Lindsay 184-186. In the early 1940s Charles Luckman (1909-1999), who had careers both as an executive of Lever Brothers and as a major architect, bought the Harper Ranch for

$57,000. He named it the **Lucky 5 Ranch**, playing on his surname and because his family had five members—himself, his wife Harriet, and their three sons. The name is still used, even though the Luckmans sold the ranch in 1955. The State of California in 2001 acquired much of the ranch to add to the California State Parks. Sometimes called **Rattlesnake Valley.** (Durham 31; Luckman, 165, 321; Stein 57)

Harrison Canyon. On the west slope of Palomar Mountain. Named for Nathan Harrison, a former slave who had a homestead here. Before 1970 it was called **Nigger Canyon;** this is when the U.S. Board on Geographic Names changed its name to Harrison Canyon. The board expressly disapproved of Nigger Canyon and Negro Canyon. For information about Harrison see **Nate Harrison Grade.** (Durham 31; Stein 87; Wood 39-42)

Harrison Park. West of Highway 79, midway between Julian and Cuyamaca Lake. A National City attorney, Ruben Harrison (d. 1941) in 1926 offered 4,000 lots here, each 20 feet by 82 feet, for $5 each. No road or utilities were available; sometimes people called them "picnic lots"—you walked to your lot and had a picnic. These tiny lots have been combined over the years to provide room for some spacious homes. The 2004 Cedar Fire did extensive damage in this area. (Durham 31)

Hartley Hill. Seven miles southwest of Morena Village at Lake Morena. Named for Frank Paul Hartley (d. 1965) settler in Potrero for 50 years. (Durham 31; *SDU,* February 4, 1965)

Hatfield Creek. Three miles east of Ramona. Named for Abraham Hatfield, settler, gold miner, and owner of a gem mine near this site. Not to be confused with Charles Hatfield, the rainmaker. (Jasper, *Trail-Breakers,* 263-264)

Hauser Canyon, Creek, Mountain, Wilderness Area. Between Barrett Lake and Lake Morena. Named for Jacob Hauser, early German immigrant and settler. He is on the 1880 U.S. Census (129) as Jacob Howser. In October 1943 nine enlisted Marines were killed fighting a fire in Hauser Canyon. A plaque in their memory was dedicated in 1949. (*SDU,* May 10, 1949; Stein 57)

Hawley. A station on the San Diego Cuyamaca & Eastern Railroad in the El Cajon Valley. Probably named for George M. Hawley (d. 1934), pioneer rancher in the valley. (Berlo Map 47)

Hayden Valley. See Jewell Valley.

Hearn, Camp. Near Imperial Beach at the junction of Silver Strand and Palm City Road. Named for Major Lawrence J. Hearn of the 21st Infantry. Why he was granted this distinction is unknown. Rifle range and headquarters of the commanding officer of the Southern California Border District, U.S. Army. Established July 1916 and closed August 1920. Authorities feared the Mexican Revolution would spill across the U.S. border and established the camp as a precaution. (Davidson Place Name File; Hinds 35-36)

Hedionda. See **Agua Hedionda.**

Helix, Mount. (Latin *helix* "spiral") Two theories explain the origins of the name of the prominent hill east of La Mesa, the trail theory and the snail theory. According to the first, the mountain was named for the circular trail that hikers made around and up the mountain. But hikers rarely circle a hill; they prefer a straight line. The spiral road to the summit dates only from 1919 (Adema 133.) According to the snail theory, the name resulted from a visit made by the eminent Swiss-born scientist Louis Agassiz, who came to San Diego in August 1872 aboard the research vessel *Hassler.* He made a collecting trip into the hinterland, including the Spring Valley area, where he collected specimens of *Helix aspersa,* a snail never recorded before in the region. According to Adema (33) Rufus K. Porter named the hill in his honor, giving it the snail name. Rufus Porter's daughter, Rufina Porter Crosby (b. 1854), had a simpler explanation for the name. In her *Reminiscences* (72), written in the 1930s, she gave credit for naming the mountain to her father: "In traveling over the mountain one day he picked up some snail shells, and in Latin Helix means snails—thus the name." As to the trail up the peak, she wrote: "I rode up on top of the mountain [in an automobile] a few years ago where I used to climb up on horseback without even a trail." The snail theory is well authenticated and convincing. For **Helix Settlement** see **Spring Valley.** (Gudde 163; Salley 92)

Hell Creek. In the Pauma Valley. Perhaps because it was difficult to cross, or because the name was a pendant to Paradise Creek, also in this area. (Durham 31; Stein 58)

Hellhole. A name for an isolated and forbidding canyon. There are two of these in the west county in addition to one in the Anza-Borrego area. One is east of San Ysidro near Ranchita, and the other is east of Valley Center. The latter may have gotten its name to match Paradise Mountain, not far away. It is now known as Hellhole Canyon Open Space Preserve. Durham refers to this area as **Lower Hellhole** and **Upper Hellhole.** (Durham 44, 79)

Helvetia Mine. Between Whispering Pines and Kentwood east of Highway 79 south of Julian. Helvetia was the Latin name for Switzerland. Perhaps Sebastian Southiermer, one of its claimants in August 1870, named it. This was one of the Julian district's largest mines. From its 450-foot inclined shaft, miners removed $450,000 in gold when it was $20.67 an ounce. On the 1997 Julian 7.5' Quadrangle. (Fetzer, *Good Camp,* 24-27)

Henshaw, Lake. On upper San Luis Rey River. The dam was completed in 1924 and the reservoir was named for William G. Henshaw, land owner and promoter. (Stein 68)

Heriot Mountain. Two miles northeast of Pala. Also spelled **Hiriart.** Named for a miner of Basque descent, Bernardo Heriot, very active in early gem mining. See, for example, **Chief Mountain** and **Tourmaline Queen Mountain.** It is on the 1997 Pechanga 7.5' Quadrangle. (Durham 32)

Hidden Glen. Off Japatul Valley Road eight miles southwest of Descanso. The Glen Lonely Truck Trail is nearby. (Durham 32)

Hidden Mesa. The mesa between Interstate 8 and Montezuma Road in east San Diego near San Diego State University. A private airport was once located there. Later developed as **Alvarado Estates** 1952-1953. (Davidson Place Name File)

Hide Park. See **La Playa.**

Hideaway Lake. Seven miles north of Escondido. (Durham 32)

Higgins Point. On Coronado Peninsula near the whaler's camp at the entrance to the bay. As the area around La Playa developed, whalers moved their operations over to North Island. Named for T.J. Higgins, an early San Diego whaling captain. His ship was the *Amelia. (SDU,* January 29, 1884)

High Knob Mountain. In the San Marcos Mountains northeast of Vista. An unusual name for a mountain, but also see **Gobblers Knob.** Since a knob is a mountain, the last word in the name is redundant. (Durham 66)

High Mountain. See **Mount Whitney.**

High Peak Mine. See **Eagle-High Peak Mine.**

High Point. The summit of Palomar Mountain at 6,126 feet elevation. (Durham 32, 55)

Highlands. A district southeast of Chula Vista. This name appears on the cover of the anonymous 1895 booklet *San Diego: Our Italy,* published by the San Diego Chamber of Commerce. (Pourade, *Glory,* 192)

Highway to the Stars. This was a catchy name for the new road up the south slopes of Mount Palomar needed to haul the giant telescope lenses and other materials to the Palomar Observatory. Surveyed in 1934 and completed in 1935. Also known as **South Grade.** There is also an **East Grade** up the mountain. See that entry. (Bawden 77)

Hill. Five miles southeast of Del Mar. Near, but not the same place as Sorrento. Had its own post office from May 1909 to Dec. 1927. Maybe named for an individual, but more probably because it was on a hill. (Durham 72; Salley 94)

Hillcrest S.D. Western Neighborhood. An older subdivision name. The Hillcrest Amended Subdivision dates from 1907 with William Wesley Whitson the developer. Supposedly, his sister-in-law, Laura Anderson, suggested the name. This neighborhood has evolved into the center of San Diego's gay community. (Security Title 20; Weisberg)

Hillsdale. A district south of El Cajon Valley north of the Sweetwater River. A Hillsdale School was established here in 1894. The conventional name survives as street names and Hillsdale Middle School. (Adema 161, San Diego County School Records Inventory)

Himalaya Mine. A gem mine on the northwest slope of Gem Hill about two miles northwest of Mesa Grande. It is on the 1997 Mesa Grande 7.5' Quadrangle. This was a popular name for a mine—there were at least four in California. This was by far the richest gem mine in the county; its tourmaline production probably equaled that of all the other mines in the county combined. Children had long noticed the pretty stones here; in 1898 Gail Lewis claimed the mine. Its best years were 1904-1912, with many gems exported to China. After the Chinese Revolution of 1911, Chinese demand collapsed and so did the Himalaya Mine. Total production has been estimated at $2,500,000. If so, it was perhaps the richest mine ever in today's San Diego County. (Foord 16-168; *Mining;* Weber 91-92)

Himmel Canyon. Along San Vicente Creek seven miles southeast of Ramona. Originally called Black Horse Canyon. Named for Charles Himmel who homesteaded here in 1898. Also see **Mount Gower.** (BLM website; Durham 32)

Hinton, Mount. Eight miles northeast of Oceanside. Named for Francis "Jack" Hinton, rancher and landowner. He had land on the Santa Margarita Ranch. (Durham 50, Rush 90, SDHS Biographical Files; *SDU,* July 7, 1870)

Hipass. See **Tierra del Sol.**

Hiriart Mountain. See **Heriot Mountain.**

Hodges, Lake. Five miles south of Escondido. Completed in 1918. Originally the place was called **Carroll Dam** and **Reservoir** for the brothers James and Thomas Carroll, who had adjoining ranches at the site that are now under water. However, after the dam was completed, it and the lake were renamed for W.E. Hodges, vice president of the Santa Fe Railroad. The water in the lake, from the San Dieguito River, was stored for communities along the coast developed by the Santa Fe Land Improvement Company, a subsidiary of the railroad. There was a post office with this name from 1924 through 1926. Before the dam was built the place was called **Crescent Valley.** (Perkins; Ryan 152; Salley 112; Stein 68-69)

Holabird. See **Grantville.**

Holcomb, Camp. See **Camp Elliott.**

Holcomb Village. Seven miles northwest of Warner Springs on Highway 79. First appears on the Warner Springs 1939 15' Quadrangle. Many Holcombs played roles in nineteenth century San Diego history, but the use of the generic term village has the ring of modernity about it. Named for an unknown Holcomb. (Durham 32)

Hollenbeck Canyon. Opens to Dulzura Creek four miles southeast of Jamul. Named for A.H. Hollenbeck, Jamul rancher. He is listed in the 1899-1900 *San Diego City-County Directory* 54.

Hollister Valley. See **Thing Valley.**

Hollydale. Area near the junction of Market Street and Imperial Ave., generally considered part of Encanto. A station of the San Diego, Cuyamaca & Eastern Railroad. Once, an effort was made to develop it as a moving picture center, San Diego's answer to Hollywood. (Davidson Place Name File; Hanft, map inside front cover)

Home Ranch. See **Ranch House.**

Homelands. Three miles east of Spring Valley near Jamacha Junction. May have been only a subdivision, but it is on the Jamul Mountains 1955 7.5 ' Quadrangle. (Durham 32)

Homestead. Seven miles west of Campo. This place had its own post office 1878-1880, 1892-1893. The name suggests that there was a cluster of homestead claims at this location. (Durham 11; Salley 96)

Honey Springs. Just past Jamul and off Highway 94. Home of Mr. and Mrs. G. D. Love in 1895. Not named for the quality of the water but because bee keepers placed hives here. (*SDU,* August 15, 1895)

Hope. See **Mount Hope Cemetery.**

Hormiguero. (Span. "ant nest"). A small community three miles north of Pala in Castro Canyon. On Pechanga 1950 7.5' Quadrangle, but gone from the 1968 quadrangle. The Spanish name invites conjecture—were there many ants here, or did this describe the community? (Durham 32)

Horno Canyon, Hill, Summit. (Span. "oven, or a cavity in which bees lodge") A cluster of names near San Onofre Mountain. (Durham 32)

Horseshoe Bend. South of Sweetwater Reservoir. A ridge with a horseshoe shape. In a district with colorful names. See nearby **Gobblers Knob** and **Wild Man's Canyon.** (Durham 33)

Horsethief Canyon. There are two of them in the county. The first is near Rodriguez Mountain east of Valley Center. The second, south from Japatul Valley, is better known. Supposedly horse thieves collected stolen horses here to drive them south into Mexico. (Stein 59; Durham 33)

Horton Plaza Central S.D. Neighborhood. Broadway between Third and Fourth Avenues. Named for Alonzo Horton (1813-1909), city father. He sold the land for the plaza to the city for $10,000. When he sold it in 1894 he was promised $100 a month in payments. One story is that the payments continued until his late death, yielding him a nice profit. But MacPhail says the payments ceased in 1903 when the sum reached $10,000. Irving J. Gill designed the fountain in the plaza; it was dedicated in 1910. City authorities named the plaza for Horton only in 1925. Ernest Hahn developed the new Horton Plaza in the 1980s. Supposedly, its design emulates an Italian hill town. (MacPhail 128, 148, 153)

Hot Springs Mountain. Named for Warner Hot Springs, Spanish *agua caliente,* not so far away. Highest peak in the county at 6,533 feet elevation. An earlier name was **Rabbit Peak** from the Cupeño name "rabbit's house." (Gudde 308; Stein 60)

Hourglass Field. From 1954 to 1956 the U.S. Navy maintained a base at what is now Hourglass Field Community Park in Mira Mesa. Officially it was called **Miramar Outlying Field.** It probably got its name from the pattern of the runways. (Hinds 97)

Howard, Camp. Established by Colonel Joseph H. Pendleton, USMC, on North Island near Spanish Bight on July 3, 1914. The Mexican Revolution had alarmed the American military and so they established this base, and others. Named for Rear Admiral Thomas B. Howard. Closed in 1917. (Hinds 41-43)

Howe. Four miles northwest of Fallbrook on the California Southern Railroad. Post office established 1882, discontinued 1891. The *San Diego City-County Directory* for 1889-1890 lists 14 adult residents at Howe. This is a railroad name that is difficult to identify with certainty. (Durham 26; Salley 97)

Hual-Cu-Cuish, Camp. Boy Scout Camp on Middle Peak in Cuyamaca Rancho State Park, founded in 1940. In Hero Eugene Rensch's *Indian Place Names of Cuyamaca* (38) this is Kumeyaay *Jual-Cu-Cuilsch,* "tough strong" the name for Middle Peak. Couro and Hutcheson (98) have *'ekwiish* meaning "tough." The camp closed in 1998 because of high maintenance costs, and was burned in the 2003 Cedar fire.

Hubbert Lake. Two miles northeast of Oceanside. Named for pioneer San Luis Rey rancher Matthew Hubbert who arrived here in 1873. (*Memoirs of Ben F. Hubbert,* in Biography Files, SDHS)

Huerta de Clement. See **San Clemente Canyon.**

Hulburd Grove. (Pronounced "Hubbard") One mile north of Descanso on the Sweetwater River. Ebenezer Wallace Hulburd established a ranch here in 1884. For a time it was a center of spiritualism with medium Justin Robinson at a house called "Searchlight Bower." Later it became a popular resort under the management of Hulburd family members. Closed after World War II. (J. Davidson, "Descanso Place of Rest, Repose," *SDET,* August 30, 1935; Friends, *Descanso,* 71-77)

Hut Cut Valley. See **Cutca Valley.**

- I -

Imperial Beach. At south end of San Diego Bay on the ocean. In 1906 E.W. Peterson, manager of the South San Diego Investment Company, invented this name to attract visitors from the Imperial Valley. The place was originally called **South San Diego**; this was the name of the post office from 1888 to 1902. Judge George Puterbaugh developed South San Diego on 2,000 acres in 1887 (*SDU,* August 21, 1887). The post office took the name Imperial Beach only in 1909. (Durham 33; Salley 100; Stein 60)

Imperial Highway. The 1950s saw a movement to create a high-speed road, the Imperial Highway, from Los Angeles by way of Oak Grove, Warner Springs, Earthquake Valley, and Sweeney Pass to Highway 80. The Imperial Highway Commission promoted the route with the goal of attracting visitors from Los Angeles. Of course, it was never built. Also known as the **Cannon Ball Road.** (Davidson Place Name File)

Iñaja Indian Reservation. (Often spelled Inaja). (Kumeyaay *'enyehaa* "my water" (or "my tears"), from *'iny-* "my" plus *'ehaa* "water." Margaret Langdon in Gudde 176). On the west slopes of North Peak in the Cuyamaca Mountains. The reservation dates from 1875 and includes 846 acres. American settlers often called the place **Anahuac,** and this was the name of the school on the reservation dating from 1889. An Aztec place name in Mexico, it was also a Texas town near Galveston, pronounced Á-na-wak. Many early settlers here were Southerners, no doubt familiar with the Texas town, and they modified the strange reservation name to fit their English-speaking tongues. For a durable misspelling of the name see **Maja. Inaja Memorial Park.** In 1956 a Santa Ana-driven fire, beginning on the reservation, swept southwest almost as far as Lakeside. Eleven men, most of them prisoners at a county honor camp, fighting the fire near the San Diego River, lost their lives. In 1957 county authorities created the park to honor their memories. It is on Highway 79-78 west of Julian. (San Diego County School Records Inventory; Stein 61)

Indian. There are at least nine of these features in the western part of the county with four more in the desert. **Indian Creek,** four miles long, joins Pine Creek near Pine Valley. **Indian Flats** are northwest of Warner Springs. **Indian Head Peak** and **Indian Head Spring** are north of El Cajon Mountain. Probably they are named for a rock formation. **Indian Point** is on San Diego Bay at 26th and National Avenues. At this location in the nineteenth century there was an Indian village (Davidson Place Name File). On the 1845 Fitch map of San Diego the point is called **Punta Verde** (Span. "green point"). **Indian Rock Spring** is two miles west of Escondido. There are notable petroglyphs in the area. **Indian Springs** was a private museum and resort two miles north of Jamul run by W.G. Honnell. Established in 1919, and closed down in 1936. For **Indian Potrero** see **Potrero.** (Durham 33-34; Stein 61)

Interbergen P.O. A curious mix of Latin *inter* "among" and German *bergen* "mountains." About five miles north of Foster. On the 1908 Hubon Map of San Diego and Imperial Counties. Salley shows no post office in the county with this name. Then where did it come from and was it ever a working post office?

International City. On the beach near the Mexican border. According to Menzel this was one of the boomtowns of the late 1880s. Consisted of only a few buildings. "Monument City and International City became noted for their prize fights, confidence men, gamblers, and drunks during the boom times...." (Menzel 90.) On T. D. Beasley's 1889 San Diego Map.

Iron. These names came from red stained soil or water. They are fairly common in the county. **Iron Mountain** is three miles east of Poway, elevation 2,696 feet. The mountain takes its name from an old iron mine on the south side of the peak (Schad 81). There are **Iron Springs** ten miles north of Descanso and three miles north of Jacumba. There's also an **Iron Spring** and **Iron Canyon** on Palomar Mountain. Edward H. Davis of Mesa Grande once owned the spring, and so it is also known as **Davis Spring.** (Davidson Place Names File; Durham 34)

Ironton. In 1889 Charles Eames chose a site near Point Loma to build a plant to manufacture nails and wire cloth, calling the place Ironton. He also laid out a subdivision with the same name in October 1891. The plant actually manufactured some goods, but soon closed. Wild talk circulated that the district would become a western Pittsburgh. Bessemer Street near Shelter Island marks the spot today. (Kooperman II 572; Security Title 22)

Irvings Crest. Presumably in the 1930s someone came up with this imaginative name for a small settlement on a spur road off Mussey Grade Road southwest of Ramona. It appears to celebrate an unknown Mr. Irving. It's not on the Blackburn 1931 County Map, a good source for locating small settlements, but it is on the El Cajon 1939 15' Quadrangle. The generic, Crest, is unusual. (Durham 34)

Isham Creek. Flows into El Capitan Reservoir from the north. Named for David C. Isham, apiarist and partner in the Atkinson Toll Road. (Durham 75; U.S. 1880 Census, San Diego 120)

Isham's Spring, Isham's California Water of Life. See **Sweetwater Spring.**

- J -

Jacques Farm. See **Admiral Baker Recreation Center.**

Jacob Dekema Freeway. Interstate 805 from Sorrento Valley to near the Mexican border. Named for Jacob (Jake) Dekema, Director, District 11 of CalTrans 1955-1980. (Reading 32)

Jamacha. District five miles north of Jamul, five miles south of El Cajon. (Kumeyaay *hemechaa* "a type of [native] gourd used to make soap" Margaret Langdon in Gudde 182). There are many variant spellings. **Jamacha Rancho,** 8,881 acres granted to Apolinaria Lorenzana. In 1895 authorities established a post office here called **Daviston**, probably for someone named Davis (Davis town?), but that same year they changed the name to Jamacha post office. It operated from 1895 to 1922. Early records sometimes refer to the ranch as **San Jacome de la Marca** (Spanish for Italian San Giacomo della Marca, "St. James of the March," 1394-1476). A march is a border region, and it's tempting to think that the ranch had this name because it was on the edge of Mexican control over the Indian population. **Jamacha-Lomita Southeastern S.D. Neighborhood** (Span. *lomita* "little hill") adjoins Lemon Grove. Jamacha Road separates the two communities. **Jamacha Springs.** See **Sweetwater Springs.** (Cowan 41; Gudde 182; Stein 62)

Jamatayume. See **Samagatuma.**

Jamul. On Highway 94 ten miles southeast of El Cajon. (Kumeyaay *hemull* "foam, lather" Margaret Langdon in Gudde 182). There was a post office here with this name from 1880. **Jamul Rancho** had 8,926 acres of land. Cowan (41) says, "In 1845 this [land grant] was sought by [Pio] Pico in a petition to himself, from himself, then granted to himself by himself." **Jamul Indian Reservation.** Six acres. Dates from 1975. **Jamul Creek** and **Mountain** are not far away. (Gudde 182; Pryde 64; Salley 103; Stein 63)

Janal. In the general area between Rancho Jamul and today's Chula Vista. (Kumeyaay. Edward Davis [n.p.] says this is *Ha-nal a ha* "rippling water") Sometimes cited as **Janat. Janal Rancho,** 4,436 acres, was granted as part of the Otay Land Grant to José Antonio Estudillo in 1829 and 1846. A ranch house never stood on this land. Now the location of vast subdivisions, including Eastlake. (Cowan 41; Webster 33-34)

Japacha Creek, Peak. (Kumeyaay *hapechaa* "handstone for grinding," Span. *mano de metate.* Margaret Langdon in Gudde 182) .On east slopes of Cuyamaca Peak in Cuyamaca Rancho State Park.

Japatul Valley. Kumeyaay. "The name probably preserves the name of the Indian village Japatai which was still in existence in the early 1800s. Perhaps from *hatepull* 'woodpecker'." (Margaret Langdon in Gudde 182)

Jaybird Creek. Flows into Pauma Valley west of Boucher Hill. Unusual ornithological name with a western twang. (Durham 36)

Jeff Valley. Five miles southeast of Boucher Hill near Mount Palomar. Unusual because it is derived from a given name, Jeff Cook, father and early settler. See nearby **Will Valley.** (Durham 36; Wood 55)

Jennings, Lake. Two miles east of Lakeside behind Chet Harritt Dam. Named for William H. Jennings, water expert and lawyer (d. 1983). Authorities named the reservoir for him in 1964. (*SDU,* February 16, 1983)

Jesmond Dene. Five miles north of Escondido. A classic European transfer name. Repeats the name of a public park in Newcastle-upon-Tyne in northeastern England. In older English a dene was a deep wooded valley. Originally this was a cabin subdivision of 160 acres developed in the late 1920s. Jesmond Dene Subdivision was recorded in 1927 (Security Title 60). Had its post office from 1933 to 1935. W.G. Morgan, with W.G. Moore his manager, developed the site. It seems likely that someone in the company that developed the property was familiar with the English Jesmond Dene. (J. Davidson, "San Diego County Gazeteer," *SDET,* May 25, 1942; Salley 104)

Jessee. Seven miles southeast of Nellie (Mt. Palomar) in Mendenhall Valley. It had a post office from 1896 to 1904. Named for its first postmaster Harriet L. Jessee. (Durham 55; Salley 104)

Jesús María Creek. See **Cottonwood Creek.**

Jewell Valley. South of Boulevard. Formerly was known as **Hayden Valley** for J. S. Hayden, proprietor of the Campo Hotel (J. Davidson, "San Diego County Gazeteer," *SDET,* February 6, 1942). In 1961 the U.S. Board on Geographic Names adopted this name, rejecting Hayden Valley or Jewel Valley. San Diego had several prominent businessmen named Jewell at the end of the nineteenth century, and this place might have been named for one of them. (Durham 36; Stein 63)

Jim Green Creek. Flows into Coleman Creek two miles southeast of Santa Ysabel. Named for an English immigrant miner and farmer with a small ranch north of Julian. (Durham 36; Jasper, *Trail-Breakers,* 142-144)

Jofegan. Six miles southwest of Fallbrook. An acronym constructed from the name of General Joseph Fegan (Jo-fegan), the first Camp Pendleton commander in 1942. Was first called **Stock Pen** when it was a shipping point for the O'Neill Ranch, once the Rancho Santa Margarita y Las Flores. (Durham 36; Stein 63-64)

Johnson. Johnson Canyon is five miles north of Warner Springs, opening into the San Luis Rey Valley. Another Johnson Canyon opens into Otay Valley west of Otay Mountain. Named for two reclusive brothers, early settlers (Stein 64). **Johnson Creek** flows into Boulder Creek eight miles north of Descanso. Supposedly named for a man that Indians killed (Davidson Place Name File). James A. Jasper describes the murder in his *Trail-Breakers* (50-53), but says the man's name was James Stewart Johnston. (Durham 36)

Johnstown. On Highway 80 east of El Cajon between Glen View and Flinn Springs. Possibly this is a transfer name from Johnstown, Pennsylvania, or it may have been named for someone called John. According to Lay (68), it existed in 1916.

Jollita Spring. (Span. "little hole") Located on or near the Fortuna Ranch north of the San Diego River west of Santee. Shown on the Partition of Rancho Mission of San Diego, 1885. An English rendering of this Spanish name was **Wahita Spring,** mentioned in some early memoirs.

Joy Meadow. South of Sunrise Highway near Crouch Ranch. Pleasing name whose origins are unknown. (Durham 36; Stein 64)

Juaquapin Creek. Enters Sweetwater River near Highway 79 in Cuyamaca Rancho State Park. Rensch in his *Indian Place Names* gives this as *Wa-Ku-Pin,* saying it means "warm house" (36). Not to be confused with Jacupin, "hot water." Langdon thinks the two place names are the same, but that seems doubtful. (Durham 36; Gudde 187)

Juch Canyon. Along Jim Green Creek two miles southeast of Santa Ysabel. Named for Arthur Juch who homesteaded in this canyon about 1890. (Jasper, *Trail-Breakers,* 105-107; Durham 36)

Judson Reservoir. Four miles northeast of Imperial Beach. It was named for Lemon Judson who owned a nearby ranch south of Chula Vista (Gudde 187). The same man also owned **Judson's Mineral Springs**, five miles from De Luz Station on the California Southern Railroad. Also see the entry for **Lemon.** (Anonymous, *History,* 73; Durham 36)

Julian City. On Highway 78-79, 60 miles northeast of San Diego. Post office established August 8, 1870. (Salley 105) Drury (Drew) D. Bailey had surveyor

John McIntyre lay out the town site in March 1870, having earlier taken out a preemption claim for the land that was not recognized officially for many years. Bailey, something of a wag and trickster, said on numerous occasions that he named the town for his cousin Michael S. Julian, claiming that he did so because Julian was handsomer than he was. Michael Julian was his mining partner and recorder of *The Julian Mining Records*. Both were Georgian Confederate Army veterans. Many documents record the full name of the town as Julian City, but the complete name has been employed only sporadically. (The term "city" was popular in mining circles. See Nevada City, California, and Virginia City, Nevada, and many other mining towns.) Unlike Bailey, the name Julian has classic associations; see the Roman emperor Julian. In spite of countless repetitions of the story (including Stein 64) Julian never had any hope of becoming the San Diego County seat. This was the result of confusion over a sub-election held there and because the story is so compelling; many yearn to believe. (See LeMenager, *Julian City,* 43-52, 109-113, for information about the founders' Civil War careers and Julian's non-candidacy for the county seat.)

- K -

K-Q Ranch. Private resort on Highway 79 about five miles south of Julian. Named for the nearby Gold King and Gold Queen Mines discovered in the late 1880s. At first, miners thought these promising mines would revive the Julian Mining District that had fallen onto hard times, but they never amounted to much. They are on the 1997 Julian 7.5' Quadrangle. (Fetzer, *Good Camp,* 52-54)

Kanaka. Gudde (189) says that the term Kanaka, Hawaiian, apparently occurs as a place name only in northern California counties, but here is one in the south. **Kanaka Flat** is abut two miles northwest of Julian on the Julian 1960 7.5' Quadrangle. I have never been able to find the name of the Hawaiian memorialized by this place name, and there is a chance it is a distortion of an unknown Kumeyaay word. Before the Coleman Grade was constructed, the route to Julian was by way of the **Kanaka Trail**. It went up Santa Ysabel Creek, then north of the Julian townsite and so to the town. (Durham 37; Jasper, *Trail-Breakers,* 10)

Kearchoffer Flat. Nine miles southwest of Descanso. Another example of the problem English-speaking people have with a foreign name, in this case Emanuel Kirchhofer (German "man from the church yard"). Resident of Alpine, according to the *San Diego City-County Directory* of 1910. In 1981 the U.S. Board on Geographic Names rejected a proposal to rename this place Sunrise Valley, probably because there were already too many places named Sunrise in California. (Durham 37)

Kearny, Camp. About eight miles north of San Diego City center. World War I army training base consisting of 3,254 acres of city land and 9,466 acres of county land (Pourade *Glory,* 226), or about 20 square miles. The base post office was established July 18, 1917; during its lifetime the camp trained more than 60,000 men. During World War II it was a naval base with emphasis on aircraft with the base post office opening on December 10, 1942. The name honors General Stephen W. Kearny (1794-1848), leader in the conquest of California during the Mexican-American War. The area of the camp is generally described as **Kearny Mesa.** Now the location of **Kearny Mesa S.D. Eastern Neighborhood.** (Hinds 71; Salley 32)

Keen Valley. A surburb of National City named for Alfred Keen, an early settler here. (Davidson Place Name File; *SDU,* May 20, 1890)

Kelly Ditch. Just north of Cuyamaca Reservoir. It passes under Highway 79. In 1894 the San Diego Flume Company dug this mile-long collecting ditch, to collect runoff from North Peak, on a ranch belonging to James Kelly, hence the name. The ditch brought the water back to the reservoir for storage. However, it promptly washed out and was abandoned. It is now a hiking trail. (Fetzer, *Year,* 180-182)

Kelly, Mount. A hill on the Rancho Agua Hedionda. Named for Robert Kelly who owned the ranch around 1900. (Davidson Place Name File; Durham 50)

Kensington S.D. Mid-City Neighborhood. A transfer name from a west London district. "In 1909, this area was selected by executives of the Santa Fe Railway Company for the building of a luxury subdivision….The man in charge, G.A. Davidson, was a Canadian with an affinity for English place names" (Pryde 224). Hence street names like Marlborough and Edgeware and the name Kensington itself. Many houses were built later, from 1924 to 1926 and in the 1950s. (Security Title 23)

Kentwood-in-the-Pines. Three miles south of Julian on the east side of Highway 79. Henlunt Kent from Los Angeles developed this 2,300-lot subdivision—one of the largest in the Cuyamacas. Most lots sold for about $100. The plat map was filed June 16, 1926. (Durham 37)

Kessler Flat. Six miles south of Santa Ysabel. Probably named for Conrad Kessler, listed as a retired resident of Julian in the *San Diego City-County Directory, 1899-1900.* (Durham 37)

Keys Canyon, Creek. Five miles south of Pala. Named for William Keyes (sic), apiarist, born in Ireland, listed in the U.S. 1880 Census in the Pala district. (Durham 37)

Kidd, Camp. On December 10, 1941, the U.S. Navy took over Balboa Park, naming the facility for Admiral Isaac C. Kidd who died in the Japanese attack on Pearl Harbor. The buildings were used as hospital wards. (Hinds 61-62)

King Creek. Heads on the west slopes of Cuyamaca Peak and empties into El Capitan Reservoir. Probably named for George T. King, 48-year old farmer in the Descanso area, according to the U.S. 1880 Census, 103. (Durham 37)

Kitchen Creek, Valley. Five miles east of Pine Valley. This is a case where English speakers had difficulties with a presumably English word. Named for August Caesar Kitching (sic), prominent rancher in both the San Luis Rey and the Laguna Mountain areas. "Kitchen" was more familiar and easier to pronounce than "Kitching." (J. Davidson, "Texas Cattleman First Settler," *SDET,* October 28, 1939; *SDU,* January 16, 1877)

Klauber Park. See **Encanto.**

Klondike Creek. Flows into San Vicente Creek near San Vicente Reservoir. Named for the Canadian gold mining district, active 1896-1906. LeMenager (*Ramona* 117) says placer mining was practiced here. Gold miners certainly worked in this location in the 1920s. (Durham 37; Stein 66)

Knox's Corners, Knox's Station, Knoxville. See **El Cajon.**

Kolb Valley. See **Colb Valley.**

Kosoyi. See **Cosoy.**

Kuka. See **Cuca.**

Kumpahui Creek. Flows into Lake Henshaw from the west. Probably a Luiseño name, but its meaning is unknown. (Durham 38)

Kwaay Paay Peak. In Mission Trails Regional Park, elevation 1,194 feet. Kumeyaay *kwaaypaay* "chief, captain, judge." (Couro and Hutcheson 28; Schad 98)

Kwaaymii Point. Near the Sunrise Highway in the northern Lagunas. Not far from the Laguna Ranch of the late Tom Lucas. He said he was a member of the Kwaaymii, a family or sub-band of the Kumeyaay Indian tribe, hence the name. On the 1997 Monument Peak 7.5' Quadrangle. (see Carrico "A Brief Glimpse")

Kwellyemak. See **El Capitán Grande.**

- L -

La Barrenda. See **Paradise Creek.**

La Carbonera. See **Switzer Canyon.**

La Costa. (Span. "the coast") Midway between Encinitas and Carlsbad. The earliest settler at this place was Oliver H. Borden and his family who home-steaded in 1879. It is mentioned in the *SDU,* January 1, 1893, and there was a La Costa post office from 1896 to 1905. Inland there is now a resort, **Rancho La Costa**. This place got a post office in 1976 as a rural branch of the Carlsbad post office. (Salley 111; Stein 66)

La Cresta. See **Crest.**

La Honda Spring. (Span. "deep"). Just north of Jamul off Highway 94. (Durham 38)

La Jolla, Point La Jolla. The town is fifteen miles up the coast from San Diego where it is officially **La Jolla S.D. Northern Neighborhood** and **La Jolla Village S.D. Northern Neighborhood.** According to Gudde (185) the name comes from a geographical term. "[Joya, also spelled hoya or jolla] is a common Mexican Spanish geographical term referring to a hollow in the moun-tains, a hollow worn in a river bed, or a hollow on the coast worn by waves." The same term can be seen in the name of the **La Jolla Indian Reservation,** a Luiseño reservation in the San Luis River Valley, 7,957 acres, founded in 1892, and in Jollita Spring near the San Diego River, as well as place names in Fresno, Santa Barbara, and Ventura Counties. The first settlers came to La Jolla in 1869; the name was first used in 1871 (Schaelchlin 30-31). The first post office at the site was called **La Jolla Park** in 1888; this was after Frank T. Botsford with his partner George W. Heald subdivided the area in 1887. The post office be-came La Jolla in 1894. Gudde also says "The popular tradition that the name is derived from the Spanish word *joya* 'jewel' sounds plausible..., but it is supported by no evidence." Margaret Langdon asserts that the word's origin may lie in Kumeyaay *matku-laahuuy* "place that has holes or caves." For **La Jolla Amago** see **Amago.** (Gudde 185-186; Pourade *Glory,* 45; Salley 110; Schaelchlin 16-19)

La Mesa. Between San Diego and El Cajon. There is no mesa in La Mesa. The place was first called **Allison Springs** or **Allison Station** for sheep rancher Robert Allison who bought 4,000 acres of land here in 1869. (The springs are in today's Collier Park, just south of downtown La Mesa.) In March 1887 the San Diego Flume Company developed a subdivision it called La Mesa Colony on the nearby mesa north of University Avenue and east of 61ˢᵗ Street, now mostly in the city of San Diego. Someone decided to merge the two names, La Mesa Colony and Allison Springs; the result was La Mesa Springs, then La Mesa. When the place got its first post office in 1891 it was as Lamesa because at the time the post office authorities required one-word names, but the two-word La Mesa triumphed in 1905. C.C. Park and S.C. Grable developed the area vigorously in 1906; one 200-acre development was called Park Grable. In World War II there was a large army training base in the general area of Lake Murray Blvd. and Navajo Road called **Camp La Mesa**. (Hinds 117-118). **La Mesa Reservoir** was the predecessor of Lake Murray. See that entry. **La Mesa Ditch,** open to the sky, brought water from Eucalyptus Reservoir (now Briercrest Park) to La Mesa Reservoir. (La Mesa, 1-14; Salley 110; Security Title 25; Stein 69-70)

La Nación Land Grant. See **National City.**

La Paleta Valley, Creek. (Span. "shovel, shoulder blade, artist's palette.") Just north of National City. Probably refers to the shape of the valley, but it may refer to color—see the reference to the artist's palette. The name was on the 1859 U.S. map of San Diego Bay. (Durham 39; Gudde 203)

La Playa. (Span. "beach") Beach extending north of Ballast Point, now partially blocked by Shelter Island. Before 1848 this was the center of the hide trade for all southern California. Local people sometimes referred to it as **Las Barracas** "the shacks" for the unsightly warehouses at the site. Alfred Robinson in his *Life in California* called it **Hide Park,** punning on London's Hyde Park. (Durham 39-40; Gudde 295)

La Posta Creek, Valley. (Span. "relay station, post") Ten miles north of Campo on old Highway 80. Stein (70-71) says there was once a stage coach station here. The Cameron Corners 1959 7.5' Quadrangle has a **La Posta Service.** Could this refer to a gasoline station? **La Posta Indian Reservation,** 3,566 acres, was founded in 1893. (Pryde 64)

La Presa. (Span. "dam") Named in 1887 for the nearby Sweetwater Dam. Terminus of the National City & Otay Railroad. Post office 1888, 1889-1895. One of the 1887 boom towns; the San Diego Development Company put it on the market and sold $45,000 worth of land the first week. (Salley 111, Stein 71)

La Punta. The extreme southern end of San Diego Bay on the road to Tijuana. On the 1782 Pantoja map marked as *R[io] y Ranc[heria] de la Punta*. The name in Spanish can mean "end," hence "end of the bay." Site of the salt works that commenced in 1872. **Rancho La Punta** in the South Bay was supposedly granted to Santiago Emilio Argüello in 1834, but the U.S. Land Commission rejected his claim. This opened the area for homesteading and the emergence of towns such as Otay, Nestor, Oneonta, and others. Argüello had a ranch house dating from the 1830s overlooking the bay, but the construction of Interstate 5 annihilated it. The rancho was often called **Rancho Milijo,** which apparently is a misspelling of **Milejo.** Two theories account for this name. The most plausible is that Milejo was an Indian village just south of the bay. Engelhardt (*San Diego* 350) spells the village name as Melijo. Milejo was one of the rancherias that sent participants to the San Diego Mission uprising of 1775 (Carrico, "Sociopolitical" 149). Thus it is assumed that the name is Kumeyaay with an unknown meaning. Another theory proposes that there was a rancher Agustín Melijo, and therefore Melijo is a Spanish surname. This Melijo, if he existed, is elusive. (Rush 5) To add to the confusion, Carlin (21) reproduces an English translation of the San Diego (Coronado) Land Grant that says the grant is bounded "on the east by the point of land on the Ranch of San Augustin Metijo [sic]." To the best of my knowledge there has never been a saint by this name. The theory that Milejo was the name of an Indian village is convincing. (Durham 40; Gunn, Guide, "Border;" Pourade *Silver,* 65; Webster 34)

La Purisima. See **National City.**

La Viñita. See **Flinn Springs.**

La Zanja Canyon. (Span. "irrigation ditch") Four miles south of Rancho Santa Fe leading towards Rancho Bernardo. It is not clear where the ditch led, if it existed. Perhaps the name comes from the shape of the canyon. (Durham 40)

Ladrillo. (Span. "brick") Station on the Santa Fe Railroad north of Atwood and south of Elvira. Center of a brick-making district going back to the 1850s. This was the location of the Union Brick Company and its strange leaning chimney, built in 1888. The chimney collapsed in 1962. (J. Davidson, "San Diego County Gazeteer," *SDET,* June 27, 1942; Durham 38; *SDU,* January 21, 1962)

Laguna Mountains, Summit. (Span. *laguna* "lake") Mountain range extending from Interstate 8 north at least to the junction of Sunrise Highway and Highway 79. The name comes from two small lakes near the center of the range, **Big** and **Little Laguna Lakes.** Because they are not on paved roads, many people do not know they exist. Never very large, they have low dams to increase their storage capacity. The name has been in use since the 1870s. On the Cuyamaca Rancho *diseño* the mountains are called **Sierra de Jacupin,** "Hot Spring Mountains" for small hot springs near the lakes. (For an analysis of the Kumeyaay word for "hot springs" see **Warner Springs**.) For this reason the district was sometimes called **Agua Caliente. Laguna Indian Reservation** is on the west side of Sunrise Highway west of Garnet Peak. Always associated with the late Tom Lucas. See **Lucas Creek.** For the settlement on the mountain see **Mount Laguna.** (Durham 6, 41; Gudde 200; Stein 67)

Laguna Seca. (Span. "dry lake") In fact, sometimes called **Dry Lake** by English speakers. Also known as **Laguna que se seca** (Span. "Lake that dries up") A string of ponds now under Cuyamaca Dam and Reservoir, dating from 1887. Every summer the ponds indeed disappeared with the heat.

Lake. See under specific names, for example, **Hodges, Lake.**

Lakeside. Northeast about ten miles from El Cajon on the San Diego River. Named for a small natural body of water, **Lindo Lake,** a Spanish-English hybrid name, "Pretty Lake." Perhaps the name of the lake was supposed to be Lindo [Lago] or more correctly Lago Lindo, but indecision triumphed. The town was platted in June 1886 by El Cajon Valley Company. The post office was established in 1887. **Lakeside Farms,** about a mile northwest of Lakeside, appears on the El Cajon 1967 7.5' Quadrangle. (Durham 39; Salley 113; Stein 201)

Lakeview. See **Glenview.**

Lancaster Mountain. Four miles southwest of the Pala Indian Reservation, elevation 1,485 feet. Named for Alford H. Lancaster or George M. Lancaster, Pala farmers, whose names appear on the 1880 U.S. Census (253). (Gudde 202; Stein 70)

Lane Field. Baseball field at the foot of Broadway. Named for William H. Lane, 1860-1938, former mining engineer who owned the first San Diego Padre franchise. The first season opened in 1936 and the last game was played here in 1957. (J. Davidson, "San Diego County Gazeteer;" *SDET,* August 2, 1942)

Lanoitan. A district three miles southeast of National City. Had its own post office from 1925 to 1928. The only reverse-spelled name in the county—see National City. (I suspect, however, that there are more than a few street names of this type lurking in the county. See, for example, Nobel and Lebon Drives which intersect in University City.) Ruben Harrison, National City attorney and the father of Harrison Park, may have invented this name. See **Lincoln Acres.** Just over the line in Riverside County is the community of Radec, also with reverse spelling. It is ingenious, but not as appealing as Lanoitan, which sounds, to me, vaguely Latin, Romantic, maybe French Canadian. (Davidson, Place Name File; Durham 41; Salley 114)

Lark Canyon. In McCain Valley north of Boulevard. Unusual bird name. Was it named for horned larks? Meadowlarks? Did the namer know the difference? (Durham 40)

Larkinville. Fifteen miles east of Campo, near present Boulevard. Had a post office for two months in 1876. Named for Peter Larkin, the first postmaster. (Durham 8; Salley 114)

Las Bancas. (Span. "little flats or benches") Between Pine Valley and lower Descanso Valley west of Guatay Mountain. Descanso early had a large Spanish-speaking population, so place names like Descanso and Las Bancas should be expected. (Durham 40)

Las Barracas. See **La Playa.**

Las Flores. (Span. "flowers") Six miles southeast of San Onofre. Fr. Juan Crespí named this place **Cañada de Santa Praxedis de los Rosales**, "Canyon of Saint Praxedis of the Rose Gardens" (for a second century martyr whose feast day was July 21), when he was on the Portolá expedition in July 1769. This was because of the numerous wild roses growing here. Padre Pedro Font in 1776 called it Las Flores, probably on the basis of Crespí's name, and the place became known as the Rancho Las Flores. In 1844 the Pico family bought the ranch and combined it with their Rancho Santa Margarita y San Onofre to form Rancho Santa Margarita y las Flores. There was an *asistencia* here, founded about 1823, for the Indian community under the jurisdiction of the San Luis Rey Mission. **Las Flores Creek** in **Las Flores Canyon** flows into the sea five miles southeast of San Onofre Mountain. **Las Flores Station** is on the Santa Fe Railroad in this location. (Gudde 133; Hanna 107; Stein 71)

Las Lomas Muertas. (Span. "barren hills") According to Gudde, when the Spanish word *muerto* is used with a generic name it means "barren." (251) A ridge five miles southeast of Escondido. (Durham 40)

Las Posas. (Span. "wells"). In Spanish California, no distinction was made between *pozo* and *poza,* and they were sometimes spelled *poso* or *posa,* according to Gudde (301). This was the name for a cluster of homesteads about fifteen miles east of San Luis Rey settled in 1881-1882 by James F. Barham and William Couch. (J. Davidson "Las Posas 'Written Up' by Early-Day Scribes," *SDET,* August 13, 1937)

Las Pulgas Canyon, Camp, Lake. (Span. "fleas") Opens to the sea midway between San Onofre and Oceanside. Now on Camp Pendleton. This was the site of a farm for the San Luis Rey Mission as early as 1828. (Durham 40; Gudde 304; Stein 71)

Lawson Valley, Creek, Peak. About eight miles northeast from Jamul. Named for John Lawson, a settler in the 1870s. Had its own post office 1890-1891. (Durham 40; Salley 117; *San Diego County Assessment Rolls for 1873-1874*).

Lee Valley. Four miles east of Jamul on Jamul Creek. Named for Albert Lee who homesteaded at Honeysprings and Deerhorn Valley Roads in 1895. (Turley 11)

Lemon. Six miles east of Otay. Named not for the fruit but for Lemon Judson, pioneer rancher. Had its own post office 1892-1895. The *San Diego City-County Directory, 1895,* lists 19 male adults, some no doubt with families, living here. See also **Judson Reservoir** and **Judson Mineral Springs.** (Durham 54; Salley 117)

Lemon Grove. Immediately southeast of San Diego. The Allison brothers named it for the numerous lemon groves in the area. The brothers subdivided it into mini-farms of 10 or 20 acres. Water came from the San Diego Flume. On the San Diego Cuyamaca & Eastern Railroad. Sometimes called **The Grove.** Got a post office in 1893. (Durham 41; Gudde 208; Hall; Salley 117; Stein 72)

Letterbox Canyon. Seven miles southeast of Oceanside. Obviously, there was a mailbox somewhere near the site. (Durham 41)

Leucadia. Three miles north of Encinitas. Named for a Greek Ionian Island, today called Levkada. The name comes ultimately from Greek *leukos* "white." In the 1930s Cave Couts Jr. wrote a letter to Mrs. Evelyn Sands in which he said that the town was founded by a group of British spiritualists who came to the U.S. seeking religious freedom (Anonymous, "Leucadia") This statement has been repeated often. Spiritualism, however, has never been persecuted in England. See, for example, the careers of Annie Besant, Madam Helena Blavatsky (resident in England 1891-1895), and the earnest spiritualist appeals of Sir Arthur Conan Doyle in the early twentieth century. Besides, no one has ever been able to identify the members of this group. Credit for founding the town should go to the Leucadia Company, which developed the town in 1887-1888. According to an article in the *SDU,* October 25, 1887, "Mr. [Thomas] Fitch, an officer of the company was to appear at a gala opening for potential buyers to deliver a speech entitled 'Greek Gods and California Boomers…'

and then the auction of 200 lots will begin." Like Cardiff with its British and Irish street names, Leucadia had an ethnic theme, and so got Greek street names, surviving today, such as Eolus Ave., Plato Place, etc. Hanna says the developer of the town was of Greek ancestry, but I have never found any evidence to support this. The town got its first post office in 1888. (Gudde 208; Hanna 171; Kooperman 272; Salley 117; Stein 72)

Liberty Station. See Rose (Louis Rose).

Lilac. Six miles northwest of Valley Center. Named for the California lilac, *Ceanothus,* not the garden lilac. Had a post office 1898-1912. (Durham 41; Salley 118; Stein 73)

Lillian Hill. Nine miles northwest of Descanso. Unknown origin. Like Juan Flat or Mildred Falls, a place name derived from a given name is particularly difficult to trace. (Durham 41; Stein 73)

Lincoln Acres. South of National City on north side of Sweetwater River. Ruben E. Harrison of National City developed this area in 1922-1924. Got its own post office in 1927. Presumedly, developers named the development for President Abraham Lincoln, but there was a developer in the area named Lincoln Moore. (Durham 41; Salley 118)

Lincoln Park S.D. Southeastern Neighborhood. The Bartlett Estate Company first developed this area in 1888, presumably naming it for President Abraham Lincoln. It was once called Frary's Addition. (Security Title 26)

Linda Vista. (Span. "pretty view") There are two of these, an old Linda Vista and a new Linda Vista. In 1886 Colonel W.C. Dickinson developed a Linda Vista along the California Southern Railroad not far from Rose Canyon and Soledad Canyon (*SDU,* May 1, 1887). Had its own post office in 1886. The development failed. During World War II, authorities built a new Linda Vista, a vast housing project mostly intended to house Consolidated Aircraft employees; this was on Kearny Mesa north of the San Diego River. During the war in 1944 when German troops destroyed a Greek Village named **Distoma**, Linda Vista residents held an election to change their community name to Distoma, but the measure failed. (MacMullen "San Diego") After the war, the area was privately developed, especially from 1952 to 1955. Now **Linda Vista Western S.D. Neighborhood.** (Durham 41; Gudde 210-211; Salley 118)

Lindbergh Field. Named for Charles Lindbergh, whose plane "The Spirit of St. Louis" was built in San Diego in 1927. San Diego's municipal airport, it was built up in 1930 with silt dredged from the bay, and dedicated on July 28,

1932. On that occasion Amelia Earhart gave the main address. (Kooperman 63-64)

Lindo Lake. See **Lakeside.**

Linwood. According to Christian Brown (interview at SDHS) this was a station on the National City & Otay Railroad in the Sweetwater Valley. Nearby was a 20-acre popular picnic ground called **Linwood Grove** (also spelled Lynwood Grove) owned by Frank Kimball. It washed away in the 1916 Hatfield flood. Not to be confused with the district called Lynwood Hills south of the Sweetwater River. (Phillips, *National City,* 50)

Lion Creek. On Palomar Mountain two miles northwest of Boucher Hill. This is apparently the only mountain lion place name in the county. (Durham 41; Stein 73)

Little Chief Mountain. Two miles northeast of Pala, just south of Chief Mountain. Named for the nearby Pala Chief gem mine. (Durham 41)

Little Italy Central S.D. Neighborhood. North of downtown San Diego. Named for the Italian immigrants and their descendents who live in the area. Interstate 5 plowed through the district, and most of what survived of Little Italy is now west of the highway. Has recently become a fashionable residential district.

Little Landers. Just north of the Mexican border in the Tijuana River Valley. On the Rodney Stokes 1910 map of San Diego County. William E. Smythe founded the colony in 1908 on 500 acres, subdivided into lots of about one acre. Smythe believed that a family could live well on this acre, if irrigated. "A Little Land and a Living Surely is Better than Desperate Struggle and Wealth Possibly," he said. About 300 families bought lots for about $350. The 1916 Hatfield flood on the Tijuana River destroyed 25 houses and damaged the land so drastically that the colony never completely recovered. Officially closed in 1922. See **San Ysidro**, the town on higher ground that the Little Landers established. (Kooperman 41-42)

Little Libby Lake. Five miles east of Oceanside. Named for the Libby family, Benjamin, Charles, and William, and spouses, with children. Sometimes spelled Libbey. (J. Davidson, "San Diego County Gazeteer," *SDET,* September 12, 1942)

Little Texas. See **Campo.**

Little Three Mine. About four miles east of Ramona near Hatfield Creek. In 1903 H.W. Robb discovered this gem mine. He had two partners, Dan

McIntosh of Ramona and Charles F. Schnack of Escondido, hence the name of the mine. It prospered in its early years but never fully recovered from the Chinese Revolution of 1911 and the collapse of the Chinese luxury market. Famous for its topazes and garnets. (Foord 165-166)

Live Oak Springs. See Oak.

Lockett, Camp. Near Campo. Established December 10, 1941, this camp eventually covered 7,108 acres. Honors Colonel James Lockett, U.S. Army, twice cited for gallantry in action in the Philippines in 1899. Earlier nearby there had been an **El Campo Camp** whose purpose was to defend the Mexican border. Camp Lockett was a training site for cavalry and armored units. The cavalry units came from Fort Riley Kansas and included "buffalo soldiers," black soldiers of the 10th Cavalry Regiment. Post office 1942-1944. (Hinds, Supplement, 1; Salley 32)

Locksville. See San Luis Rey.

Lockwood Mesa, Lockwood's Station. See Solana Beach.

Logan, Barrio Logan S.D. Central Neighborhood. (Span. "neighborhood"). Named for General John A. Logan, Civil War hero (1826-1886). Formerly part of Logan Heights, this evolved as a neighborhood west of Interstate 5 with many Spanish speakers. (J. Davidson, "San Diego County Gazeteer," *SDET,* October 6, 1942; Durham 42)

Logan Heights S.D. Central Neighborhood. Between Interstates 5 and 15. Like Barrio Logan, named for Civil War General John A. Logan. Developed first in 1886, and then sporadically to 1906. Several major streets are named for Spanish-American War admirals such as Sampson St. for Admiral William Thomas Sampson. (Showley)

Loma Alta Settlement, Creek, Mountain. (Span. "high hill") Six miles east of Oceanside. There was a small settlement here with this name on the Santa Fe Railroad (Durham 42; Stein 73).

Loma Portal. (From Latin *porta* "gate") On the eastern slopes of Point Loma. Had its own post office from 1915 to 1928. Now is **Loma Portal S.D. Western Neighborhood.** (Gudde 214; Salley 121)

Lomaland. Obviously derived from Point Loma. This was the name of the Theosophical Society headquarters on the ridge of Point Loma 1899-1942. (J. Davidson, "San Diego County Gazeteer," *SDET,* November 7, 1942)

Lomita. See **Jamacha-Lomita S.D. Southeastern Neighborhood.**

Lone Fir Point. Off Nate Harrison Grade on Palomar Mountain. A rare reference to the high-altitude native white fir, *Abies concolor*, sometimes cut for lumber. (Stein 73)

Lone Tiger Spring. Three miles north of Jacumba. The name may come from a striking rock formation. (Durham 42)

Long Potrero. See **Potrero.**

Long Range Mountain. See **Cowles Mountain.**

Lookout Mountain. See **Dictionary Hill.**

Loop's Beach. The beach north of Torrey Pines near the mouth of Peñasquitos Creek. Named for Theodore Murray Loop, associated with the development of Del Mar. Sometimes incorrectly spelled Loup's Beach. Also called **Cordero Beach.** See **Cordero.** (J. Davidson, "San Diego County Gazeteer," *SDET,* December 14, 1942; Ewing 44)

Lopez Canyon. Tributary to Peñasquitos Canyon, merging just east of Interstate 5. The Lopez family homesteaded here early in the twentieth century. Yet remaining is an inscription in concrete "RAMONA LOPEZ, Oct. 25, 1947." (Schad 84, 88-89)

Los Angeles Junction. Two miles north of Oceanside. Where the Fallbrook line connected with the main line of the Santa Fe Railroad. This must have been one of the county's more confusing railroad names—a place called Los Angeles in San Diego County. Sensibly, now named **Fallbrook Junction.** (Durham 43)

Los Gatos Ravine. (Span. "cats") Seven miles northwest of Buckman Springs. This could refer to domestic cats or the wild variety. The generic ravine is not common in the county. (Durham 43)

Los Pinos Mountains. (Span. "pines") North of Morena Reservoir and west of Pine Valley. Elevation 4,807 feet. These mountains do in fact have a cover of pines. Gudde (291-292) says that English speakers (including Stein) sometimes misspell this term as piños because the correct form pinos is dangerously close to the English word penis. (Durham 43, Stein 75)

Los Terrenitos. (Span. "little bits of land") West of Descanso on Sweetwater River. Early in the twentieth century the Stanley Groome family operated a resort here with this name. (Durham 43; La Force 366)

Los Tules. See **Tule.**

Los Vallecitos. (Span. "little valleys") Seven miles north of Rancho Santa Fe along San Marcos Creek. Perhaps a vestige of the name of San Marcos land grant, Los Vallecitos de San Marcós. (Durham 44)

Lost. Not really lost, but a name for a remote feature. **Lost Lake** is an ephemeral lake that becomes "lost" as it dries up. It is just west of Warner Springs. **Lost Valley.** Six miles northeast of Warner Springs. Jasper says Jim Stone of Mesa Grande named it because of its isolation. **Lost Islands.** This is the common name for Cortes Bank and Tanner Bank, submarine islands a hundred miles off the San Diego Coast. (Gudde 218; Stein 75-76; *U.S. Coast Pilot* 41-42)

Lotus Pond. This was a farm pond on Hervey Parke's Alta Ranch in the 1890s. So named became the owners planted it with exotic aquatic plants. It survives at Anthony's Restaurant not far from Grossmont Summit. In general, county residents do not like the generic name pond; no matter how small a body of water, it's usually called a lake. (Guy 49-50)

Louis Rose Point. See **Rose (Louis Rose).**

Love Valley. On the East Grade on Palomar Mountain. Named for John A. Love, prominent early rancher. (J. Davidson, "Love Valley Returning Gradually to Conditions of Indian Age," *SDET,* April 26, 1930; Durham 44)

Loveland Reservoir. Three miles south of Alpine on the Sweetwater Reservoir. Named for Chester H. Loveland, president of the California Water and Telephone Corporation, the company that built the dam 1943-1945. (*SDU,* September 12, 1945)

Lovett's Bee Ranch. See **Glen Oak** (under **Oak**).

Lowe. Station on the San Diego Cuyamaca & Eastern Railroad between Hollydale and Chollas in 1919. There were several prominent San Diego businessmen with this name at the end of the nineteenth century. (Hanft, inside front cover)

Lower Otay Reservoir. See **Otay.**

Lucas Creek. Four miles northwest of Monument Peak in the Lagunas. Named for Tom Lucas, last of the full-blooded Laguna Kumeyaay. See **Kwaymii Point.** (Durham 44)

Lucky 5 Ranch. See **Harper Valley.**

Lusardi. The name of a family of nineteenth century Italian immigrant farmers and sheepherders who worked and lived in the Rancho Santa Fe-Black Mountain area and elsewhere in North County. **Lusardi Canyon** opens into San Luis Rey River Valley seven miles southeast of Boucher Hill. **Lusardi Creek** is two miles east of Rancho Santa Fe. The family sold land to Douglas Fairbanks Sr. for his Zorro, later Fairbanks, Ranch. There was a settlement called **Lusardi** on Lusardi Creek five miles south of Lake Hodges and three miles northwest of Black Mountain. It had a post office as of 1889, and sporadically until 1911. Peter (Pietro) Lusardi (1838-1929) was the first postmaster. On the Escondido 1901 15' Quadrangle. Presumably, the Lusardi School, open from 1890 to 1904, was at this community. (Durham 45; Ewing 34; San Diego County School Records Inventory; Salley 125; Stein 76)

Lux Valley. Two miles east of Encinitas. Manchester Ave. passes through Lux Valley. Named for John and Christiana Lux, early settlers from Germany who lived here. (Durham 45; Land)

Lycuan Indian Reservation. When the notice establishing the Sycuan Reservation was published on December 27, 1875, as the result of a typographical error (the printer misread an S for L), it was printed as Lycuan Reservation. This error will not die. In Pourade, *Glory,* 147, 90 years later, we read that the Lycuan Reservation was established in 1875. Also see **Maja Reservation.**

Lynwood Grove. See **Linwood Grove.**

Lyons Creek, Valley, Peak. Five miles east of Jamul. In 1851 young Captain Nathaniel Lyon helped survey this area for a possible route between San Diego and Yuma. He also apparently acquired land here. Very early in the Civil War General Lyon was killed at the Battle of Wilson's Creek. Some early accounts say he left all his property to the U.S. government, but according to his biographer Ashbel Woodward (357), "The newspaper statement that Gen. Lyon gave his property by will to the Government, is erroneous." (Davidson Place Name File; Durham 45, Stein 76-77; Turley 1-3)

- M -

Mack Mine. About two miles southeast of Rincon. This is the best-known gem mine in the Rincon District. It is named for John M. Mack, who discovered it in 1903. It is on the 1997 Boucher Hill 7.5' Quadrangle. (Weber 106)

Mackinnon's Landing. See **Cardiff-by-the-Sea.**

Magee Creek. Northeast of Pala. It flows into the San Luis Rey River. Named for John Magee, 54-year old merchant listed on the 1880 U.S. Census, 73. (Durham 45)

Magnesia. Near Chula Vista. A nearby plant produced magnesium chloride from the waters of San Diego Bay. Briefly it had a post office in 1915. (Salley A3)

Maja Indian Reservation. When the authorities published a list of new San Diego County Indian reservations on December 27, 1875, the typesetter misread the first two letters In- or Iñ- in the name of the Inaja reservation as M-, so that he set the word as Maja, later confounding several historians. Hero Eugene Rensch (*Indian* 38) said Maja was "the southern part of what was later the Inaja Indian Reservation." Pourade, *Glory,* 147, lists a **Maja Reservation**, with the wrong acreage, among the 1875 reservations. See **Lycuan Reservation** also.

Malava Valley. See **Mendenhall Valley.**

Manzanita Indian Reservation. North of Interstate 8 in southeastern San Diego County. Manzanita is a common chaparral shrub. In Spanish, it means "little apple." The reservation, founded in 1893, has 4,580 acres of land. (Pryde 64)

Marbello. (Span. "beautiful sea." There is a Marbella in southern coastal Spain) In 1959 an unsuccessful attempt was made to form a new town by merging Encinitas, Cardiff, and Leucadia. A contest was held to choose a name for the united town and Marbello was declared the winner. Besides the obvious suggestion to preserve one of the three town names as the name for all, many other names were submitted. Here are the other final candidates: Mar Linda, Mar Cresta, Sans Beach (Sand Beach?), Crescent Beach, Sea View, Los Palermos (?), Moonlight Bay, Poinsetta Bowl, Moonlight Beach, Via Mar, Playa Encantado, Reinas (Span. "Queens"), Alta Mar, Del Oro, El Fresco, Tri-City, Solamar, San Dieguito, Encardia (the most ingenious, the only acronym, formed from the three town names—but it sounds like a heart disease), Cresta Mar, Marsaille (Marseille?), Las Olas (Span. "waves"), Miramar, Arena Mar, and Portola (but there's already one in Northern California). Note how many of the names, including the winner, are Spanish—the spirit of Helen Hunt Jackson's *Ramona* lives on. None of them seem truly inspired. For other town-naming contests see **Coronado** and **Serra Mesa.** (*SDET,* September 23, 1959)

Mariette Creek. Flows into Jim Green Creek one mile northwest of Julian. An error for what should have been Marlette Creek, for Joseph H. Marlette, Julian farmer in the 1880 U.S. Census. (Durham 45; Jasper, *Trail-Breakers,* 136-137)

Margarita. See **Ranch House.**

Marina Central S.D. Neighborhood. West of the Gaslamp District on the harbor. It does in fact have a marina, a mooring place for small boats. There's a Marina district in San Francisco and a Marina del Rey in Los Angeles.

Marion Canyon. Enters the San Luis Rey Valley two miles east of Pala. Stein (78) says it was named for the Marion family who homesteaded in the Pala District. (Durham 45)

Marmarosa. A station on the San Diego Arizona & Eastern Railroad on the shore of San Diego Bay near Chula Vista. This may be the prettiest name in the county. Probably from Greek *marmaros* "marble." It sounds as though it was intended as a shipping point for rock products. (Hanft, inside front cover; Blackburn's 1931 San Diego County Map)

Marron. There is a **Marron Valley** between Vista and Oceanside, named no doubt from the prominent Marrón family, and particularly Juan María Marrón, grantee of Rancho Agua Hedionda. **Mount Marron** is eight miles southeast of Oceanside, with probably the same source for its name. **Marron Canyon**, however, is four miles east of Otay Mountain on the Mexican border. Named for a different Juan Marrón, an 1880s settler. (Durham 45, 50; Schmid 118-122)

Marston. Several San Diego places were named for San Diego merchant and philanthropist George Marston (1850-1946). **Camp Marston** is a YMCA camp in Pine Hills named for him in 1920. **Marston Point** is on the western side of Balboa Park. It was once (before tall trees and taller buildings intervened) known for its fine views of the harbor. **Marston Meadow** is six miles south of Julian on the west side of Cuyamaca Peak. (Durham 11, 45)

Matacawat, Mataquequat. See **Cameron Corners.**

Mataguay. (Kumeyaay *Mataahway* "place that has white clay." Couro and Hutcheson 31) A cluster of place names at the north end of the Volcan Mountains above Lake Henshaw. Boy Scout **Camp Mataguay,** on private land, dates from the early 1960s. **Matagual** (sic) **Valley, Creek.** In 1962 the U.S. Board on Geographic Names ruled that this was the correct spelling for these features, not Matagua, Mataguay, or Matajuae. The decision seems contrary to the conventional spelling for the places. Kroeber (47) says Matagual is a misprint. Margaret Langdon in Gudde (230) submits different interpretations of this place name. She believes that the name means either "battleground" or "ground-red." (Stein 78; Durham 45)

Matthews, Camp. Marine Corps base dating from 1917, but most active after 1942. On the mesa above La Jolla, 577 acres. Now the site of UCSD. It survived until the 1960s. Named for General Calvin B. Matthews USMC (1882-1939). (Durham 11; Hinds 90-91)

Maxcy's (Maxey's) Vineyard. See **Vineyard.**

McAlmond Canyon. Opens to Cottonwood Creek two miles north of Barrett Junction. Named for Captain C.G. McAlmond, early settler in the Potrero district. He was also pilot commissioner for the port of San Diego. (Durham 46; Stein 77)

McClellan-Palomar Airport. Five miles southeast of Carlsbad. Opened in 1959, it is operated by San Diego County. Originally called Palomar Airport, in 1982 its name was expanded to honor Gerald McClellan, a private pilot and community leader. (Gaona)

McGee Flat, Post Office. Five miles southeast of Santa Ysabel. The post office here operated from 1891 to 1893. It was named, like the Flat, for Richard W. McGee, the first postmaster. (Durham 37; Salley 132)

McGinty Mountain. Five miles southeast of El Cajon, elevation 2,183 foot. According to Stein it was named for a miner who produced some kind of ceramic product here in the early 1900s. (Durham 46; Stein 77)

McGonigle Canyon. Canyon running from Soledad east towards Black Mountain. Takes its name from the McGonigle family, of Soledad, Irish immigrants, who lived here as early as 1874 (*SDU,* January 31, 1874). They appear in the 1880 U.S Census, San Dieguito Township, 246. McGonigle Road survives near Torrey Pines Beach. An early name for the place was **Cordero Valley.** See **Cordero** and **Carmel Valley.** (Durham 46; Ewing 36-37; Gudde 222; Stein 78)

McKellar Stage Station. See **Cocktail Springs.**

Medanos Point. (Span. "sand dune or bank") Just north of the entrance to Mission Bay at Mission Beach. Sometimes misspelled as Meganos. On Fitch map of 1845. Also see **Ocean Beach.** (Durham 58; Gudde 232)

Melijo. See **La Punta.**

Memorial S.D. Southeastern Neighborhood. In 1922 Memorial Junior High School was named in memory of San Diegans who died in World War I. The neighborhood was probably named for the school. There is also a Memorial Community Park. (*SDU,* March 23, 1947)

Mendenhall Valley. On the eastern slopes of Palomar Mountain. Named for the Mendenhall family, long-time ranchers on the mountain. The family founder, Enos Mendenhall, came here about 1870, followed by his three sons. An earlier name for the place was **Malava Valley,** a Luiseño name whose meaning is unknown. There was a Malava School 1877-1903. For another Mendenhall property see **Cuca.** (San Diego County School Records Inventory; Wood 61-64)

Meridian District. In east El Cajon. The north-south San Bernardino Meridian, the basis for mapping all land titles in southern California, passes through El Cajon Valley just west of Third St., hence the name. There was a Meridian School here as of 1887. (Durham 8; San Diego County School Records Inventory)

Merigan. See **Sumac.**

Merle. Three miles north of Encinitas on the Santa Fe Railroad very close to today's Leucadia. The authorities established its post office in 1888, and discontinued in 1909. It was named for the son of the first settler, a youngster named Merle Scott. There was a Merle school from 1889 to 1903. (Davidson Place Name File; Durham 46; Salley 134; San Diego County School Records Inventory)

Merriam Mountains. A range of hills four or five miles in length northwest of Escondido. Major Gustavus F. Merriam was the first settler in this area in 1875. He had a famous feud with Cave Couts, and apparently won. (Durham 46; Gudde 235; Stein 79)

Merton. Eight miles south of Bernardo at the southwest end of Poway Valley. Had its own post office from 1890 to 1902. The place got a Merton School in 1907. English settlers in the district probably named it for fourteenth century Merton College, part of England's Oxford University. (Durham 46, Salley 134, San Diego County School Records Inventory)

Mesa Grande Indian Reservation. (Span. "large tableland") Northwest from Santa Ysabel. The reservation was founded in 1875, and consists of 920 acres. The post office was established for seven months in 1879, then re-established as **Mesaville** in 1883. Local residents disliked the name intensely, and the authorities changed it to **Mesa Grande** the same year. Its Kumeyaay name is **Tekemak** (Couro and Hutcheson 45) meaning literally "behind the ridge" from *teke* (?) "ridge" and *'emak* "behind." Compare with place name Cuyamaca "behind the clouds." (Salley 79-80; Stein 79-80)

Mesa, The. A ridge seven miles southwest of Alpine. How such a generalized name appeared at such a remote location is unknown. (Gudde 235; Stein 138)

Mesaville. See **Mesa Grande.**

Mexican Canyon. Parallel and east of Highway 94 between Jamul and Jamacha. Probably got its name as a route for immigrants moving north from the border. On AAA 1996 San Diego County Map.

Middle Peak. The middle of the three Cuyamaca peaks. John Davidson and Stein confused Middle and North Peaks. Read them with care. Stein also calls this peak Middle Mesa Peak, a name which I have never seen elsewhere. The Kumeyaay name, as interpreted by English speakers, is also muddled. See Camp Hual-Cu-Cuish for one theory. (Durham 47; Stein 80)

Middletown. As the name indicates, on the bay midway between Old Town and New Town. In 1850 Agoston Haraszty, Cave Couts, and W.H. Emory bought 687 acres on the bay to connect the two communities. The development, Middletown, never prospered. (J. Davidson, "San Diego in Four Units in 1850," *SDET* April 5, 1935; Pourade, *Silver,* 163; Smythe 321)

Midtown S.D. Western Neighborhood. This appears to be a reduced version of what was once called Middletown. Interstate 5 separates Midtown from the Midway District.

Midway S.D. Western Neighborhood. Immediately west of Interstate 5. May have taken its name from Midway Drive which bisects the district.

Miguel. See **San Miguel.**

Mildred Falls. A waterfall on Ritchie Creek. It flows into the San Diego River west of Julian. Mildred was a surprisingly common name in Julian about 1900. I have found a Mildred Williams, a Mildred Taylor, and a Mildred Price Hoskings living there. Stein favors Mildred Williams as the girl for whom the falls got its name. From a local citizen, Stein heard that an Indian girl named Mildred committed suicide here by leaping into the falls. This must be the most common place-name myth in America—I heard a story about a supposed Indian maiden's suicide (sometimes she was a princess) from a local "Suicide Rock" when I was a child living far away from San Diego. (Durham 47; Stein 80)

Milejo, Milijo. See **La Punta.**

Mills Crossing Station. See **Tierra del Sol.**

Milpitas. See **Buena Vista.**

Milquatay. See **Campo.**

Mine Canyon, Creek. The canyon opens into Cottonwood Creek southeast of Otay Mountain close to the Mexican border. Prospectors discovered gold here in the 1880s. Stephen A. Donohoe (See **Donohoe Mountain**) was the most important figure in the district. The very small district revived about 1908 and in the 1920s. The biggest mines were the Golden Artery, the Golden Chief, and the Comet. (Durham 47; Schmid 11-21)

Mineral Hill. This was at the heart of the Boulder Creek Mining District along Boulder Creek west of Cuyamaca Peak. Small gold mines operated here from 1890 to about 1940. (Durham 47; Fetzer, *Year,* 126-129)

Minneapolis Beach. Between Carlsbad and La Costa. The developers, Dwight L. Robinsons (Sr. and Jr.) supposedly came from Minneapolis. A failed development in 1894-1895. Promoters claimed that the site was ideal for producing silk, and said they had hired Japanese experts who would help the lucky people who bought lots here become rich cultivating silk worms. Also see **Seda.** (J. Davidson, "Minneapolis Beach Fiasco Told," *SDET,* August 23, 1935; Pourade, *Glory,* 233)

Minnewawa, Camp. On Otay Lakes Road four miles west of Jamul. According to Schmid (138), when E.S. Babcock owned Jamul Ranch, his son Arnie built Minnewawa Lodge here with an enclosure for his polo ponies. Not a San Diego name, but an upper midwestern one, like Minnesota or Minneapolis. In the 1930s the CCC had a camp here, and now it is the site of a large RV camp. (Durham 11)

Mira Mesa S.D. Northeastern Neighborhood. North of Miramar Marine Corps Air Station. The name appears to mean in Spanish "view of the mesa" and it is probably modeled on nearby Miramar, "view of the sea." Pardee Construction Company began building this subdivision in 1969.

Miramar. (Span. "view of the sea," but more correctly it is "(it) looks at the sea," Gudde 240) About 1890 E. W. Scripps, press magnate, investor, and colossal grouch, bought 400 acres (this later grew to 2,000 acres) of land about 11 miles north of San Diego to build an isolated estate. He took the name and the neo-Gothic architectural style for his home, about a mile east of today's Interstate 15, from a seacoast palace "Miramar" that Maximilian, Emperor of Mexico, built in 1854-1856 for his Carlotta near Trieste on the Adriatic, then part of the Austro-Hungarian Empire. (Now that Trieste is Italian the palace is called "Miramare.") Scripp's Miramar got its own post office in 1892. The nearest point on the railroad was miles away at Linda Vista Station (*not* the San Diego suburb). Scripps died in 1926, after spending 34 years at Miramar, interrupted by trips in his yacht. The last of Scripps' 47-room home, abandoned and thoroughly vandalized, was torn down in 1973. **Camp Miramar** began as a Marine Corps base in September 1942 on 324 acres, with more land added from adjacent Camp Elliott; the Navy took over in 1947 when it became **Miramar Naval Air Station**. According to a 1950s publicity brochure, it was originally called **Mitscher Field** for Admiral Marc B. Mitscher, naval flyer and World War II hero. It became a Marine Corps Air Station in the 1990s. Also see **Scripps Ranch.** For **Miramar Outlying Field** see **Hourglass Field.** Also **Miramar S.D. Northeastern Neighborhood.** (J. Davidson, "Miramar Takes Name From Ranch," *SDET,* n.d.; Gudde 240; Hinds 86-90; Salley 137; Stein 81)

Mission. Originally **Misión San Diego de Alcalá** was located below the Presdio near an Indian village named **Cosoy**. However, the friars decided to move it about five miles east up the San Diego River to another village called **Nipaguay** to get away from the Presidio's soldiers and to find better farm land. Therefore the mission sometimes is called **Misión San Diego de Nipaguay** (Pourade, *Time,* 20). The mission has given its name to a number of features in the area. **Mission Bay,** like San Diego Bay, is a swathe of land that has subsided west of the Rose Canyon Fault; it is largely filled with sediment, especially from the San Diego River. On the 1782 Pantoja map of San Diego, Mission Bay is called **Puerto Falso,** "False Bay," possibly because it seemed to repeat San Diego Bay. English speakers also called it **False Bay.** Padre Pedro Font called it **Puerto Anegado** in 1776 (Gudde 240) "Flooded Bay." Rose Hardwick Thorpe said that she and Harr Wagner renamed it Mission Bay in 1888. In August that year she wrote in *Golden Era* (457), "Fair Mission Bay/ Now blue, now gray,/ Now flushed by sunset's afterglow." In 1915 the U.S. Board on Geographic Names officially changed the name to Mission Bay; in 1933 the board refused to change the name back to False Bay. (Durham 48; Gudde 240; MacPhail *Story* 93-94;

Stein 81). **Mission Beach** was the last of San Diego's three beach towns to be developed. Brothers John and Adolph Spreckels purchased the land in 1914 and put it on the market in 1919, running an electric train line through it to La Jolla in 1925. They built a wooden bridge over the channel draining the bay to connect Mission Beach with Ocean Beach. They also developed the **Mission Beach Amusement Center**, presenting the land to the city. The park included a dance hall, roller-skating rink, and a roller coaster, the "Big Dipper," that opened in 1925. An amusement center was called **Luna Park** from the Coney Island resort of the same name. In 1955 the park's name was changed to **Belmont Park**, from New York state's Belmont Race Track (*SDU,* December 16, 1955). There is now a **Mission Beach S.D. Northern Neighborhood** (Durham 48; Pourade, *Gold,* 179-180; SDHS Subject File "Mission Beach"). **Mission Gorge** was originally called **Portillo de Cajon** (Span. "Box Pass"), but English speakers called it **Cajon Gap.** This may be the only use of the generic, gap, in the county. When it first became known as Mission Gorge is hard to say (Durham 48). George W. Marston and Charles S. Hamilton apparently filed the first plat map for **Mission Hills**, east of Presidio Hill, in 1908, continuing to sell lots here into the 1920s. It is now **Mission Hills S.D. Western Neighborhood** (Gudde 241; Durham 48). **Rancho de la Misión San Diego de Alcalá**, a land grant with a total of 58,875 acres, was ceded to Santiago Argüello in 1846. Eventually, much of this land would be annexed into the city of San Diego (Cowan 75; Durham 48). **Mission Valley.** The Spanish name for this place was **Cañada de San Diego** (Engelhardt, *San Diego,* 56), but by 1870 it was called Mission Valley (J. Davidson, "Canada de San Diego Former Name of Valley," *SDET,* September 24, 1937). Mission Valley is now the site of two San Diego Neighborhoods: **Mission Valley West** and **Mission Valley East.** For **Mission Mountain** see **Cowles Mountain.**

Mitchell Convalescent Hospital. At Camp Lockett near Campo. Established in July 1944, it was named for Civil War surgeon Silas W. Mitchell. Declared surplus in 1946. (Hinds 1)

Mitscher Field. See **Miramar.**

Monkey Hill. East of Lake Henshaw. During high water it is an island in the lake. There are two theories for this name, neither of them very convincing. According to one (Lindsay 240) the name came from a troop of escaped monkeys. Stein (82) says that monks once were here and somehow the monks became monkeys, because the words are similar. The solution to the problem may lie in an entry in Edward H. Davis's *Diegueño Indian Words: Place Names.* He wrote "Koo-rook. Images or monos—used in death ceremonies." Davis is referring to the funeral images made for the Kumeyaay Karuk ceremonies—

yard-high effigies of the deceased that are burned at the conclusion of the ceremony. (The Luiseño also make them under a different name.) He indicates that they are called "monos" in Spanish, which means both "monkeys" or "images." If an informant told a mapmaker that a hill was called "El Cerro de los Monos" the mapmaker might well understand this as "hill of the monkeys, monkey hill," while the intended meaning was "hill of the (funeral) images, image hill." On the 1903 Ramona 30' Quadrangle. See the following entry, **Monos Canyon.** (Durham 48)

Monos Canyon. (Span. *monos* "images" "image canyon") A canyon enclosing Agua Hedionda Creek east of Oceanside. (Durham 43)

Monserrate Land Grant, Mountain. (Span. "jagged mountain") Monserrat is a famous mountain and monastery in Catalonia, Spain. (There are variant spellings.) In 1846 Isidro M. Alvarado claimed this 3,323-acre land grant, Rancho Monserrate, located on both sides of today's Interstate 15 in north county. Had its own post office 1874-1876, 1889-1891. The mountain is on the rancho. (Cowan 49, Gudde 245, Salley 139, Stein 82)

Montezuma Valley, Mining District. Along S-22 north of Anza-Borrego Desert State Park. Ranchita is located in this valley. Named for a Montezuma Mine on the south slope of San Ysidro Mountain. (J. Davidson, "San Diego County Gazeteer," *SDET,* April 3, 1943; Weber 156)

Montgomery. John J. Montgomery (1858-1911) will always be remembered for his gliding flight of perhaps 600 feet in 1883 at his father's farm south of Chula Vista. Unfortunately, he took no photographs of the flight, nor were there reliable witnesses, so there have been doubters. The site of the experiment is now **Montgomery Waller Community Park.** The Waller was Luckie S. Waller, a developer who donated much land for public use (*SDU,* December 17, 1965) **Montgomery Field,** belonging to the City of San Diego, is located on Kearny Mesa. This field was originally called **Gibbs Airport**, for William H. Gibbs, owner of Gibbs Flying Service. He opened this private field in 1937. The city took over the field in 1947 and in 1949 changed its name to Montgomery Field (*SDU,* September 2, 1949). **Montgomery Freeway** is the name of Interstate 5 below Chula Vista (Webster 34). San Diego City has two Montgomery Middle Schools and one Montgomery High School (Kooperman II 564). In 1985 the city of Chula Vista annexed **Montgomery,** a district with three-plus square miles of land and 23,000 people (Webster 37). **Montgomery Hill** in Santa Clara County is also named for John J. Montgomery. (Gudde 247)

Monument. A settlement near the monument marking the Mexican border. The monument itself, dating from 1851, was renovated in 1895. A Monument School opened here in 1870. In 1888 the voting precinct in the area embracing the towns of Otay and Tia Juana was also called Monument. The *San Diego City-County Directory 1884-1885* listed five heads of households in Monument. **Monumentville** was a judicial district that appears on the U.S. 1880 Census. It must have included much of the south bay since it listed 260 inhabitants. (Alvarez 126-127; J. Davidson, "Monument City Unrealized Dream," *SDET,* August 7, 1936; San Diego County School Records Inventory)

Monument Peak. In the Lagunas, the fourth highest mountain in the county at elevation 6,272 feet. Stein (82) says that this is a typical name for a place where surveyors erected a stone monument to fix a location. (Durham 48)

Moosa Settlement, Mountain. Nine miles northwest of Escondido. Shortened from **Pamoosa** or **Pamusi.** This may be a Kumayaay word, but its meaning is obscure (Gudde 248). According to an oft-repeated story, post office officials rejected Pamoosa or Pamusi because both were too close to an existing post office name, Pomona. This sounds reasonable. Moosa had its own post office from 1881 to 1912. The original settler was a John Brown, but the best known settler was Washington E. Irving, nephew of the writer. The story that the name Moosa has some connection with an old man's beard should be allowed to die a quiet death. (J. Davidson, "Did the PO Dept. Reject Pamoosa Because It Was Too Close to Pomona?" *SDET,* April 13, 1934; Durham 48)

Moreno, Morena. This place name presents problems because it may have originated as a Spanish surname Moreno, or it may be a descriptive term meaning "brown." Three districts show clusters of this name. **Morena Village, Butte, Valley, Reservoir, Dam** are all about five miles east of Barrett Lake. The Southern California Mountain Water Company began construction on the dam on Cottonwoood Creek about 1895; the city of San Diego bought the reservoir for $1,500,000 in 1912 (J. Davidson, "San Diego County Gazeteer," *SDET,* April 19, 1943). Stein (83) repeats J. Davidson in saying that it was named for Felipe Morena, a minor character in *Ramona.* **Moreno,** above Mission Bay, was laid out in 1887 by James McCoy and others. North of Old Town and south of Atwood on the Santa Fe Railroad. Possibly it was named for Mathias Moreno, former governor of Lower California (Anonymous, "Moreno"). Morena Blvd. survives in this area. Now it is **Moreno S.D. Western Neighborhood. Moreno Valley.** One mile north of Lakeside on the San Diego Cuyamaca and Eastern Railroad. According to one source it was named for early settler Manuelo Moreno from Descanso. Also see **Dexter Valley.** (Friends, *When,* 34; Gudde 248; Stein 83)

Morettis Junction. One mile southeast of Lake Henshaw on Highways 76 and 79. Named for the Moretti family from Switzerland who had a 2,000-acre dairy farm here in the late nineteenth century. (J. Davidson, "San Diego County Gazeteer," *SDET,* April 19, 1943; Durham 49)

Morgan Hill. Two miles west of Palomar Observatory. Probably named for James E. Morgan (b. 1833) farmer and preacher, on the 1880 U.S. Census, 109. (Durham 49; Stein 83)

Morley Field. Athletic field in Balboa Park. Named for John Morley (d. 1940), superintendent of San Diego City parks for 27 years. The name was used as early as 1945. (*SDU,* December 23, 1945)

Mormon Coal Mine. About two miles north of the Coast Guard Lighthouse. The modern sewage treatment plant obscures the site of the mine. Dates back to the late 1840s when Mormons attempted to establish a coal mine here. Abandoned when the so-called Utah War began in 1857. Further attempts were made to mine coal here in the 1880s and 1890s, but the coal was of poor quality and seawater infiltrated the mine. Never much more than a solitary shaft; never a source of commercial coal. (J. Davidson, "San Diego County Gazeteer," *SDET,* April 24, 1943; Pryde 106)

Morro Hill. (Span. "crown-shaped rock or hill") Five miles south of Fallbrook. Sometimes spelled as Moro. With this spelling it would mean "Moor, Muslim" or possibly "roan-colored." (Durham 49; Gudde 249; Stein 83-84)

Mother Grundy Peak. Three miles east of Dulzura. In her book *Pioneering in Dulzura* Dorothy Schmid (3) wrote this about the origins of the name, "Louis Harvey was homesteading a valley north of a mountain which had once been called 'Madre Grande' because its great rocks looked like a woman's face. He thought pert Claire Hagenbuck was mighty cute when she tossed off, 'Madre Grande looks more like Mother Grundy to me,' thereby renaming the venerable mountain." The name, then, is folk etymology, rendering a Spanish original into familiar English, with a dash of flirtation. Since the eighteenth century Mrs. Grundy has been the by-name for a proper neighbor. "What would Mrs. Grundy think?" was the tag. A prominent early Dulzura settler, Lila Collins Clark, was from Grundy County, Illinois. (Schmid 44)

Mother Miguel Mountain. South of Sweetwater Reservoir. This strange hermaphroditic name may have taken its Mother from Mother Grundy Mountain and its Miguel from San Miguel Mountain. (Durham 49; Stein 84)

Mount. See under specific names. For example **Helix, Mount.**

Mount Ecclesia. (Greek "church") This is what Mr. and Mrs. Max Heindel named their Rosicrucian Fellowship Headquarters on 46 acres of land a mile east of Oceanside in 1911. (J. Davidson, "San Diego County Gazeteer," *SDET,* May 3, 1943)

Mount Hope Cemetery. South of Interstate 94 in east San Diego. In 1871 the San Diego City Board of Trustees set aside 200 acres here for the first San Diego municipal cemetery in the American period. Also **Mount Hope S.D. Southeastern Neighborhood.** (Pourade, *Glory,* 90)

Mount Laguna. Eight miles east of Pine Valley on the Sunrise Highway, S-2. This is the resort area in the Laguna Mountains. It had its own post office from 1920-1930 under the name of **Resort,** and then the authorities changed it to Mount Laguna. See also **Laguna Mountains.** (Durham 50; Gudde 250; Salley 143, 178)

Mountain Lily Mine. Four miles southeast of Oak Grove. This is the best-known gem mine in the Aguanga Mountain District. Bert Simmons of Oak Grove and Charles Gordon of San Diego discovered this mine in 1903. It was noted for its tourmalines and beryls. Later names for the mine were **Emeralite Mine,** which sounds like a play on the word emerald, and **Ware Mine,** named for J.W. Ware of San Diego. With the name Ware Mine it appears on the 1997 Palomar Observatory 7.5' Quadrangle. (Weber 102)

Mountain View S.D. Southeastern Neighborhood. Named for Mountain View Park. In turn, the park's name may have been inspired by Ocean View Blvd., which bisects the park. The neighborhood has an outstanding view of San Miguel Mountain.

Mule Hill. Located east of Interstate 15 not far from Lake Hodges. A historical marker stands on Pomerado Road to mark the location of the hill some distance away. After the Battle of San Pasqual, American troops took refuge on this knoll on December 7, 1846, where, desperate for food, they killed and ate mules. It has been called Battle Mountain and Starvation Hill. (J. Davidson, "Light Shed on Mountain's Identity," *SDET* n.d.; Durham 50; Gudde 28; Hinds 117; Stein 85)

Murphy Canyon. Enters Mission Valley eight miles east of Ocean Beach. Interstate 15 runs through it. Named for John Murphy, Irish immigrant, farmer, and teamster. Offered his property for sale in 1875. (*SDU,* May 20,

1875) (J. Davidson, "Irish Immigrant..." *SDET,* August 5, 1938; Durham 50; Stein 86)

Murray Canyon, Ridge. Extends from Mission Valley onto Linda Vista Mesa. Was once called **Cañada de Osuna** for a member of the large Osuna family. Named for John Savage Murray, pioneer settler in this area. He is listed in the 1880 U.S. Census with 160 acres of land; his home survived as late as 1934. (Durham 50)

Murray, Lake. Opens into Alvarado Canyon three miles northwest of La Mesa. Named for James A. Murray (d. 1921), a partner (he put up most of the money) with Ed Fletcher in the Cuyamaca Water Company. Before investing in San Diego, he made a fortune in private water companies and land speculation. Originally much smaller and called **La Mesa Reservoir,** it was the final destination of water from Eucalyptus Reservoir and the San Diego Flume. In 1919 the dam was much enlarged; it was given Murray's name in 1924. Now the center of **Lake Murray S.D. Eastern Neighborhood.** There was also a small **Murray Hill Reservoir** near Grossmont High School; it survives as a street name. (Davidson Place Name File; Durham 50)

Music Mountain. Three miles southeast of Manzanita. The origins of this poetic name are, unfortunately, unknown. It might have been a personal name. The repetition of the "M" makes the name of the mountain more memorable. (Durham 50)

Mussel Beach, Mussel Beds. See **Ocean Beach.**

Mussey Grade, Grove. This was a toll road leading from what is today San Vicente Dam towards Ramona. Taking the place of the steep Atkinson grade, the road was constructed in 1887 (*SDU,* May 1, 1887) and survived until the construction of the dam. Later became a county road. The grove is now under the waters of San Vicente Reservoir. Both were named for Albert Mussey, who built the road with partners. A farmer from Vermont, he appears in the 1880 U.S. Census. (Durham 50)

Mussey-Matthews Canyon. Canyon leading out of Lakeside. Albert Mussey lived at one end of it, and Mrs. Charles Matthews at the other. She ran a hotel there. (*San Diego City–County Directory, 1895*)

Muth Valley. Three miles north of Lakeside off Wildcat Canyon Road. Named for A.M. Muth, prominent bee-keeper in the El Cajon and Alpine districts. The 2003 Cedar Fire killed several residents here. (Stein 86; Durham 50)

- N -

Nancy Jane County Park. Located in Crest. Named for Nancy Jane Cornelius. Her father, Barney Cornelius, a developer in La Cresta, donated the land
for the park in 1928. (J. Davidson, "San Diego County Gazeteer," *SDET,* June 7,
1943)

Nate Harrison Grade. On the west shoulder of Mount Palomar. Named for
Nathan Harrison, a former slave (d. 1920). The 1880 U.S. Census lists him as
50 years old, born in Alabama. The county constructed the road about 1900. It
was steep and dusty and Harrison was known for aiding the rare traveler who
drove it. Before July 17, 1956, when the county supervisors officially changed
its name at the request of the NAACP the road was called **Nigger Nate Grade.**
See also **Harrison Canyon.** (Gudde 258; Stein 87; Wood 39-42)

National City. Between San Diego and Chula Vista. This was originally
pastureland belonging to the San Diego Presidio. It was called **La Purisima
[Virgen]** or **Rancho del Rey** ("King's Ranch"). When Mexico became inde-
pendent in 1821 the name King's Ranch was no longer acceptable and it became **Rancho de la Nación** ("Nation's Ranch," or less happily, "National
Ranch"). In 1845 John Forster claimed **La Nación Land Grant** with its 26,632
acres. He sold it in 1868 to Frank A. and Warren C. Kimball. In turn they subdivided it into lots, many of them agricultural, as National City. In 1869 the
place got its own post office. For many years National City was a rival to San
Diego. (Durham 50; Gudde 256; Salley 145; Stein 87-88)

Nebo, Mount. In the city of La Mesa. Biblical mountain from where Moses
saw the Promised Land and where he died. Developer Sherman C. Grable named
it some time after 1906 when he began his subdivisions in La Mesa. (La Mesa
Historical Society, *La Mesa,* 91-92)

Nellie. See **Palomar Mountain.**

Nelson Canyon. Opens into Pine Valley Creek four miles south of Descanso.
Possibly named for Nelson Overmier who lived in Alpine, according to the
1880 U.S. Census (116).

Neptunia. From Neptune, the Roman god of the sea. In 1898 Dr. and Mrs.
John Mills Boal planned a 1,300-acre community on the seaward side of Mount
Soledad in La Jolla. The development failed but its distinctive name survives
as Neptune Beach and Neptune Street. (Schaelchlin 28-29)

Nestor. Two miles east of Imperial Beach. Named for Nestor A. Young, state assemblyman 1887-1893. Another boomtown; it got its post office in 1890. Now the site of **Nestor S.D. Southern Neighborhood.** (Durham 51; Gudde 258; Salley 148; Stein 88)

New Boston. See **Bostonia.**

New Encinitas. See **Green Valley.**

New Hope Rock. In the ocean one mile west of Point Loma. Named for the schooner *New Hope,* active at San Diego 1869-1884. (Gudde 259)

New London. See **Witch Creek.**

New Texas. See **Campo.**

New Town. American promoters could see that Old Town San Diego had an impossibly cramped location, and so as early as 1850 William Heath attempted unsuccessfully to shift the center of the community to "New Town," its present location on the bay. Alonzo Horton, "the father of San Diego" is usually credited with this accomplishment. For **New Town Park** see **Pantoja Park.**

Newton Canyon. Opens into Santa Margarita River three miles north of Oceanside. Probably named for the Newton family of Santa Margarita Ranch. Jesse Newton was president of Oceanside's First National Bank. (Durham 51; *SDU,* November 22, 1934)

Nigger Nate Grade. See **Nate Harrison Grade.**

Nigger Canyon. See **Harrison Canyon.**

Nipaguay. See **Mission San Diego.**

Noble Canyon. Opens into Pine Valley Creek five miles east of Pine Valley. Named for Thomas Noble Sr. and his sons Thomas Jr. and John Noble. Mining gold in the canyon named for them, they resided in Descanso. (Durham 51; Friends, *When,* 45; Stein 89)

Noonan's Point. See **Swami's.**

Normal Heights S.D. Mid-City Neighborhood. North of Monroe St. and east of Boundary St. Named for the State Normal School on 11 acres at Normal St.

and El Cajon Blvd., dedicated in 1899. The word "normal" has had a strange history. Originally, when related to education, it was a translation of French *école normale,* the first teacher-training school in France (1794.) This school was intended to serve as a model, a norm, for all other teacher-training institutions in France. In English, somehow, this was transformed into the idea that "normal" colleges trained teachers. This sense is always confused in the public mind with the more general meaning of "healthy, average, not abnormal." For a similar situation elsewhere see Normal, Illinois.

North City S.D. Northern Neighborhood. This is the most northwesterly neighborhood of the city of San Diego adjoining Del Mar and Solana Beach.

North Island. All maps of San Diego bay before about 1920 show that the tip of Coronado Peninsula was an island connected tenuously with the peninsula only along the sea beach. According to Phillips (*Around* 3) on early maps the French called the place **St. Etienne** (in 1782), the Italians called it **San Stefano** (in 1824), and the Spanish called it **Peninsula de Estevan** (in 1824), but the name St. Steven for this place did not persist. The body of water separating the island from the peninsula was called **Spanish Bight.** See that entry for information about this inlet, now filled in. North Island is now a naval air base, but until the 1930s the U.S. Navy and Army shared it. (Durham 51, Stein 90)

North Park S.D. Western Neighborhood. More correctly, the area east of Balboa Park centered along University Avenue. Development began in this area about 1910 and accelerated after the Panama-California Exposition of 1915. (Security Title 33)

North Peak. The northernmost of three prominent peaks in Cuyamaca Rancho State Park, elevation 5,593 feet. Benjamin Hayes visited the area in 1870 and left a description of the mountain. Arthur Woodward (*Notes* 150) in his notes to Hayes' description said the Indian name of the peak was the same as the rancheria on its east slope, *Iguay-ee,* "the buttocks." Couro and Hutcheson say that *ewaay* means "rear end" (18). The meaning comes from the rounded shape of the mountain. Hayes stated that his Kumeyaay guide, Chono, also told him there was a cave on the mountain to which deer fled in great numbers when in distress. Mary Elizabeth Johnson read this, and in the foreword to her *Indian Legends of the Cuyamaca Mountains* wrote that the Indian name for North Peak was *E-yee'* "nest" because of a "big nest or den" into which wild animals disappeared when hunted. Rensch agreed with her (*Indian Place Names* 35). Of course, such a cave does not exist, and deer or wild animals don't flee to caves when in danger. Woodward, with support from Couro and Hutcheson, is probably correct, and Johnson's nest theory for the Indian name of North Peak is untenable. (Durham 51; Stein 90 with errors)

North San Diego. This was the official designation for Old Town. There was a post office with this name from 1870 to 1889. (Durham 51; Salley 160)

Nuevo. See **Ramona.**

Nuvida Springs. See **Sweetwater Spring.**

- O -

Oak. Probably the most common place-name element in San Diego County. In nearly every case the oak in question is the coast live oak, *Quercus agrifolia.* Providing welcome shade the year round, it thrives from sea level to about 4,000-foot elevation on better moist soil. Natural features with this name include **Oak Canyon,** on the lower San Diego River Valley near Mission Gorge; **Oak Flats,** northwest of Mesa Grande; **Oak Grove Valley,** where the settlement of Oak Grove is located (see below); **Oak Lake,** along Agua Hedionda Creek; **Oak Ridge** and **Spring,** three miles south of San Felipe; and **Oak Valley** and **Oak Valley Creek,** five miles southeast of Descanso. A number of settlements in the county have oaks in their names. **Glen Oaks,** also known as **Oak Glen,** is two miles west of Alpine. It was a popular site for beehives and was also known as **Lovett's Bee Ranch,** for apiarist Elden Lovett (J. Davidson, "San Diego County Gazeteer," *SDET,* December 14, 1942). Also see **Boulder Oaks. Live Oak Springs** was a small cabin resort near Campo Indian Reservation settled by Charles Hill in 1868 (Stein 73). **Oak Grove** is a settlement on Highway 79 not far from the Riverside County line. From 1858 to 1861 it was a stop on the Southern Immigrant Trail and later on the Butterfield Overland Stage Line. It had its own post office from 1870 to 1900 (Durham 52, Salley 153). **Oak Park S.D. Mid-City Neighborhood** in east San Diego north of Highway 94 was named for Oak Park subdivisions dating from 1922 and 1923. (Security Title 33) **Twin Oaks** was a settlement five miles northeast of San Marcos. Major G.F. Merriam was the first settler here in 1875. It had its own post office from 1889 to 1901, and a school from 1889. Nearby is **Twin Oaks Valley.** For more about Major Merriam see **Merriam Mountains.** (Durham 78; Salley 219 San Diego County School Records Inventory)

Oakzanita. The name combines oak with manzanita, an attractive chaparral shrub. **Oakzanita Springs Resort** is south of Cuyamaca Rancho State Park on Highway 79. **Oakzanita Peak** not far away, first appeared on the 1960 Cuyamaca Peak 7.5' Quadrangle, while the resort is on the 1931 Blackburn San Diego County Map, suggesting that the mountain was named for the resort. (Durham 52; Gudde 266; Stein 91)

Oasis Spring. Two miles northwest of Monument Peak in the Laguna Mountains. A rather poetic name (Durham 52).

Oat Hills. Between Twin Oaks and Burnt Mountain. Presumably named for invasive European wild oats. (Stein 91; Durham 52)

Ocean Beach. Between Mission Beach and Point Loma. Earlier names were **Mussel Beach, Mussel Beds, Medanos** (Span. "dunes"), **Palmer's Place, Palmer's Ranch** (*San Diego Herald* June 11, 1856), and **Palmiro's,** the last three for a forgotten Mr. Palmer (Kooperman 272). William H. Carlson (mayor of San Diego 1893-1896) and Alfred E. Higgins laid out this community with a hotel in 1887. The name, like those of all three beach communities, is insipid. Mussel Beach would have been better (many people would have thought it was Muscle Beach), or Palmiro's, or best of all would have been Medanos. In 1889 there was a "gold discovery" on the beach here which reeks of a publicity stunt. The place did not get its own post office until 1909. Now **Ocean Beach S.D. Western Neighborhood.** (Durham 52; Gudde 267; Salley 154)

Ocean Crest S.D. Southern Neighborhood. Located on distant Otay Mesa far from the ocean, this neighborhood has very few residents.

Oceanside. Two theories explain the name of this place. One has it that it "named itself," as they say, as a generally accepted name for the place, originator unknown. Another theory has it that about 1882 A.J. Myers, J. Chauncey Hayes and Cave Couts suggested La Playa or Orilla del Mar (Span. "beach" or "edge of the sea, oceanside") as names for the town. Myers, however, insisted on an English name, Ocean Side (Sully 28). The town was first laid out in 1883 on the new California Southern Railroad line. An early unofficial name for the town was **Carnation City** for a flower field near the station (Sully 37). Briefly in 1888-1889 there was a post office two miles further southeast called **South Oceanside.** (J. Davidson, "Oceanside Early County Railroad Hub," *SDET,* September 29, 1939; Durham 72; Gudde 267; Salley 155, 202; Stein 91-92)

Old Castle. See **Castle.**

Old George Mountain. Three miles southeast of Manzanita. This is very probably a reference to George Washington McCain, patriarch of a large family that settled near Campo. (Durham 52; McCain 68-82)

Old Ironsides County Park. In Harbison Canyon. According to Lynne E. Christenson, county historian, the park was originally called Iron Springs Park. This more than suggests that Old Ironsides does not refer to the famous old warship but to a spring with iron stains. The park was a gift from Joseph E. Shreve (*SDU,* January 21, 1947).

Old Landing. See **Spanish Landing.**

Old Spanish Lighthouse. A classic misnomer for the lighthouse high on Point Loma. The U.S. Government built it in 1854, but local guides wanted something more romantic, so gave it this name.

Old Town. Below Presidio Hill. The name dates from about 1850 and the American conquest, and referred to the original settlement of San Diego dating from 1769. Lieutenant Cave Couts named its streets in honor of Mexican and American generals of the Mexican-American War. Now **Old Town S.D. Western Neighborhood.** (J. Davidson, "San Diego County Gazeteer," *SDET,* August 21, 1943; Durham 52-53)

Olive. A few miles northeast of Moosa. Never had a post office but it is on the Irving Hubon 1898 county map. The Olive School was open from 1896 to 1900. According to the *San Diego City-County Directories,* Olive had five adult male residents in 1906 and 12 in 1907. (SDHS *School Records Inventory)*

Olivenhain. Four miles east of Encinitas. (German "olive grove" The German word *Hain* has ancient and romantic associations, something like *woods* in English.). An organization founded in Denver in 1884 brought together a group of German immigrants who came here to buy land from Frank Kimball of National City. Kimball was an advocate of olive culture, and his advice to grow olives may be the source of the name. Erroneously said that the original name of the settlement was Olivenheim (possibly the result of contamination from the name Anaheim), but the copy of the colony's original charter at SDHS, in German, of course, shows that it was once and forever Olivenhain. (see Bumann; Gudde 269; Stein 92)

Oliver, Camp. Between Descanso Junction and Descanso. Named for Lawrence Oliver, prosperous Portuguese businessman in the fishing industry, who donated the land in 1949 for a Catholic children's camp.

Olivewood. A short distance south of National City. This was the city residence of Warren Kimball and also a station on the National City & Otay Railroad. Dates from 1886. (Christian Brown Interview; Durham 53)

Olmsted Lodge. See **Fletcher.**

Olympus, Mount. Three miles northwest of Pala. In Greek mythology the home of the gods. Gudde doesn't bother to list all the places with this name in California, but they must be numerous. (Durham 50, Stein 85)

O'Neal Canyon. Opens into the Otay River near Otay Mesa. Obviously named for a settler, possibly south county farmer James C. O'Neal. (Durham 53; *San Diego City-County Directory 1930* 1259; Stein 93)

O'Neill Home Ranch. See **Ranch House.**

O'Neill Lake. Located on Camp Pendleton near the Santa Margarita River. Jerome O'Neill and James Flood of San Francisco bought the Santa Margarita Ranch in the 1880s. The lake was named for the O'Neill family. (Durham 53, Gudde 269)

Oneonta. Between Imperial Beach and Mexican border. A transfer name from Oneonta, Delaware County, New York. The name means "protruding stone" in Onondaga. (Gudde 270). There is also an Oneonta in Alabama. The town was established in 1887, and its developers probably included at least one New Yorker. Had a post office from 1888 to 1900. There are also references to an **Oneonta Slough** on the Tijuana River, and even an **Oneonta Beach.** (Durham 53; Phillips *San Diego* 62-64; Salley 156)

Opata Creek. In the Miramar area. Gudde says this is the name of an Indian tribe in Sonora. (270)

Orcutt. See **Grantville.**

Orinoco Creek. Three miles south of Santa Ysabel near Pine Hills. How the name of a South American river attached itself to this place is unknown. There was also an Orinoco School in the same area that opened in 1890. Could the name be from a misunderstood Kumeyaay word? (Durham 53; San Diego County School Records Inventory)

Oro Fino Mine. See **Escondido Mine.**

Orosco Ridge. Five miles northeast of San Pasqual on 1996 AAA San Diego County map. It may be named for José María Orozco (sic) who claimed the Rancho Guejito in 1845. (Stein 94)

Osgood. See **Bonsall.**

Osuna Valley. One mile south of Rancho Santa Fe. Juan María Osuna was the grantee for the Rancho San Dieguito. This place could have been named for him or one of his heirs. (Cowan 38-39; Durham 53)

Otay. Appears in a cluster of names in the inland south bay area. Everyone assumes it is a Kumeyaay word. Kroeber (53) says it is *otai* or *otaya* "brushy." Edward H. Davis says (n.p.) it is *Tou-ti* "big mountain," while Margaret Langdon in Gudde 273 seems to agree with Davis, saying "perhaps from Diegueño *'etaay* "big." José Antonio Estudillo claimed **Otay Rancho,** 6,658 acres, in 1829 and 1846. **Otay River, Mesa, Valley, Mountain** are local features. **Upper Otay Reservoir** is on San Miguel Creek and **Lower Otay Reservoir** is on the Otay River. Lower Otay Dam washed out completely in the 1916 Hatfield flood, and the city of San Diego rebuilt it in 1919. In 1933 the U.S. Board on Geographic Names rejected a proposal to change the name of Otay Valley to Ohjai Valley, no doubt because it would have very close to the name Ojai in Ventura County. The town of **Otay** was south of Chula Vista; developers laid it out in 1887. Chula Vista absorbed the town by about 1900. For a time it had a newspaper, the *Otay Press,* and a famous watch factory, never very successful, which operated 1889-1890. Otay had a post office 1870-1872, 1887-1925. Now the sites of **Otay Mesa S.D. Southern Neighborhood** and **Otay Mesa West S.D. Southern Neighborhood.** (Cowan 55-56; Durham 53-54; Salley 159; Stein 94; Webster 34)

Overlook. On the bluff north of the San Diego River overlooking Mission Bay. At one time there was a large sign here reading "Overlook." The Overlook Realty Company filed a plat map for this subdivision in 1914. (Durham 54; Davidson Place Name File)

Owens Mine. Located about a mile or so northeast of Julian. It is on the 1997 Julian 7.5' Quadrangle. Named for Barney Owens, one of its discoverers. This was the richest gold mine in Julian's immediate vicinity. Miners from its 350-foot vertical shaft with drifts removed $450,000 in gold at $20.67 an ounce. Production came early 1870-1875, then little more gold was found. For safety's sake, the mine was bulldozed long ago. (Fetzer, *Good Camp,* 20-24)

- P -

Pacific Beach S.D. Northern Neighborhood. Northernmost of San Diego's three beach communities. In 1869, the site of the district's first race track, Agricultural Park. With a great flourish, during the boom years, promoters founded Pacific Beach Subdivision in 1887. Here they erected the San Diego College of Letters, accompanied with great cultural and educational aspirations. When it failed, its buildings became the Hotel Balboa. The community did not really thrive, but became a lemon-growing center for many years. (Durham 54; Gudde 275)

Paine Bottom. A canyon four miles south of Santa Ysabel. Probably named for Fred Paine, who was a rancher in the Santa Ysabel district. The generic, bottom, is rare in the county. (Jasper, *Trail-Breakers,* 375-376)

Painted Rocks. Near the south shore of Lake Hodges. Outstanding collection of Kumeyaay rock art. Many images are geometrical and are assumed to have religious significance. Also known as **Piedras Pintadas,** a Spanish translation. See Ruth Alter *Painted Rocks.* (Pryde 54-55)

Pala. Cluster of place names on the San Luis Rey River east of Interstate 15. Probably from Luiseño *páala* "water" (Gudde 276). The older theory that it took its name from Spanish *pala* "shovel" is not convincing. There have been two **Pala Indian Reservations.** On January 31, 1870, President U.S. Grant allocated a 46,000-acre Pala reservation extending north of Pala. When local settlers protested, Grant rescinded the reservation on February 17, 1871. (Carrico, *Strangers,* 65-69). For other rescinded reservations see **Potrero** and **San Pasqual Indian Reservations.** In 1875 Grant established a second 12,117-acre Pala Reservation. Here now live Luiseño Indians, and Cupeño Indians who came here in 1903 when the government expelled them from their traditional lands at Warner Springs (Pryde 64.) Since 1816 at Pala there has been a station of Mission San Luis Rey, **Asistencia San Antonio de Pala**, named for St. Anthony of Padua (1195-1231), a favorite of the Franciscans. Pala has had a post office since 1875. Nearby are **Pala Mountain** and **Creek.** For **Pala Chief Mine** see **Chief Mountain. Pala Mesa** is a small settlement, not at Pala, but near the intersection of Interstate 15 and Highway 76. It was first developed in 1958. (Durham 54-55; Salley 160; Stein 95)

Palm City. South of Chula Vista off Interstate 5. The community was originally called **Palm Avenue** because its major street was palm-lined, but the post office authorities would not approve this name, believing it might confuse mail deliveries. This name does appear on maps such as the San Diego 1902 15' Quadrangle. Had its own post office 1914-1956. Now the location of **Palm City S.D. Southern Neighborhood.** (Salley 160; Stein 95-96)

Palmer's Beach, Palmer's Ranch, Palmiro's. See **Ocean Beach.**

Palomar Mountain. (Span. "pigeon roost" probably from the large numbers of band-tail pigeons that live on the mountain.) The earliest reference to this name is on the 1846 *diseño* for the Camajal y Palomar land grant. American settlers called it **Smith Mountain,** for Joseph Smith, native of South Carolina, 40 years old, according to the 1860 U.S. Census, early settler on the eastern slope of the mountain. In May or June 1868 Rufus K Porter (founder of Spring Valley), a correspondent for the *San Francisco Bulletin* wrote, "An Englishman shot Smith dead as he worked. The murderer did not flee, but stayed in the area. Neighbors discovered the body and the presumed murderer returned. He confessed the deed....Next morning the murderer was found hung to a tree in the neighborhood." (Porter) Many have conjectured about this event. What was the motive for the killing? Why didn't the murderer flee? Who lynched him and where? (J. Davidson, "Palomar Called Smith Mountain," *SDET,* June 30, 1939, and "Lynch Slayer of Mountain's Namesake," *SDET,* July 7, 1939; Gudde 279; Wood 47). After about 1870 the place was called both Smith Mountain and Palomar Mountain, but in 1901 the U.S. Board on Geographic Names rejected the name Smith Mountain in favor of Palomar Mountain. The first post office on the mountain was called **Nellie** from 1883 to 1920 when it became **Palomar Mountain.** The Nellie was Nellie McQueen, first postmaster. (Durham 55; Gudde 279; Stein 96)

Pamo Valley, Canyon. Northeast from Ramona. (From Kumeyaay *paamuu,* meaning unknown. Couro and Hutcheson 37). For years the authorities have proposed building a dam on Santa Ysabel Creek in the canyon, but opposed by conservationists, their plans have foundered. See also **Santa Maria** for information about the **Valle de Pamo** or **Santa Maria Land Grant.** (Durham 56; Gudde 279; Schad 70-71; Stein 97)

Pamoosa or **Pamusi.** See **Moosa.**

Pantoja Plaza or **Park.** Bounded by F, G, Columbia, and India Streets. Created in 1850 by William Heath Davis and others as the heart of their New Town. Named for Juan Pantoja y Arriola, early Spanish sea captain. He made the first good map of San Diego Bay in 1782 (Reproduced in Pourade, *Time,* 80). Sometimes called **New Town Park.** (J. Davidson, "Plaza de Pantoja," *SDET,* December 21, 1934)

Paradise. This place name occurs in two districts. The first is near Rodriguez Mountain northeast from Valley Center where **Paradise Creek** and **Mountain** are located. **Paradise Valley** and **Paradise Creek** are within National City limits. Originally the stream was called **La Barrenda** (Span. *barreño* "wash basin"). On the 1859 U.S. Government map of San Diego Bay it is called Valley of La Berrenda (sic). Later, Americans called it **Salt Creek,** probably because it was a tidal stream. Landowner and National City Constable J.C. Crain, for promotional reasons, gave it and the valley its present name in the 1870s. (Durham 56; Phillips, *National City,* 117; Pourade, *Glory,* 208-209)

Park West S.D. Central Neighborhood. West of Balboa Park. Vaguely reminiscent of Manhattan's Central Park West.

Pauma. A district along the San Luis Rey River. Possibly from Luiseño *páamay* "little water" (Gudde 283). **Pauma** or **Rancho de Potrero** (Span. "meadow ranch") was a land grant of 13,310 acres given to José Antonio Serrano and others in 1844. The **Pauma-Yuima Indian Reservation,** Luiseño, 5,877 acres, dates from 1891. (The much larger Pauma Reservation completely surrounds the tiny Yuima Reservation. There is also a **Yuima Creek.** This name is probably Luiseño, but its meaning is not certain). **Pauma Creek** flows off Palomar Mountain. What is usually called the Pauma massacre occurred in this area when Manuelita Cota and other Luiseño Indians killed 11 Californios after the Battle of San Pasqual. (Bancroft, I, 563; Cowan 59; Durham 56; Pryde 64; Stein 97)

Pechstein Reservoir. Located between Vista and San Marcos. Named for William Pechstein, an early land and water developer in the Vista District. (Stein 98)

Peerless Valley. Just north of Bostonia in the El Cajon Valley. Peerless Drive survives in this district. (Lay 30, 35, 43)

Peik Airport. See **Pike Airport.**

Pelican Point. Where the water-level Point Loma lighthouse is located. Could be named for the brown pelicans common along the coast or a suggestive rock formation. On the 1855 San Diego Pueblo Lands Map. An early name for the site is **Vallado,** (Span. "stake, palisade"), presumably from the shape of the rocks here. (J. Davidson, "Pelican Point Last Outpost of America," *SDET,* August 2, 1935)

Peñasquitos. (Gudde 285 says Span. "small crags") West of Interstate 15 and south of Rancho Bernardo. This was a land grant **Rancho Santa María de Peñasquitos** given to Francisco María Ruiz and Francisco María Alvarado in 1823 and 1834. There is also a **Peñasquitos Canyon** and **Creek.** The creek enters the sea just south of Del Mar. The marshes at its mouth are sometimes called **Peñasquitos Slough** or **Lagoon.** An early name for this feature was

Cordero Slough. See **Cordero. Rancho Peñasquitos.** In 1962 developer Irvin J. Kahn bought the ranch for $10,000,000. After it was annexed to San Diego its development began in the late 1960s. Location of **Rancho Peñasquitos S.D. Northeastern Neighborhood.** (Cowan 94; Durham 43; Stein 74-75)

Pendleton, Camp. Marine Corps base on the coast between Oceanside and San Clemente. About 125,000 acres. Purchased in 1942 for $4,239,062 from the owners of the Santa Margarita y Flores Ranch. Named for Major General Joseph H. Pendleton (1860-1942), who long led the campaign to establish a Marine Corps base in San Diego County. (Gudde 285; Hinds 19-20; Stein 119-120)

Peninsula de San Diego Rancho. See **Coronado.**

Penny Pines. On Sunrise Highway in the Laguna Mountains and on Palomar Mountain near Fry Creek Campground. In 1970 the Cleveland National Forest set up a fund to purchase trees to plant here after the Laguna Fire. School children contributed "pennies for pines." (*SDU,* October 9, 1970; Schad 133, 138)

Perez Cove. In Mission Bay. One of the few historical references in the twentieth century bay. Juan Pérez was the captain of the *San Antonio,* which came to San Diego Bay on April 11, 1769. Later he sailed along the California coast. (Harlow 8-9)

Peutz Valley. Two miles northwest of Alpine. Nikolas Peutz was a German immigrant charcoal-maker who arrived here in 1880. He sold his product, made from coast live oak, to smoke hams and other meats in San Diego. (La Force 209; Stein 98)

Pico's Lake. See Whelan Lake.

Piedra de Lumbre Canyon. (Span. "flintstone") Opens into lowlands about four miles south of San Onofre Mountain near Las Pulgas. (Durham 57; Gudde 289)

Piedras Pintadas. See **Painted Rocks.**

Piermont. North of Poway at Twin Peaks Road and Community Road. Hanna (232) calls it Peermont. According to the *SDU,* May 6, 1887, "This tract lies at the base of a bold and rugged ridge that pushes out into the valley like a pier. This ridge is called Piermont, and has given [its] name to the townsite." In 1887 developers Orlando S. Chapin and S. J. Baird (both born in the U.S.—see *The Great Register of Voters 1890*) laid out a townsite here. The street names were given British names, perhaps because there was British money invested in the project. Some of the original street names still survive; for example, Aubrey, Edgemoor, and York. According to the *San Diego City-County Directory 1892-93,* 12 adult males lived here, no doubt some with families. For another development by Baird and Chapin see **Stowe.**

Pike Airport. At southeast corner of Mission Bay. Arnold H. Peik had a **Peik Airport** here as of 1935, but in 1953 it became Pike Airport. It closed in 1957. On the La Jolla 1953 7.5' Quadrangle. (*SDU,* September 26, 1946, and April 7, 1957)

Pilgrim Creek. Flows into the Santa Margarita River five miles north of Oceanside. Named for Charles M. Pilgrim who farmed on the Santa Margarita ranch in the 1890s. (Durham 57; *SDU,* June 23, 1942; Stein 98)

Pill Hill. Many American cities have a height with hospitals, medical clinics, doctors' offices, etc. In San Diego Pill Hill is in Hillcrest on 4th, 5th, and 6th Avenues. (Pryde 223)

Pine Hill. See **Torrey Pines State Reserve.**

Pine Hills. Three miles southwest of Julian. Ed Fletcher laid out this second-home mountain subdivision in 1912, centering it around Pine Hills Lodge designed by Richard Requa, still standing today. Fletcher sold large lots for about $600, targeting as buyers wealthy San Diegans who owned their own cars to drive to Pine Hills, something only the rich could afford at the time. Got its post office in 1913. (Salley 166)

Pine Valley, Canyon, Creek. On Old Highway 80 eight miles east of Descanso. Its early name was the Spanish **Valle de los Pinos.** The district does indeed have many handsome Jeffrey and Ponderosa pines. First settler in 1869 was Captain William S. Emery from Rockland, Maine. During World War II there was a Marine Corps truck driving school here at a former CCC camp, called **Pine Valley Camp.** (Durham 57; Hinds 51; Redman 23-29; Stein 98-99)

Pinery, The. Heavily wooded north slopes of North Peak in the Cuyamaca Mountains. This is the best timber tract in the county, and the site of several sawmills over the years. Western cedar and white fir grow robustly here. The Cedar fire of 2003 did extensive damage in this district.

Pinezanita. Resort between Cuyamaca Lake and Julian on Highway 79. Perhaps modeled on the name of Oakzanita resort, combining, as it does, a tree and a shrub, pine and manzanita.

Piñon Point. In the Lagunas near Kwaaymii Point. According to Schad, two kinds of piñon grow here. These are unusual trees for the Lagunas. (Durham 57; Schad 206)

Pinos Mountain. See **Los Pinos Mountain.**

Pio Pico, Fort. An army base at the northern end of the Coronado Peninsula. Intended for coastal defense, it dated from 1906 to 1919. Named for Pío Pico (1801-1894), last governor of Mexican California. (Durham 84; Hinds 43)

Pioneer Mail Picnic Grounds. On the Sunrise Highway in the northern Lagunas. When this place was named in the 1930s it was believed the Birch "jackass" mail line, 1857-1861, came through here. Now it is agreed that it crossed the ridge further north and went down Oriflamme Canyon. There was no pioneer mail at Pioneer Mail Picnic Grounds.

Pirate Cove. At Gumbo Slough at the mouth of Switzer Creek in San Diego Bay. From around 1880 to 1900 guano pirates lived here. They illegally raided Mexican offshore islands for bird guano, which they sold in the U.S. No swashbucklers, no swingers of cutlasses these, but thieves who fled with suspect booty. (Pourade, *Glory,* 242)

Plaisted Creek. Flows into Potrero Creek two miles south of Boucher Hill. L. H. Plaisted was a well-known San Diego printer at the end of the nineteenth century. Because of health problems, he was known to visit the north county regularly. (Durham 58; *SDU,* August 19, 1882 and August 17, 1886)

Planwydd. See **Butterfly Farm.**

Poggi Canyon. Leads north from Otay. Named for Joseph Poggi (1881-1968), Italian immigrant. (Durham 58, Stein 99)

Point Loma. English version of the Spanish *Punta de la Loma de San Diego.* A translation might be "Hill Point." Crucial in the creation of the harbor because it shields the port from northwestern winds. It appears on the 1782 Pantoja San Diego Bay map. Site of **Point Loma Heights S.D. Western Neighborhood.** (Durham 58; Gudde 214)

Pomerado Road. It may look Spanish but it isn't. Originally the name of Pomerado School District, made from combining the names of three earlier districts, POway, MERton, and bernArDO; later the name of the road. For another early acronym see **Gravilla.** (Kooperman II 594)

Ponto. (According to Gudde (298) this is poetic Span. for "sea.") Just north of Batequitos Lagoon. Often confused with La Costa, which got a post office as early as 1896. See **La Costa.** Ponto was a station on the Santa Fe Railroad and never had a post office. Ponto Drive is near South Carlsbad State Beach. (Gudde 298)

Porter's Valley. See **Spring Valley.**

Portillo del Cajon. See **Mission Gorge.**

Poser Mountain. East of Viejas. Named for Heinrich von Poser, an early settler who was on the military rolls for 1881. (Durham 58, Stein 99)

Potash Station. On the Coronado Belt railroad line north of Marmarosa on San Diego Bay just west of Chula Vista. This was the station for the Hercules Powder Plant, which treated kelp to recover potash and other chemicals. On Blackburn's 1931 map of San Diego County.

Pothole Canyon. Opens into Pine Valley Creek four miles southeast of Descanso. No doubt it has water-worn potholes. (Durham 58)

Potrero. The Spanish name, for the most part, supplanted English "meadow" in the county. Ultimately, the word is derived from Spanish *potro* "colt" (Gudde 300). **Potrero Creek** flows into the San Luis River four miles southwest of Boucher Hill. The settlement of **Potrero** is five miles east of Barrett Junction. It got a post office in 1876. The area of the settlement saw an explosion of nearby potreros: **Potrero Creek, Little Potrero Creek, Potrero Peak,** and of potreros proper, **Little Potrero, Long Potrero** (once called **Big Potrero,** but the U.S. Board on Geographic Names rejected this name in 1962), and **Round Potrero.** There are also **Indian Potreros** near Santa Margarita Peak and Monument Peak in the Lagunas. In 1875 President Grant created the **Potrero Indian Reservation** (It is now the La Jolla Indian Reservation, dating from 1892.), but Pres. Rutherford B. Hayes revoked it in 1877. **Potrero del Tenaja.** See **Tenaja.** (Carrico *Strangers* 84, Durham 59, Gudde 300, Salley 171, Stein 100)

Pottery Canyon. At the 2700 block of Torrey Pines Road in La Jolla. Mexican immigrant Cornelio Rodríguez founded the La Jolla Canyon Clay Products here in 1929. Associated with pottery since that date. (Murray)

Pound Canyon. See **Cabrillo Canyon.**

Poverty Gulch. Four miles northwest of Descanso. This sounds like a Depression name but it is on the 1903 Cuyamaca 30' Quadrangle. In 1891 cowboy Bob Womack discovered gold in Poverty Gulch, Colorado, near Pike's Peak, leading to the founding of the fabulous Cripple Creek Mining District. Perhaps the San Diego namer had the same hopes for his Poverty Gulch. Gold mines were nearby at Boulder Creek and Descanso. The generic, gulch, is a mining term unusual in the county. (Durham 59; Fetherling 92)

Poway. Twenty miles north of San Diego. Also **Poway Creek, Grove,** and **Valley.** One of the most contentious names in the county. However, everyone agrees that it is a Kumeyaay name. It first appears on an 1828 mission document as Paguay. In the American era spellings for the town proliferated. Kooperman (II 556) says the name has been spelled at least 21 ways. However, debate over the name ended when the town got its Poway post office in 1870. There are even two different pronunciations. Old-timers say Pow-wye, but more recent citizens say Pow-way. The definitions of the Indian name are also multitudinous. Stein (100) says it is "place where the valley ends." Hanna (243) said it mean "meeting of the valleys." Couro and Hutcheson (38), whose authority is respected, say it is Kumeyaay *pawiiy* meaning "arrowhead." William Bright, in Gudde (300) thinks the meaning of arrowhead is just a coincidence, and the name may mean something else. Just as the natives of Norway are Norwegians, some say the natives of Poway should be Powegians. Only time will tell if the name will take root. (Durham 43; Salley 172; Stein 100-101)

Powderhouse Canyon. A branch of Switzer Canyon in or near Balboa Park. In 1884 John G. Capron got the city's permission to build a powderhouse here. A previous name for the place was **Slaughterhouse Canyon.** The Point Loma 1967 7.5' Quadrangle calls it Powerhouse Canyon. (J. Davidson, "Switzer Canyon Once Farm Site," *SDET,* October 18, 1935; Durham 59; *SDU,* December 27, 1884)

Presidio Hill. (Span. *El Presidio.* In European Spanish, "prison.") Four presidios were founded in California, with official dates: Monterey 1770, San Diego 1774, San Francisco 1776, Santa Barbara 1782. Gaspar de Portolá established San Diego Presidio in 1769 to protect Father Serra's nearby mission. (Gudde 302)

Pringle Canyon. Opens into Dulzura Creek a mile north of Dulzura. Named for Ben Pringle who came to Dulzura about 1890. (Durham 59; Schmid 91)

Prisoner Canyon, Creek. About five miles west of Lake Henshaw towards Palomar Mountain. Although I have not seen it documented, it's tempting to identify this place name with the Pauma Massacre, when Luiseño Indians killed 11 Californios after the Battle of San Pasqual. The Californios were taken prisoner and held briefly before their deaths. (Durham 59; Pourade, *Silver,* 114-116)

Proctor Valley. Between Jamul and Otay Lakes. In 1890 the American widow of the English astronomer (best known as a popularizer), Richard Anthony Proctor (1837-1888), arrived in San Diego with a project to create an observatory on the summit of San Miguel Mountain. She led several excursions to the peak (There is a vivid description of one of these excursions in Adema 103-107). After taking the National City & Otay Railroad to its terminus at La Presa, her party rode to the base of the mountain up an unnamed valley. Later it was called Proctor Valley to honor the astronomer and maybe his fetching widow. "Her eyebrows are as black as her widow's weeds," the *Union* wrote. She later hoped to build the observatory closer to San Diego, but support from local citizenry was not forthcoming. In the late 1960s and early 1970s the Proctor Valley Monster was said to haunt the valley in the small hours of the night. Observers differed in their stories of what they thought they saw, but most said it was a kind of cow-like thing. Ranchers complained that late-night drivers, accompanied by their wide-eyed girl friends, were disturbing their cattle along Proctor Valley Road, even shooting at them. (Durham 49; *SDU,* June 10, 1890; *SDU,* June 15, 1890, and November 19, 1968; Stein 101, but he has the wrong dates)

Pueblito. See **Ysidora.**

Pueblitos Canyon. Opens into the Santa Margarita River ten miles southwest of Fallbrook. Probably named for Pueblito, the place later known as **Ysidora.** See that entry. (Durham 59; Stein 101-102).

Pueblo. (Span. "town," perhaps meant ironically for such a remote place). Station on the San Diego Arizona & Eastern Railroad six miles northeast of Campo. Between Clover Flat and Tierra del Sol. (Durham 59; Hanft, inside front cover)

Puertecito de San Juan. See **Spanish Bight.**

Puerto de la Cruz. (Span. "pass of the cross") About five miles north of Warner Springs. Named by Fathers Mariano Payeras and José Sanchéz in September 1821. They erected a cross here. Supposedly was to be the site of an *asistencia* but it was never built because of Mexican independence, which was on its way. It has been the site of a California conservation camp. (Durham 60; Engelhardt, *San Diego* 201; Gudde 303; Hill 42)

Puertezuelo. (Span. "little pass") Often misspelled; on the Cuyamaca 1845 *diseño* it is *Portesuelo.* This was the high point on the trail, now a gravel road, between Viejas and Descanso. Pedro Fages was the first European to cross it in 1772. He left a description of his 1782 crossing. (Gudde 303; see Rensch "Fages' Crossing")

Puerto Anegado. See **Mission Bay.**

Puerto Falso. See **Mission Bay.**

Pulgas. See **Las Pulgas.**

Pump House. Surfing site in La Jolla between Marine Street and Little Point. Named for a conspicuous nearby San Diego City pump house. The most famous surfing place in the county because New York writer Tom Wolfe wrote a breathless but perceptive essay in two parts about it in 1966 called "The Pump House Gang Meets the Black Panthers—or Silver Threads among the Gold in Surf City" and "The Pump House Gang Faces Life." Both were reprinted several times as "The Pump House Gang." Wolfe's essay is mysterioso, *Dionysian.* Little did you know, but at Pump House the sun over the surf is like God's very own dentist lamp!

Punta de los Arboles. See **Torrey Pines State Reserve.**

Punta de los Guijarros. See **Ballast Point.**

Punta de los Muertos. See **Deadman.**

Punta Verde. See **Indian Point.**

Pyle's Peak. On the shoulder of Cowles Mountain in Mission Trails Regional Park, elevation 1,379 feet. Apparently the name dates only from the park's early years after 1989. Probably named for a member of the Pyle family who are active in San Diego conservation circles. Possibly it is also a word play on the much more famous Pike's Peak in Colorado.

-Q-

Quail Canyon. Three of these are in the county. One opens into Santa Ysabel Creek five miles west of Mesa Grande. Another opens into Sycamore Canyon north of Santee. A third is one mile east of Lakeside; Lake Jennings is located in this canyon. California quail were unbelievably abundant in early days, and hunters pursued them everywhere. Mountain quail are also common at higher altitudes in the county, but no one has named a canyon for them. (Durham 60)

Quanai Canyon. One mile southeast of Santa Ysabel. From Kumeyaay *kwa'naay* "wire grass used in basket making." (Couro and Hutcheson 28)

Queermack. See **Cuyamaca.**

- R -

Rabbit Peak. See **Hot Springs Mountain.**

Rainbow Valley. Off Interstate 15 just south of the Riverside County line. Got a post office in 1889. Named for James P. M. Rainbow, 1879 settler and member of the San Diego County Board of Supervisors. (Durham 60; Salley 174; Stein 103)

Ramona. Forty miles northeast of San Diego. In the earliest days it was called **Santa Maria** for the Santa Maria Rancho on which the town grew up. Got its first post office as **Nuevo** (Span. *Nuevo [Pueblo]* "New [Town]") in 1883, but the name was changed to Ramona in 1886. Because of rivalry with a town in Los Angeles County for the name, the name Ramona reverted to Nuevo in 1887. Finally, when the name Ramona was free once more in 1895, the town took and held the name of Ramona in perpetuity. Named for the title of Helen Hunt Jackson's novel, 1884. Ramona's name, in turn, was based on the Spanish given name *Ramón*. French immigrants, some in the sheep business, founded the town. The Santa Maria Land and Water Company developed it on a large scale in the late 1880s. (Durham 60; Gudde 309; Salley 153; Stein 103-104)

Ranch House. Near Santa Margarita River on Camp Pendleton. Originally called **Margarita** because it was on the Rancho Santa Margarita y las Flores. Changed to Ranch House because it was near the ranch house of the Pico family, one-time owners of the place. It was also called **Home Ranch** and **O'Neill Home Ranch** when the O'Neill family owned the ranch before 1942. See San Luis Rey 1901 30' Quadrangle. (Gudde 269; Hanna 249)

Ranchita Mine. In Rodriguez Canyon four miles southeast of Banner. In 1895 a vaquero named Leandro Woods discovered gold just a few feet from the ranch house of the Lopez family, hence the name. Cave Couts Jr. bought the mine for $5,500; eventually it produced $150,000 in gold at $20.67 an ounce. This was the last major find in the Julian-Banner Mining District. It is on the 1997 Julian 7.5' Quadrangle as the Ranchito Mine. (Fetzer, *Good Camp,* 76-80)

Rancho del Rey. See **National City.**

Rancho La Costa. See **La Costa.**

Rancho Santa Fe. Inland five miles from Solana Beach. In 1906 the Santa Fe Railroad (hence the name) bought the San Dieguito Rancho for $100,000 for the experimental planting of eucalyptus trees. In 1922 the railroad, under the direction of W.E. Hodges, began to develop much of the land. The place got its post office in 1924. In 1944 the railroad got out of the development business, selling the land to developers who kept the original name. (Durham 61; Gudde 310; Salley 175; Stein 105-106)

Rancho Viejo. (Span. "old ranch") South of the San Luis Rey River near Interstate 15. Not very old at all—this is a dairy and housing development dating from 1950. (Durham 61; Rush 88)

Rattlesnake. Since there are rattlesnakes nearly everywhere in the county, it's no surprise that the name is common. There is a **Rattlesnake Canyon** and **Creek** northeast of Poway, a **Rattlesnake Canyon** six miles southwest of Fallbrook, **Rattlesnake Creeks** near Barrett Junction and Boucher Hill. **Rattlesnake Mountain** is ten miles east of Campo. For **Rattlesnake Valley** see **Harper Valley.** (Durham 61)

Ready Relief Mine. Located about a quarter-mile up Chariot Canyon north of Highway 78 in the Banner District. It is across Chariot Creek from the Redman (Banner) Mine. The name suggests rescue from a perilous situation, riches relieving poverty. (There was another Ready Relief Mine in Kern County.) Drury Bailey, founder of Julian City, claimed this mine in August 1870. Over the years he took $500,000 in gold from it, and so it was one of the richest mines in the Banner District. Located on a steep hill, the mine had three tunnels (adits) one above the other. It is on the 1997 Julian 7.5' Quadrangle. (Fetzer, *Good Camp,* 45-49; *Mining)*

Ream Field. South of Imperial Beach. A flying field where the army taught aerial bombing in the 1920s. Named in 1918 for Major William R. Ream, a reserve army military aviator and the first flight surgeon killed in an aircraft crash. (Hinds 36)

Reba. On Blackburn's 1931 map of San Diego County. Railroad siding on the Santa Fe Railroad four miles south of Del Mar. Called Rheba on the Del Mar 1953 7.5' Quadrangle. A classic short railroad name. (Durham 72)

Reche's Grove. See **Fallbrook.**

Recluse. Four miles northwest of De Luz. Surely the most isolated settlement in the county. It had its own post office from 1893 to 1898 and its Recluse School in 1895-96. The *San Diego City-County Directory 1897* listed six male adult residents here, no doubt some with families. (Durham 20; Salley 176)

Red. Nine miles northeast of Barrett Junction is the distinctively named **Red Top,** while there is another in Anza-Borrego Desert State Park. **Red Mountains** are three miles northeast of Fallbrook and eight miles north of Escondido. (Durham 61; Stein 106)

Redman Mine. See **Banner.**

Redondo Flat, Spring. (Span. "round, circular") Eight miles northwest of Jacumba. (Durham 61)

Redwood Villages. See **Darnall.**

Reidy Canyon. Five miles north of Escondido. Named for early homesteader Maurice Reidy who was here in 1869. (Stein 106-107)

Resort. See **Mount Laguna.**

Rice Canyon. One such feature opens to the San Luis Rey River seven miles southeast of Fallbrook. There was a Mang Rice Ranch not far from Bonsall; perhaps there is a connection with the canyon (SDHS Subject File "Bonsall.") Another Rice Canyon opens into the Sweetwater River Valley three miles southeast of National City. It may have been named for Julius A. Rice, educator and school board member. (Anonymous, "Julius")

Rice Mining District. Usually called the Grapevine Mining District because it is in the Grapevine Mountains in Anza-Borrego Desert State Park (see Lindsay 181). Named for William Rice. (*SDU,* June 22, 1898)

Richland. On the eastern edge of today's San Marcos on the Escondido branch of the Santa Fe Railroad. Early farming community, as the town's name hopefully announced. Got its own post office in 1894, but it was discontinued in 1905. The school came earlier in 1887. The *San Diego City-County Directory 1897,* listed 63 adult male residents here. (Carroll 53; Salley 179; San Diego County School Records Inventory)

Riley, Camp. In 1849 Lieutenant W.H. Emory established a camp at the southeast end of San Diego Bay at La Punta. He named it for General Bennett Riley, military governor of California at the time. From here surveyors from both the U.S. and Mexico went out to establish the Mexican border. Personnel from the camp also constructed the border monument, dedicated on July 4,1851. (J. Davidson, " 'Fourth' Gives Community Start," *SDET,* August 14, 1936; Hinds 99; Pourade, *Silver,* 149-151)

Rincón. Spanish *rincón* "an inside corner or a small portion of land" Gudde 317, so a possible translation might be "Devil's Corner" for **Rincón del Diablo Rancho.** Consisting of 12,653 acres, it was in the Escondido area and northeast through Valley Center. Granted to Juan B. Alvarado in 1843. The rancho passed through several hands until Edward McGeary, and Matthew, John and Josiah Wolfskill bought it. For a time people referred to the rancho as **Wolfskill Plains**, a generic name unique in the county. In 1883 the partners sold it to the Escondido Company which developed the town of Escondido. The nearby **Rincon Indian Reservation.** Luiseño, 4,200 acres, dates from 1875. (Cowan 32; Gudde 317; Pryde 64; Stein 108)

Rincón Refugio. See **Valle de los Amigos.**

Rios Canyon. Opens into Coches Creek three miles southeast of Lakeside. Named for the Rios family who farmed here for generations. (Durham 62; Lay 64-65)

Ritchie Creek. Flows into the San Diego River eight miles southwest of Santa Ysabel. Named for George Ritchie who settled between Wynola and Julian in the 1890s. Farmer and school teacher. (Durham 62; Jasper, *Trail-Breakers,* 155-156)

Riverford Crossing. At the bridge over the San Diego River north of Lakeside. The term ford is unusual among the county's place names. The generic term, crossing, is rare in the county, but see Scissors Crossing in the desert (see Lindsay 313-314). (Lakeside 12)

Riverview. A station on the San Diego Cuyamaca & Eastern Railroad four miles northwest of El Cajon. **Riverview Farms** was a mile southwest of Lakeside. Riverview Farms Mutual Water Co. was organized in 1916 to serve 1,290 acres. Still functioning in 1933. Both places are on the El Cajon 1976 7.5' Quadrangle. (Lakeside 28)

Roblar Creek. Flows into De Luz Creek four miles west of Fallbrook. From the Spanish word *roblar* "place where deciduous oaks grow" (Gudde 319). This is perhaps the only reference to the high-altitude California Black Oak in the county. Outnumbered by place names derived from *encino,* "live oak." (Durham 62; Gudde 319; Stein 108)

Rock Haven Spring. Near Woodson Mountain off Highway 67. A spring in a very rocky place. (Stein 108; Durham 62)

Rockville. On the National City & Otay Railroad. This was near the end of the line at La Presa where the Excelsior Paving Company quarried rock. (Menzel 80)

Rockwell Field. From 1912 until 1939 this was a U.S. Army air field on Coronado Island. That year the army relinquished control of the area to the navy. It was named for Lt. Lewis C. Rockwell, 10th Infantry, who was killed in an airplane crash on September 28, 1912. (Hinds 44-50)

Rockwood Canyon. Enters San Pasqual Valley from the north. Named for the B.B. Rockwood family, early settlers. A member of the family, Mary Rockwood Peet, wrote the standard history of the district, *San Pasqual: A Crack in the Hills.* (Stein 109)

Roden Canyon. See **Boden Canyon.**

Rodeo Grounds. Five miles northeast of Buckman Springs on the Mt. Laguna 1960 7.5' Quadrangle. In early days before fences ranchers held an annual round-up to sort out branded and unbranded cattle. This event was called a rodeo, and this name may be a survival from those days. (Durham 63)

Rodriguez Mountain. Between Valley Center and Lake Wohlford. On the Ramona 1942 15' Quadrangle this feature is identified as **Roderick Mountain,** but on subsequent maps beginning with the Rodriguez Mountain 1948 7.5' Quadrangle, it is called Rodriguez Mountain. And so to the present. Possibly named for Ramón Rodríguez, a well-known Spanish rancher at San Luis Rey. The 1850 tax rolls show him owning $635 in property. (*San Diego Herald* April 3, 1858; *SDU,* October 25, 1884; Stein 109-110)

Rolando S.D. Mid-City Neighborhood. This development was put on the market in the late 1920s, but most of it was not developed until after World War II. The name plays on the phrase "rolling land." (Security Title 39)

Ron Packard Freeway. Freeway 78 between Oceanside and Escondido. Named for Ron Packard (b. 1931), congressman 1982-2000. He was elected in the fourth successful congressional write-in election in U.S. history.

Rose. Louis Rose (1807-1888), early settler, gave his name to two sites close to San Diego. **Rose Canyon** leads north from Mission Bay to Torrey Pines. Its Spanish name was **Cañada de las Lleguas** ("mare canyon"). Rose had a tannery here for many years; because of the smells and sights, tanneries were located far from residential areas. Geologists keep a close eye on the **Rose Canyon Fault,** which runs along the canyon and into La Jolla. Rose also developed **Roseville,** close to the bay below Loma Portal and east of La Playa, now obscured by Shelter Island. It had a wharf, a store, and a Rose Hotel at Addison and Byron that survived until 1931. Rose hoped to persuade a transcontinental railroad to build its Pacific terminus here, but he was never close to successful. After the closure of San Diego's Naval Training Center in the 1990s in what had been Roseville, the Corky McMillin Companies developed a combination residential, historical, and office complex here called **Liberty Station.** In 2004 a parcel of land on the bay front at Womble Rd. was designated **Louis Rose Point**, and a memorial to his name was dedicated here in 2005 (Harrison 219). At this location is the **Roseville-Fleetridge S.D. Western Neighborhood.** David Girton Fleet (d. 1991) founded Fleetridge Realty, naming it for himself. His company developed much of this district, hence the name Fleetridge. Mr. Fleet may have been emulating former U.S. Senator Frank Putnam Flint, who developed the community of Flintridge early in the twentieth century near Los Angeles in his own name. This was the site of five subdivisions named Fleetridge from 1950 to 1955 and a Fleetridge Drive exists today. (J. Davidson, "Roseville," *SDET,* May 17, 1935; Security Title 16; Stein 110; Williams)

Rose. Although the county has wild roses, a number of local rose place names probably had little to do with the flower; they are just pleasant traditional names. **Rosebank** was a station on the National City & Otay Railroad in National City south of Sweetwater Junction in Chula Vista. It was also the name of a subdivision dating from 1911 (Security Title 39). According to the La Jolla 1903 15' Quadrangle there was a settlement on north Kearny Mesa called **Rosedale.** It dates from 1897 (Durham 41; Security Title 39). Hinds (64) says that **Rosedale Landing Field** was located here at Balboa Ave. and Charger Blvd. Hinds also says that another name for the place was **Bootleger Field,** an intriguing but unidentifiable name. However, it may be only a faulty spelling for bootlegger. **Rosemont** is a community on Highway 67 five miles west of Ramona. On the 1938 El Cajon 15' Quadrangle. (Durham 63)

Rosecrans, Fort. On Point Loma. Honors Brigadier General William Starke Rosecrans (1819-1898). A prominent general in the Civil War, although he was defeated at the Battle of Chickamauga. He came to San Diego in 1867 as an associate of Alonzo Horton. The American fort at Point Loma dates from 1852, and it was given his name posthumously in 1899. Emphasis at the base has been on coast defense, but it was transferred to the navy in 1959. **Fort Rosecrans**

National Cemetery was established here in 1934. (J. Davidson, "Fort Rosecrans," *SDET,* July 19, 1935; Hinds 126; Stein 110)

Round Mountain. A mile north of Jacumba. A good name for a symmetrical peak that is 3,367 feet in elevation. (Durham 63; Stein 111)

Round Potrero. See **Potrero.**

Russian Well or **Springs.** George B. Hensley's 1873 map of San Diego shows a "Russian Springs" on the beach near the end of the bay. It may have got this name because Russian otter hunters favored it; their presence at San Diego is well recorded. The next event in the story of Russian Well has nothing to do with history—it is pure fiction. Arnot M. Loop, son of Theodore M. Loop, promoter of Del Mar, wrote a short story, called "The Fight of the Paso Del Mar," (publishing it in *Silver Gate,* January 1900). It is, in fact, as he says, a prequel to Bayard Taylor's poem with the same name (for more information about the poem see **Del Mar**). In the story's early passages, Loop tells of sailors finding a blonde child, a girl, alone on Coronado Island. She turns out to be Russian. She tells an interpreter that her father with six other men are "sleeping" near Russian Well. Rescuers find seven corpses surrounding the well, which the men had scraped dry in search of water. The rest of the story has more melodrama in three pages than an Italian opera—events will lead to the two deaths above the sea that occur in Taylor's poem. On June 30, 1952, an article in the *SDU* appeared describing the rediscovery of the well, where Hensley had showed it. But now the reporter recounts Loop's fiction *as fact.* In 1958 Duncan Gleason in his *Islands and Ports of California* (77) tells the story in a straightforward manner as though it is factual, but he does conclude the passage with, "This *legend* [my emphasis] inspired the poem, *El Paso del Mar,* by Bayard Taylor." Not only does Gleason have the name of the poem wrong, Taylor was not inspired by the legend, and he had no blonde waif and no seven corpses in his poem; these are Loop's contribution. Gudde (324) says "Russian Spring owes its name to a rather fantastic story." Then he describes the girl and the corpses at the spring, etc. Others have recounted Loop's story as fact or halffact. Among them, J. Davidson seems to want to believe the story. See his "Pt. Loma Fuel Depot on Historic Site." (*SDET,* March 10, 1939)

- S -

S Mountain. See **Cowles Mountain.**

Sabre Springs S.D. Northeastern Neighborhood. Adjoins Poway. I have never seen a Sabre Springs on any map. The spelling, sabre, reflects the current trend to reject the American spelling that Noah Webster advocated, saber, to return to the British sabre, possibly because it looks more exclusive, not to say snobbish. See also such doublets as theater-theatre, and center-centre.

Sacaton. This is the American spelling for the Mexican-Spanish *zacatón*, a coarse grass cut as hay all over the southwest, *Sporobolus airoides*. The name appears in two local place names. **Sacatone Spring,** seven miles northwest of Jacumba, and **Sacatero Valley,** which apparently opens into Japatul Valley, but it is not on any USGS maps. La Force (25) has two pictures of this place in her book, which she calls Sacratero (sic) Valley. This is probably an error (perhaps because of confusion with the English word sacred) for Sacatero or Sacatera (Span. "hayfield" Gudde 325) Valley. De Frate (93) also refers to this place as southeast of Flynn Springs. The *SDU* for June 11, 1880, has a reference to a "Zacatero Johnson," reflecting the Spanish spelling. In Friends of the Descanso Library, *When* (13-14) it is called **Scatero Canyon-Village.** (Bright 127; Durham 63; Gudde 325; Stein 111)

Saddleback Pass. Seven miles southwest of Santa Ysabel. The name is descriptive. This is one of the few passes in the western county. (Durham 63)

St. Malo. In south Oceanside. A transfer name from the French seaport on the Brittany coast. In 1928 Kenyon A. Keith, a Pasadena builder, established this second-home beach subdivision on 28 acres of land. The houses were designed in a "French rural" architectural style. Most of the wealthy buyers were from Pasadena or Los Angeles. It was annexed to Oceanside in 1955. Probably the county's first gated community. (*SDU,* December 3, 1934)

Salmons City. On Trujillo Creek which flows five miles to the San Luis Rey River at Pala. Named for Frank A. Salmons who located the Tourmaline Queen Mine in 1903. This was a settlement associated with gem mining. On the Pechanga 1950 7.5' Quadrangle. The inclusion of the generic term "city" is characteristic of mining communities. For Salmons Creek see **Trujillo Creek.** (Durham 63, 78)

Salt Creek. Flows into the Otay River west of Otay Mountain. Perhaps it is close enough to the bay to be salt-contaminated, a tidal stream. For another nearby Salt Creek see **Paradise Creek.** (Durham 63; Stein 111)

Salt Works. In 1919 a station on the San Diego & Arizona Railroad between Marmarosa and Coronado Heights. (Hanft, inside front cover)

Samagatuma Valley, Creek. Between Descanso and Guatay. Tongue-twister Kumeyaay place name. Margaret Langdon says that it may be *'ehaa 'emat aayum* "water place spread-in-the-sun (Gudde 32). Woodward (141) writes that Benjamin Hayes' guide Chono in the Cuyamacas in July 1870 said the place's name was **Jamatayume,** "explaining that 'jamat' is bran (of the acorn), 'agume' (to gather)." (Durham 64; Stein 111)

San Alejo. See **San Elijo.**

San Antonio de Pala. See **Pala.**

San Apolinario. See **Cristianitos Canyon.**

San Bernardo. Saint Bernard, 1090-1153, was a French mystic, Crusader, and reformer. The **Rancho Cañada de San Bernardo**, 17,763 acres, went to Joseph Francis Snook in 1842 and 1846. In the American era this name gave birth to names such as **Bernardo Mountain** and the settlement of **Bernardo,** four miles southeast of Escondido. It had a post office from 1872 until 1918. In 1961 a consortium of Texas oil men developed **Rancho Bernardo,** now a **S.D. Northeastern Neighborhood.** It got its own post office in 1976. (Cowan 73; Gudde 33, 330-331; Stein 105)

San Carlos S.D. Eastern Neighborhood. Claire Tavares, herself namesake of Clairemont and wife of the developer Carlos Tavares, suggested to him that he name this subdivision, which he developed, for himself, but adding a religious reference. Hence the name San Carlos. (Claire Tavares Interview).

San Clemente Canyon. Like the preceding entry, if the story is true, the name of this place has nothing to do with a saint. According to several accounts this canyon leading east from Rose Canyon was named for an Indian named Clemente. He had a garden here so the place was called either **Cañada** or **Huerta** (Span. "garden") **de Clemente.** The name may have become confused with that of San Clemente, early pope. ("The Canada Clemente or Huerte of Clemente," *SDU,* January 23, 1875; Gudde 332; Stein 111-112)

San Diego. When he first saw the bay in 1542 Juan Rodríguez Cabrillo named it San Miguel because the archangel's feast day was September 29, the first full day his party spent there. However, Sebastián Vizcaíno named it San Diego de Alcalá de Henares because November 11, 1602, when his party was in the bay, was that saint's feast day. *San Diego* was also the name of Vizcaíno's flagship.

The Spanish saint, San Diego (1400-1463), was named for St. James the Apostle the Greater; the name Diego was a common alternate for Santiago, also Spanish for St. James the Greater, the Spanish patron saint. In Latin the name San Diego was rendered as Sanctus Didacus. Like the majority of Europeans of his day, Diego had no family name. San Diego was a peasant who joined the Franciscan order as a lay brother. Advance in the church was impossible for him because of his low social status and because he was illiterate. He devoted his life to good works, prayer, and healing the sick, a noble calling at which he excelled. He worked many miracles. Even after his death in Alcalá de Henares, his relics cured Don Carlos, son of Philip II, of a grave illness. He was canonized in 1588 (see Case). The name San Diego is associated with many features, including a river, a bay, a peninsulS (see **Coronado**), a mission and land grant (**Rancho de la Misión San Diego de Alcalá**, 58,875 acres, granted to Santiago Argüello in 1846), a city, a county, and more. (Durham 64; Gudde 332-333; Stein 112-116) There was a **San Diego Gem Mine** located on the east slope of Gem Hill two miles west of Mesa Grande. Discovered in 1899, it mostly yielded tourmaline. It is probably a continuation of the same rich pegmatite dike as appears in the Himalaya Mine. Like most county gem mines, its best years were 1904-1912; it never really recovered from the 1911 Chinese Revolution that ended the Chinese demand for luxury items such as gemstones. It is on the Mesa Grande 1997 7.5' Quadrangle. (Foord 166-168)

San Dieguito. There never was a saint with this name; the name was created to identify an area close to San Diego, something like "Little San Diego." **Rancho San Dieguito** was a land grant of 8,825 acres given to Juan María Osuna in 1840, 1841, or 1845. The center of the Rancho would be near today's Rancho Santa Fe. The **San Dieguito River** is formed by the confluence of Santa Maria Creek and Santa Ysabel Creek northwest of Ramona. The valley along the lower stretches of the river is called **San Dieguito Valley. San Dieguito Reservoir** is just north of Rancho Santa Fe. There was once a settlement called **San Dieguito** in the Rancho Santa Fe area. It had a post office from 1874 to 1876, then again from 1877 to 1886. In 1933 the U.S. Board on Geographic Names rejected the spellings San Diegito and San Digitas for the traditional San Dieguito. (Cowan 75; Durham 65; Gudde 333; Salley 187; Stein 116)

San Elijo. North of Solana Beach. The Portolá expedition camped here on July 16, 1769. The following day was the feast day of St. Alexius, patron saint of pilgrims and beggars, so they called the place **San Alejo.** Somehow this became confused with the name **San Eligio,** St. Eligius or Eloi, the patron saint of goldsmiths, the result being the name of a saint, San Elijo, who never existed (Gudde 333). A land grant correctly had the original saint's name, **Rancho Cañada de San Alejo**, an alternate name for Rancho Encinitos (See **Encinitas**). **San Elijo Lagoon** and **Canyon** are both in the vicinity of Escondido Creek on the coast. San Elijo was an early name for Cardiff-by-the-Sea. (Durham 65, Stein 116)

San Francisco Peak. Five miles east of Carlsbad. This was located on the Rancho Agua Hedionda, which had an alternate name, Rancho San Francisco. Hence the name of the mountain. See **Agua Hedionda.** (Durham 65; Stein 2-3)

San Gerónimo. (Span. "St. Jerome") In 1846 this was a small rancho adjoining Rancho Rincón del Diablo on the southwest, but later it merged with it. It had an attractive name apparently lost without a trace. St. Jerome was a fourth century church father and translator of the Bible. (Ryan 6)

San Jacome de la Marca. See **Jamacha Rancho.**

San Jorge. See **Spring Valley.**

San José. (Span. "St. Joseph") The early name for the valley now partially occupied by Lake Henshaw. Padre Juan Mariner gave it the name of Valle de San José in 1795. **Rancho Valle de San José**, 26,689 acres, was granted to John Warner in 1844. In part, this was carved out of an earlier land grant awarded to Silvestre de la Portilla, 17,634 acres, in 1836. (Cowan 81; Durham 66; Gudde 338)

San Juan Capistrano el Viejo. See **San Luis Rey.**

San Luis Rey. The Portolá 1769 expedition named a large river valley in the north county **San Juan Capistrano Valley** and **River** for the Italian San Giovanni de Capistrano (1386-1456), a preacher and militant priest who fought the Turks in the Balkans. Expedition members believed it was a good site for a mission. In 1797 when it was reconsidered for a mission the site was called **San Juan Capistrano el Viejo** "Old Capistrano" because in the meantime a new mission further north had been founded with this name. A year later Padre Fermín Lasuén established the mission, but under the name **Misión San Luis Rey de Francia**, for St. Louis, Louis IX, King of France (1214-1270). This became the name of the river and the valley, as well as other features. In 1846 **Rancho San Luis Rey y Pala** was granted to Antonio J. Scott and José Antonio Pico, but the U.S. Land Commission never recognized the claim. In the American era there was a settlement called **San Luis Rey** near the mission. It had a post office from 1861 to 1865. For a time the place was called **Locksville** to honor Edward G. Locke who owned a store at this place (San Diego County Assessment Book, December 27, 1875) **San Luis Rey Heights** is five miles southeast of Fallbrook on the San Luis Rey River. **San Luis Rey Downs,** on the river, had its own post office from 1969 to 1979. (Durham 66; Gudde 340; Salley 189)

San Marcos. Named for St. Mark the Evangelist. **Los Vallecitos de San Marcos** (Span. "little valleys of San Marcos"), 8,975 acres, was a land grant given to José M. Alvarado in 1840. The grant gave its name to **San Marcos Creek, Valley, Lake, and Mountains,** all in the area of today's **San Marcos.** In the 1880s the San Marcos Land Company bought the Rancho San Marcos and established a town; it got a post office in 1888. The area included three communities, San Marcos, Barham, and Richland. San Marcos has emerged as the dominant community. (Gudde 340; Salley 189; Stein 117-118)

San Mateo Creek, Canyon, Point. Named for St. Matthew the Evangelist. All are at the north end of Camp Pendleton on the ocean. The *Arroyo de San Mateo* was recorded here as early as 1778 according to Gudde (341). (Durham 66-67; Stein 118)

San Miguel Mountain. Three miles west of Jamul, south of Sweetwater Reservoir. Named for the Archangel Michael. The mountain is on the 1843 *diseño* for Rancho de la Nación. Nearby **San Miguel,** south of Sweetwater Reservoir, was one of the short-lived boomtowns of 1887. Called a dream town by its developers, it never grew large enough to get a post office, but it did have a school dating from 1888. When the boomtown collapsed buyers left their land vacant. (Adema 76-79) For **San Miguel,** Cabrillo's first name for San Diego, see **San Diego.** (J. Davidson, "San Miguel 'Dream' Boom Town," *SDET,* March 20, 1936; Durham 67; Gudde 341)

San Onofre Canyon, Creek, Mountain, Beach, Bluff. About five miles south of San Clemente. Named for St. Onuphrius in Latin, Humphrey in English. An early Egyptian hermit. This was also a station on the Santa Fe Railroad. It has had a post office 1917-1919, 1920-1936, 1938-1943. The construction of Interstate 5 wiped out the settlement. Now the site of a nuclear power plant. (J. Davidson, "History Hazy on Naming of San Onofre," *SDET,* February 22, 1935; Gudde 342; Salley 189; Stein 118-119)

San Pasqual. Probably named for St. Pascal Baylon (1540-1592), a Spanish Franciscan (Gudde 342). A farming community grew up in the **San Pasqual Valley,** with a school, as early as 1875. In 1887 W.F. Thomson tried to establish a **San Pasqual City** in the valley, but it failed (Peet 83-84). Had a post office 1874-1880, 1887-1901. There have been two Kumeyaay **San Pasqual Indian Reservations.** President U.S. Grant established the first in 1870; very large, it included 92,000 acres. Because local white settlers and newspapers objected, Grant rescinded the reservation in 1871. In 1910 a second reservation of only 1,380 acres was granted, well north of San Pasqual Valley. Much of the valley is in the **San Pasqual S.D. Northeastern Neighborhood.** (Carrico, *Strangers,* 65-69; Gudde 342; see Peet; Salley 189; Stein 119).

San Simon Lipnica. See **Agua Hedionda.**

San Vicente. A cluster of names in the area between Lakeside and Ramona. There are so many St. Vincents that it is impossible to say which one the padres had in mind when they employed this name. The names stem from a land grant, **Cañada de San Vicente y Mesa del Padre Barona.** (For information about the grant see **Barona**). In the vicinity are now **San Vicente Creek, Mountain,** and **Valley. San Vicente Dam** was built in 1943 on San Vicente Creek. (Cowan 89; Gudde 350; Stein 123)

San Ysidro. Probably named for the Spaniard St. Isidore the Ploughman (d. 1130). This place name is found in two widely separated districts in the county. The first is north of Ranchita. Here are **San Ysidro Mountain** (singular) and **San Ysidro** settlement on the Los Coyotes Indian Reservation. (For more information about the reservation see Lindsay 308.) The other district is in the southwestern corner of the county at the Mexican border. Here are the **San Ysidro Mountains** (plural), which include Jamul and Otay Mountains. Although there was a Rancho San Ysidro mentioned in San Diego Mission documents as early as 1836, there was never a land grant with this name. The Little Landers revived the name **San Ysidro** for a settlement near their farms after 1909. They chose the name because they felt special affection for St. Isidore, cultivator of the land. Supposedly, William Smythe, founder of the Little Landers, rejected the name Tia Juana for the place, although the name had been in common use for decades, because it was too "sporty." San Ysidro got a post office in 1910 and a school in 1914. For more information see **Little Landers.** Also a station on the San Diego & Arizona Railroad in 1919. (Durham 69; Gudde 350-351; Hanft, inside front cover; Salley 190; Stein 123-125)

Sandia Canyon. (Span. "watermelon") Near De Luz Heights. It opens into the San Luis Rey River. (Durham 64; Stein 112)

Santa Isabel. See **Santa Ysabel.**

Santa Margarita. Cluster of names on the coast north of Oceanside. The Portolá expedition of 1769 contributed this name. Padre Crespí wrote in his diary, "Because we arrived at this place on the day of St. Margaret [of Antioch] we christened it with the name of this virgin and martyr." The name also appears in the 1841 land grant **Santa Margarita y San Onofre Rancho,** which became the **Santa Margarita y Las Flores Rancho** in 1844. The grant was given to Pío and Andrés Pico, and it was the largest California land grant ever, at 133,441 acres. Also the name of **Santa Margarita River, Peak** and **Mountains.** For the railroad station **Margarita** see **Ranch House.** (Cowan 93; Durham 68; Gudde 347; Stein 119-120)

Santa Maria. This was the name of a land grant, **Valle de Pamo** or **Santa María,** granted to Edward Stokes and his father-in-law José Joaquín Ortega in 1843. Including 17,708 acres, its center was where today's Ramona is located. Also see **Pamo.** The grant in turn gave birth to the names of **Santa Maria Creek** and **Valley.** (Gudde 347; Stein 120-121)

Santa María de los Peñasquitos. See **Peñasquitos.**

Santa Monica. See **El Cajon.**

Santa Sinforosa Ridge. Seven miles east of Oceanside. According to the chronicler Miguel Constansó when he was on the 1769 Portolá expedition his party called a place near Hedionda Lagoon Santa Sinforosa for a second century Roman martyr saint because her feast day was the next day, July 18. The name survives today as the name of this ridge. (Brown, *Gaspar* 164; Durham 68)

Santa Teresa Valley. South of Sutherland Reservoir. By all accounts, Spanish-speaking people did not introduce this Spanish name. Early American settlers, perhaps William Warnock or William Cole first employed this name in 1850. Perhaps named for St. Teresa of Avila (1515-1582). (Durham 68; Stein 121)

Santa Ysabel. West of Volcan Mountains between Julian and Sutherland Reservoir. Named for Elizabeth or Isabella of Portugal (1271-1336), daughter of the king of Aragon. This is the location of an a*sistencia* belonging to the San Diego Mission, established in 1818. The Kumeyaay name for the place is **'Ellykwanan** "crowded knolls," (Couro and Hutcheson 3). Site of a land grant, **Rancho Santa Isabel,** given to Edward Stokes and his father-in-law José Joaquín Ortega, 17, 719 acres, in 1844. The **Santa Ysabel Indian Reservation,** Kumeyaay, dating from 1875, includes 15,527 acres of land. The name of the a*sistencia* gave birth to the names **Santa Ysabel Peak** and **Valley.** The settlement of **Santa Ysabel** got a school in 1888 and a post office in 1889. (Durham 69; Gudde 350; Salley 192; San Diego County School Records Inventory; Stein 122-123)

Santee. Between Lakeside and Cowles Mountain. Originally called **Cowlestown** or **Cowlesville** for its founder George Cowles (See **Cowles Mountain**). It got a post office with the name Cowlesville in 1889, although Cowles died in 1887. His widow Jennie married Milton Santee, and Post office authorities obligingly changed the town's name to Santee in 1891, with Santee as the first postmaster. Also the site of **Santee Lakes,** man-made ponds used for recreation. (Gudde 350; Salley 192; Stein 123)

Savage Dam. In 1916 the Hatfield floods destroyed the Lower Otay Dam on the Otay River. Under San Diego City ownership, it was rebuilt in 1917. In

1934 it was named in honor of Hiram Newton Savage (1861-1934), city engineer, who had supervised the construction of the dam. (J. Davidson, "San Diego County Gazeteer," *SDET,* September 3, 1943; Gudde 352)

Sawmill Mountain. See **Cuyamaca.**

Scatero Valley. See **Sacaton.**

Scholder Creek, Grade. Two miles northwest of Mesa Grande. Named for an early settler in Mesa Grande, the German immigrant Frederick Scholder. (Durham 69; Quinn 12-13)

Schoolhouse Canyon. On the Santa Ysabel Indian Reservation, opening onto Highway 79 from the Volcan Mountains. There's still a schoolhouse at the site. (Durham 69)

Scripps Ranch S.D. Northeastern Neighborhood. East of Interstate 15 and north of the Miramar Marine Corps Air Station. Named for E.W. Scripps, newspaper magnate and owner of the original Miramar Ranch dating from the 1890s. In 1968 the Macco Corporation, a subsidiary of the Pennsylvania Central Corporation paid $4.2 million for 1,180 acres of land on the former Miramar Ranch (*SDU,* July 30 and October 2, 1968). Here it developed thousands of residences and much commercial property. In October 2003 many houses burned here when the Santa Ana-driven Cedar Fire swept into the area from hills to the east. For information about E.W. Scripps see the entry under **Miramar.**

Secret Canyon. Opens to Pine Valley seven miles south of Descanso. An intriguing name. Stein thinks it was so-named because it is inaccessible. (Durham 69; Stein 125)

Seda. (Span. "silk") Two miles south of Carlsbad. Had its own post office from 1895 to 1897. The post office was established just when **Minneapolis Beach** (see that entry) was founded. That place was touted as a silk-making center, and a connection between Seda and Minneapolis Beach seems very likely. (Durham 13; Salley 194)

Selwyn. A station on the Santa Fe Railroad southwest of Linda Vista Station. Named for George A. Selwyn, cattleman, partner of Robert Allison of La Mesa, and resident of Rose Canyon. (Durham 70; Pourade, *Glory,* 161; Chester Gunn Interview)

Sengme Oaks Water Park. On the La Jolla Indian Reservation. Luiseño, but the meaning is unknown. Appears in Engelhardt, *Mission San Luis Rey* (255) as Rancheria Senga.

Sentenac Creek. Flows into the San Diego River two miles south of Santa Ysabel. Named for the French immigrant settler Paul Sentenac (1842-1927). For information about him see Lindsay (315-316). (Durham 70)

Serra Mesa S.D. Eastern Neighborhood. Named for Junípera Serra, founding father of the California missions. An area north of Mission Valley and south of Kearny Mesa. The name dates from 1961 when a contest to rename the Mission Villages Development was held. Contestants submitted 458 names, with these finalists: Cabrillo Heights, Cabrillo Mission, Alta Mira, Cielita, Friars Heights, Northcrest, and the winner, Serra Mesa. For other town-naming contests see **Marbello** and **Coronado.** (*SDU,* June 7, 1961)

Shady Dell. This was a resting place on the old Atkinson Grade between Foster and Ramona. See **Atkinson Grade.** One of the few dells in the county. (J. Davidson, "Atkinson Grade Opened as Toll Road in 1873," *SDET,* July 23, 1937; Durham 70)

Sharp Peak. See **Stonewall Peak.**

Sheep Camp Creek. Flows into Boulder Creek nine miles north of Descanso. A reminder that from about 1870 to 1900 herding sheep on open land was a major industry in the county. (Durham 70)

Sheephead Mountain. Four miles northeast of Buckman Springs near Kitchen Valley. An unusual name. Was it named for an incident or because it resembles a sheep's head? (Durham 70)

Shelltown S.D. Southeastern Neighborhood. Joseph Poggi (1881-1968) said in an interview at SDHS, "In 1917 I built Shell Town. I had a business there, oil station, dance hall, and motel. Shell Town was along Main Street between 32nd and the National City line." Supposedly named for the shells found in its sandy soil—it is close to the bay.

Shelter Island. Early in the twentieth century a long narrow sandbar emerged off Roseville in San Diego Bay. Someone unknown named it Shelter Island because, well, it was an island and it sheltered the shore. The earliest use of the name I can find is in the *SDU* for September 2, 1937, but it is probably much older. Bringing in fill, in 1948 the Port Authority extended Byron St. to the sandbar to make the island a peninsula, changing the name of this stretch of the road to Shelter Island Drive, and developing many facilities there. Nearby **Harbor Island,** a similar development but totally artificial, dates from 1961. (Innis 147-148)

Shenandoah Mine. This was the most important mine in the Shenandoah Gold Mining District located close to Scholder Grade a few miles north of Mesa Grande. Shenandoah, a valley and a river in Virginia, was a popular mine name; there were four in California, all, perhaps, founded by Virginians. The mine was discovered in the late 1880s and worked for about ten years, then again in 1932 when gold went to $35 an ounce. It had a 175-foot shaft and 250 feet of drifts, and a five-stamp mill. It is on the 1997 Mesa Grande 7.5 ' Quadrangle. (Quinn 15-16, 67-77; *Mining*; Weber 163)

Shepherd Canyon. Opens into Murphy Canyon from the east. On the La Mesa 1994 7.5' Quadrangle. Probably another memento of the county's sheep herding days. (Durham 70)

Sherilton Valley. In 1944 H. Wilton Williams bought a large plot of land on King Creek west of Cuyamaca Peak. He named it Sherilton Valley Ranch, drawing on elements from the names of his daughter Sherrilyn and son H. Wilton Jr. The name, then, is an ingenious acronym, like **Pomerado** or **Gravilla,** and others in the county. The ranch is gone, but the name lingers on.

Sherman Heights S.D. Central Neighborhood. Named for Captain Matthew Sherman, Civil War veteran. He settled in San Diego in the middle 1860s, and was San Diego mayor 1891-1893. His Sherman Addition is sometimes described as part of Logan Heights. First subdivision dates from 1869, but mostly developed in the 1880s. The Villa Montezuma, now a SDHS museum, is in this neighborhood. (SDHS Biographical File; Security Title 42)

Siempreviva. (Span. "everlasting flower," in Latin, *sempervivum*) Perhaps named for a local plant, one of the *Dudleya*. Often misspelled. Ten miles southeast of Otay near the Mexican border. Had a post office from 1889 to 1892 when it was moved three miles west to **Lemon.** The *San Diego City-County Directory, 1893-1894,* lists 10 adult male residents. Survives today only as Siempre Viva Road parallel with the border. (Durham 54; Salley 197)

Sierra de Jacupin. See **Laguna Mountains.**

Sill Hill. Seven miles north of Descanso near Mineral Hill. A sill is a geological term for a layer of igneous rock injected into sedimentary or metamorphic rock. It's probably safe to say there is a sill on Sill Hill. (Durham 70)

Silvano. See **Sylvana.**

Silver Gate. Sometime in the nineteenth century this term emerged to describe the entrance to San Diego harbor, undoubtedly emulating San Francisco's Golden

Gate. Came into its own in the late 1880s with a ferryboat *Silver Gate* and a Silver Gate Masonic Lodge in 1889. The local magazine *Silver Gate* published its first issue in January 1899. The name probably will never be an unqualified success, because silver, as everyone knows, is second-rate.

Silver Strand. South of Coronado on the ocean. The name probably dates from the time when the Coronado Peninsula was developed in the 1880s. It has a promotional ring to it. On Dalyrimple's 1789 map the beach was called **Costa Brava** (Span. "rugged coast.") (Harlow 65-68)

Silverdome Mountain. Two miles west of El Cajon Mountain. The U.S. Board on Geographic Names approved the creation of this name in 1990. It appeared for the first time on the El Cajon Mt. 1997 7.5' Quadrangle. Silverdome is on the property of the nearby Audubon Society Silverwood Wildlife Sanctuary, dating from 1965, and this is the source of its name. There has been some silver mining in the area. See the "Old Silver Mine" just south of the San Diego River below El Cajon Mountain on the M.G. Wheeler 1872 map of the Rancho El Cajon. (Durham 24; Lakeside 35; Schad 114-115)

Simmons Canyon, Flat. The canyon opens into La Posta Creek five miles east of Buckman Springs. Source of the name is unknown. Simmons Flat is two miles northeast of Julian. It was named for 1887 homesteader Benjamin I. Simmons. (Durham 71; Jasper, *Trail-Blazers,* 69)

Sizzle Spring, Camp. This was the catchy name for a railroad camp north of Jacumba used during the construction of the San Diego & Arizona Railroad. Perhaps the spring sizzled like water on a skillet, or the name may have been a reference to the sizzling heat in the area. (Davidson Place Name File; Durham 12)

Skunk Spring, Hollow. Skunk Spring is four miles north of El Cajon Mountain near Barona Indian Reservation. **Skunk Hollow** is one mile north of Barrett Junction. (Durham 71; Stein 127)

Skye Valley. East of Barrett Lake. A transfer name. Supposedly two Scottish McLean brothers (first names unknown) named this place for the Isle of Skye off Scotland's west coast. (Davidson Place Name File; Durham 71; Stein 127)

Skyline S.D. Southeastern Neighborhood. Probably named for Skyline Community Park on Skyline Drive.

Slaughterhouse Canyon. West of Highway 67 near Eucalyptus Hills. Here Ray Gavin of Lakeside once had a slaughterhouse. Such businesses tended to be located in remote places like this. But, in early days before refrigeration, livestock had to be butchered locally. For another Slaughterhouse Canyon see **Powderhouse Canyon.** (Durham 71; Lakeside 75; Stein 127)

Sloane Canyon. The valley of the Sweetwater River below Loveland Reservoir. Hampton P. Sloane registered as a 70-year old voter and rancher at De Hesa in 1894. He was important enough to be included in Guinn's *History of California,* 1181. The name is spelled Sloan on the Alpine 1988 7.5' Quadrangle.

Smith Mountain. See Palomar Mountain.

Smuggler Canyon, Gulch. The canyon is on the east side of Point Loma. In the Spanish and Mexican periods smugglers supposedly hauled goods around the Custom House at Point Loma (J. Davidson, "Pt. Loma Early-Day Smugglers Nest," *SDET,* June 8, 1935). The gulch is south of Imperial Beach near Border Field State Park; smuggling might have been an occupation here. (Durham 71)

Snakewall. In north Del Mar. In 1925 wealthy owner Coy Bennett built a large house here, designed by Richard Requa, on 23 acres. He enclosed the house in a conspicuous meandering wall, supposedly because his daughter Valentine had a deathly fear of snakes, hence the name. Almost certainly not true, but it is an appealing story; besides, the wall itself seems to loop like a snake. (Ewing 177-178)

Soboyame. Four miles southeast of Palomar settlement. Had a post office in 1910-1911. Sometimes called Sovoyama. Probably a Luiseño name, but no one seems to be sure of its meaning. (Durham 55; Kroeber 59; Salley 200)

Soda Springs. See Buckman Springs.

Solana Beach. (Span. "sunny place") Its first name was **Lockwood Mesa,** or **Lockwood's Station,** from early settler Nathan S. Lockwood who settled here in 1889 or earlier (*SDU,* June 16, 1889; BLM website). Developed with water from Lake Hodges by Ed Fletcher who may also have named it. He filed the plat map on March 5, 1923. Its post office opened in 1924. (Durham 71; Salley 200; Stein 128)

Soledad Mountain, Valley, Land Grant. (Span. "solitude," an isolated place or a reference to the lonely Mary after Christ's death, Nuestra Señora de la Soledad). Portolá crossed the valley leading southeast from Del Mar and called it **Valle Santa Isabel,** but Crespí called it La Soledad. On the 1845 Henry D.

Fitch map it is shown as Cañada de la Soledad. Today it is usually called Sorrento Valley. See below. The name of the mountain came from the valley. **Rancho Soledad Land Grant** was given to Francisco María Alvarado in 1838 but the U.S. Land Commission never confirmed it. (Durham 71; Gudde 368-369; Stein 128)

Sorrento. Six miles southeast of Del Mar. Named for Sorrento Italy, a picturesque seaside community south of Naples, but our Sorrento is miles from the ocean. This was a boomtown dating from 1887. Post office from 1888 to 1904, re-established in 1927. The *San Diego City-County Directory 1889-1890* lists 31 adult males at Sorrento, 24 of them farmers. The names **Soledad Valley** and **Sorrento Valley** have been used almost interchangeably, but today Sorrento Valley seems to be more popular. There is a **Sorrento Valley S.D. Northeastern Neighborhood.** (Ewing 71; Gudde 370; Salley 201; Stein 129)

Sourdough Spring. Five miles northeast of Boucher Hill on Palomar Mountain. Sourdough bread is made with yeast, not spring water, but perhaps the spring has a sour smell. (Durham 72; Stein 129)

South College Neighborhood. See **S.D. East Village Neighborhood.**

South Fork. See **Conejos Creek.**

South Grade. See **Highway to the Stars.**

South Park S.D. Central Neighborhood. Actually due east of Balboa Park. Named, of course, for Balboa Park.

South Peak. See **Cuyamaca Peak.**

South Rim. Six miles southeast of Imperial Beach near the Mexican border. This refers to an extension of Otay Mesa. (Durham 72)

South San Diego. See **Imperial Beach.**

Southcrest S.D. Southeastern Neighborhood. Probably named for Southcrest Community Park. Just north of Shelltown.

Southeast San Diego. A place name that is fading away. In 1992 a group of concerned citizens led by City Councilman George Stevens held an event, complete with mock coffin and funeral, to bury this name. The participants believed that "Southeast San Diego" had become code words in police newspaper reports to identify African-American crime. They recommended that the names of local San Diego neighborhoods replace this name when describing crimes and other events, and this has happened. (Hearn)

Spalding Park. At Sunset Cliffs. Named for Albert G. Spalding, sporting goods millionaire and advocate for Lomaland. Developer John D. Mills gave this park to the city in the 1920s. Much of the park has disappeared as waves have eroded the coastline. (*SDU,* August 11, 1916; Stone)

Spangler Peak. South from Ramona, elevation 1,984 feet. Named for D.B. Spangler, land developer, who came to the district in 1869. (LeMenager, *Off,* 70-71)

Spanish Bight. This is the inlet that once separated North Island from Coronado Peninsula on the bay side. "Bight" is the name for an enclosed bay; also a loose curve in a rope. Possibly it got its name because Spanish ships anchored here. According to Phillips (*Around* 3) the early Spanish name for this place was **Puertecito de San Juan** ("little port of St. John") The name Spanish Bight appeared in the *SDU* for July 13, 1886, but was probably older. The Spanish Bight Fault leaves the Rose Canyon Fault in downtown San Diego and crosses west over the Coronado Peninsula. Land has subsided along the fault, resulting in an incursion of bay water. The military has filled in the bight to make landing fields, etc., but the fault is still there. (Scott LaFee, "Scientist Uneasy about City's Quake Construction Rules," *SDU,* July 5, 1982)

Spanish Landing. People coming by boat from La Playa landed here to proceed to Old Town. Now completely filled in; today the landing would be at Rosecrans Blvd. and Udall St. Also known as **El Desembarcadero** and **Old Landing.** (J. Davidson, "San Diego County Gazeteer," August 9, 1943)

Spencer Valley. West of Julian at Wynola. Named for its first settler, first name unknown, who located at the north end of the valley in the late 1860s. Spencer sold out in 1875 and left the district. (Jasper, *Trail-Breakers,* 186)

Spook Canyon. See **Harmony Grove.**

Spooners Mesa. Two miles south of Imperial Beach at the Mexican border. Maybe named for young couples in search of a quiet parking place—to spoon is to show affection, especially in a sentimental manner. But still, it might have been named for an unidentified Spooner family. (Durham 72)

Spring Valley. South of Mount Helix and east of Lemon Grove. Known as Meti or Neti in Kumeyaay, names whose meaning is unknown. Spanish speakers called this area **Aguaje de San Jorge** or **Fuente de San Jorge**, both meaning

"St. George Spring." When Rufus K. Porter bought land here in 1865, people sometimes called it **Porter's Valley**. Sometimes Porter called it **San Jorge**, perhaps ultimately rejecting this name because its pronunciation, San Hor-hey, is uncomfortable for some English speakers. Finally he chose to abandon Indian or Spanish names for his ranch altogether. As he said, "I like Spanish, Mexican, or Indian names, and would not have changed the name to Spring Valley, as far as I was concerned, but my folks wanted some other, hence the name." (Adema 31). Porter did something that was rare in the transition from Spanish to English place names: he translated Spanish *aguaje* or *fuente* into English Spring Valley. However, as boom times came in 1885 for some reason he chose **Helix** as the name for the post office on his ranch (See **Mount Helix**). This was also the name of a short-lived subdivision here in 1887-1888. Sometimes Porter referred to his place as **Helix Farms** and H.H. Bancroft retained this name after he bought out Porter. Officially the name of the place remained Helix until 1909 when on the same day the old name was dropped and the place became Spring Valley (see Adema; Durham 73; Salley 95; Stein 131-132).

Spur Meadow. Six miles northwest of Morena Village. A survival from the days when San Diego County was the land of the horse. (Durham 72)

Squaw Tit. Four miles northeast of Jacumba on the Jacumba 1959 7.5' Quadrangle. Undoubtedly the most questionable place name in the county. When I inquired of the U.S. Board on Geographic Names about the propriety of this name I was told politely that the board does not take moral positions on place names, with the exceptions of "Nigger" and "Jap" which cannot appear on any official U.S. maps. The term "squaw," now under heavy criticism from Indian organizations nationwide, also appears on several features in Anza-Borrego Desert State Park. (Lindsay 329)

Starvation Hill. See **Mule Hill.**

Starvation Mountain. Elevation 2,140 feet. North of Rancho Bernardo and east of Interstate 15. Probably named for the incident when U.S. troops were starving after the Battle of San Pasqual, but not to be confused with **Mule Hill.** (Durham 73)

Steele Canyon. Four miles northwest of Jamul off Highway 94. In 1888 National City businessmen Elizur Steel and John B. Steel (also spelled Steele) bought 1,700 acres on the Jamacha Ranch (*SDU,* January 4, 1884). Probably the canyon was on their property. (Durham 73)

Stephenson Peak. One mile southeast of Monument Peak. Named for James Burton Stephenson (d. 1944). He was in charge of the U.S. Forest Service Descanso District from 1921 to 1938. (Durham 73; *SDU,* June 6, 1944)

Stevens Creek. In northern Del Mar. Named for Edwin Stevens, a rancher. (Ewing 94)

Stewart (Lithia) Mine. About one mile north of Pala on Tourmaline Queen Mountain. Named for John Stewart, who had a claim here in 1883, but the mine began operations only in 1892. This was a source of gemstones as well as lithium ore—for a time this was the biggest domestic source of lithium, found here in lepidolite crystals. Tourmaline is the most important gemstone at the Stewart Mine. It is on the 1997 Pechanga 7.5' Quadrangle. (Foord 161-163; Weber 185-189)

Stewart Station. See **Farr.**

Stingaree. San Diego's red light district beginning about in the 1880s, but it closed in 1912 on the eve of the Panama-California Exposition. Centered at Third Ave. and Island Street, but expanded beyond this area. On lower 5th St. as early as 1881 there was a "collection of shacks" known as the Stingaree Block (*SDU,* November 4, 1881). This place apparently gave its name to the whole district. Stingaree is a fisherman's way of saying the word stingray—the insertion of a vowel simplifies an unusual consonant cluster, and the change brings rhyming first and last syllables. The name is exceptional, combining as it does the nautical (it's near the bay); sting, the name for a scam or a confidence game; and the erotic, perhaps best left to the reader's imagination. The best-known bordello in the district also had an exceptional name: **Canary Cottage.** (see MacPhail, *When*)

Stock Pen. See **Jofegan.**

Stockton, Fort. Above the San Diego Presidio. In 1840 Mexicans threw up earthen barricades above Old Town. When hostilities began in 1846, American sailors took them over, naming them **Fort DuPont,** for Samuel Francis DuPont, commander of the *Cyane,* a ship anchored in the bay. After the American occupation Commodore Robert F. Stockton (1795-1866) improved the works in 1846 and named them for himself. He became California's second military governor. (Gudde 375; Hinds 98)

Stockton S.D. Central Neighborhood. South of Highway 94 and east of Grant Hill Neighborhood. Probably named for Stockton Elementary School (Now

King Elementary School) on 31ˢᵗ St. Like Fort Stockton, the school was named for Robert F. Stockton, California's second military governor.

Stokes Valley. Between Barrett Lake and Lake Morena. According to the *San Diego City-County Directory 1899-1900* and *1904* there was an Edwin B. Stokes living in Campo. Probably he was the namesake for this place. (Durham 73; Stein 133)

Stone Steps. Handsome stairway to the beach located at Seaside Gardens Park in Encinitas. A popular surfing location. The steps (concrete, not stone), were constructed in the 1930s and renovated in the 1980s. Alliteration, the repeated st-, makes the name more memorable. See **Music Mountain** also. (Cleary and Stern 177)

Stonewall Peak, Creek. East of Highway 79 at Paso Picacho Campground in Cuyamaca Rancho State Park, elevation 5,730 feet. Named for the nearby Stonewall (Jackson) Mine, discovered in March 1870. Before that date it was called **Sharp Peak.** For the Stonewall (Jackson) Mine see **Cuyamaca.** (Durham 37; Stein 135)

Stowe. In Sycamore Canyon almost midway between Poway, six miles away, and El Cajon Valley. It had a post office from 1889 to 1905 and a school from 1890 to 1903. Orlando Chapin and S.J. Baird (Baird and Chapin Company) developers of Piermont, sold land here in the 1880s. They were both born in the U.S. (see *The Great Register of Voters 1890)*, but for some reason they were fond of British names. (See the street names in Piermont) It was for this reason that they probably named this place for Stowe Park and Stowe House, a grand eighteenth century estate in Buckinghamshire, England. The *San Diego City-County Directory, 1897,* listed 14 adult male residents here. Now **Goodan Ranch County Park** as part of the Sycamore Canyon Open Space Preserve. The Goodan family ran their ranch here until World War II. (Durham 73, Goodan Ranch County Park website; Salley 207; 81-82, San Diego County School Records Inventory; Schad 72)

Strand. This was the name of a post office one mile south of the La Jolla Post Office from 1924 to 1934. (Salley 207)

Stratton. See **Cuyamaca.**

Strong Castle. See **Castle.**

Stuart. Five miles north of Oceanside. Was named in 1908 for E.B. Stuart, Santa Fe railroad agent. There's also a nearby **Stuart Mesa.** Not to be confused with Stewart Station, south of Oceanside. (Durham 73; Stein 133)

Sumac. Three miles southwest of San Marcos. Probably named for a common chaparral shrub, California sumac. This was a new name, 1890-1891, for the **Merigan** Post Office, 1889-1890. It was named for the first postmaster, Michael Merigan. (Durham 66; Salley 134, 208)

Suncrest. See **Crest.**

Sunday School Flats. Two miles east of Boucher Hill on Palomar Mountain. Arriving on Palomar Mountain in the 1880s, early settler Theodore O. Bailey held open-air services at this place. (Durham 74; Stein 134)

Sunnyside. A community and station on the National City & Otay Railroad between Bonnie Brae and Avondale in the Sweetwater Valley. A post office was here from 1892 until 1974. In 1876 Judson Carter Frisbie, after making money in Chicago hardware, bought 246 acres here that he planted with lemons and other fruit. Community awareness has persisted and Sunnyside is on many recent maps. The suffix "–side" is literary and occurs often in the works of Sir Walter Scott, for example, "Tweedside." The cozy domestic name is typical of stations on the railroad. (Salley 208; Stein 134; Stewart 272)

Sunrise Highway. More officially, County Road S-1. Runs for about fifteen miles along the crest of the Laguna Mountains. A rough road was first constructed here in 1918—it was only 11 feet wide—but it was very much improved in 1937. The name is apt because the road offers many unimpeded views of the sun rising east over the desert. (*SDU,* December 7, 1937)

Sunset Cliffs S.D. Western Neighborhood. At north end of Point Loma on the ocean. In 1924 Albert G. Spalding, sporting goods magnate, owned a strip of land adjoining the Theosophical Society's Lomaland. He called it **Sunset Cliffs Park,** and so the name of the neighborhood. J.P. Mills developed it as a residential area in the 1920s. (J. Davidson, "Sunset Cliffs Oil Stories Continue Despite Denials by Early Developer," *SDET,* December 9, 1938; Security Title 45)

Sunshine Mountain, Summit. The mountain is southwest from Julian, while the summit is on Highway 79 north of Warner Springs. Good names for sunny places. (Durham 74; Stein 134)

Sutherland. Seven miles northeast of Ramona. This was a settlement named for John P. Sutherland who came to Ramona in 1886 from Kansas. It had a post office from 1895 to 1903. **Sutherland Dam,** named for the nearby settlement or its founder, on Santa Ysabel Creek, was under construction for 27 years, 1927 to 1954, thanks to engineering problems. It belongs to the city of San Diego. The official name of the reservoir, according to the U.S. Board on Geographic Names, is **Sutherland Lake.** (Durham 74; Pryde 132; Salley 209; Stein 135)

Suycott Wash. In Mission Trails Regional Park. It opens into Mission Gorge. According to Randy Hawley, first San Diego City Park Ranger, when the park was established in 1989 its board attempted to preserve existing names in the park. They found this name on a 1976 AAA San Diego County map. The name Suycott may date from the time when the locality was part of the Marine Corps' Camp Elliot. The generic, wash, is rare in coastal San Diego County.

Swami's. Surfing beach at Encinitas. Originally called **Noonan's Point** for the Noonan family who owned land there (Hartley 64). A swami is an initiate of a Hindu religious order. Not far above the beach is the site of the **Golden Lotus Temple of All Religions**, built in 1935-1938 (the temple was lost in a landslide in 1942 due to its position on the unstable ocean bluff). The property, owned by the Self-Realization Fellowship, is a retreat and ashram center. The most famous spiritual leader identified with the place in the 1930s, and later, was Swami Paramahansa Yogananda, who enjoyed swimming in the ocean. Perhaps he contributed his title to the beach. The official name of the place is Sea Cliff Park, providing an instructive contrast between a forgettable bureaucratic name and the memorable spell cast by the word "Swami's." (*SDU-T,* September 11, 2003; Kooperman 272)

Swan Lake. An intermittent lake three miles west of Warner Springs. According to Unitt's *Birds of San Diego County* (53), whistling swans have been seen at Warner Springs. (Durham 74)

Swartz Canyon. Opens into San Vicente Valley four miles southeast of Ramona. Named for William Swartz, farmer in the Ramona district. (Durham 74; SDHS Biography File; Stein 135)

Sweetwater. This is a translation of Spanish *agua dulce,* the name of good clear water anywhere where Spanish speakers lived. **Sweetwater River** runs from Cuyamaca Rancho State Park to lower San Diego Bay; it is shown with this name on the A.B. Gray 1850 map of San Diego Bay (Phillips, *Around,* 1). The river is dammed at **Loveland Dam** (1945) and at **Sweetwater Dam** (1888) built by the San Diego Land and Town Company to irrigate the National City and Chula Vista areas. Sweetwater Dam was damaged in the 1916 Hatfield Flood but did not fail. **Sweetwater Junction** was where the National City & Otay Railroad left the main line to head up the Sweetwater Valley. **Sweetwater Springs** is located at the foot of San Miguel Mountain near Sweetwater Springs Road. This place has had a long and sometimes scandalous history, as its many owners attempted to make maximum profits selling its water. In order to induce sales they have given the spring many fancy names. These include **Baldhead Spring,** because its water were supposed to cure baldness; **Nuvida Springs,** supposed to mean something like "New Life"; **Jamacha Springs,** for the ranch on which the springs were once located; **Isham's Spring, Isham's California Water of Life,** because Alfred H. Isham was one of its owners; and others. For **Sweetwater Settlement** see **Dehesa.** Also see **Hansen's Ponds.** (Adema 101-109; J. Davidson, "Spring Brings Wealth, Trouble," *SDET,* June 12, 1936; Durham 74-75; Gudde 381; Pryde 136; Stein 135-136)

Switzer Canyon, Creek. In downtown San Diego. Extends north of Broadway at 19th and 20th Streets and reaches the bay at 11th Street. Named for E.D. Switzer (d. 1909), a jeweler in San Diego in the 1870s. An earlier name for the canyon was **La Carbonera** (Span. "a place where charcoal is made.") It appears on the 1859 U.S. map of San Diego Bay. (J. Davidson, "Switzer Canyon Once Farm Site," *SDET,* October 18, 1935; Gudde 66, 381)

Sycamore. Named for the omnipresent western sycamore, found along watercourses at lower altitudes. **Sycamore Canyon** is north of Santee. **Sycamore Flats** is north of San Pasqual. (Durham 75)

Sycuan. South of Alpine in Sweetwater Valley. According to Kroeber (57) the name is derived from a Kumeyaay word *sekwan,* a kind of bush. There are many variant spellings such as Cycuan, Sekway, Secuan, Sequan, Socouan, and others. The U.S. Board on Geographic Names established the present spelling in 1977 (Gudde 382). For a persistent erroneous spelling see **Lycuan.** The Kumeyaay **Sycuan Indian Reservation,** 640 acres, was established in 1875. A **Rancho Sequan Land Grant** was given to Juan Lopes in 1839, but he never defended his claim before the U.S. Land Commission. **Sycuan Peak, Creek** are nearby. (Cowan 97; Durham 75; Pryde 64; Stein 125-126)

Sylvana. Five miles east of Valley Center on Escondido Creek above Lake Wohlford. Apparently from the Latin *silva* "wood, forest." This suggests that the settlement was among trees; my guess is that it was among coast live oaks. The spelling with "y" is an acceptable variant. Under the name **Silvano** it had a post office 1893-1894 and 1900-1901. However, from 1907 to 1912 the name was spelled Sylvana. The *San Diego City-County Directory, 1910,* lists 18 adult residents here. On the 1947 Ramona 15' Quadrangle. (Salley 198, 210)

- T -

Table Mountain. Four miles northeast of Jacumba. Obviously a name for a flat-topped peak. (Durham 75)

Talega Canyon. Four miles northeast of San Clemente on the Orange County line. Spanish "bag, wide short sack." This suggests something about the shape of the canyon. (Durham 75, Gudde 385; Stein 137)

Taliaferro, Camp. Established in 1916 at the location of today's Morley Field in San Diego's Balboa Park. Named for 1st Lieutenant Walter R. Taliaferro, killed in an aviation accident in 1915. At times it was the headquarters for the Army's Southern California Border Patrol District. (Hinds 52)

Talmadge S.D. Mid-City Neighborhood. Originally called **Talmadge Park.** North of El Cajon Blvd. and east of Kensington. The Southern California Realty Corporation developed this subdivision beginning in 1925. Hollywood film figures, among them producer Joseph Schenk, financed the company. His wife was the movie star Norma Talmadge, and so the name. The district has streets named for her and her sisters, Constance and Natalie. Dedicated January 3, 1926. No, none of the three sisters ever lived in Talmadge. (Bawden 81-82; Kooperman 284; Security Title 45)

Tanner Bank. One of the two submerged **Lost Islands** 100 miles off the Coronado Islands. The other is **Cortes Bank.** Tanner Bank is named for a Captain Tanner, USN. (Gudde 218; Davidson Place Name File, *U.S. Coast Pilot,* 41)

Tapawingo, Camp. In Cuyamaca Rancho State Park near Cuyamaca Lake. A girl scout camp from 1931 to 1975. The name, apparently suggesting tappings and wings, was also used in the Adirondacks, so it is not local. (Durham 12)

Tecate. At the Mexican border, inland 20 miles from the sea. Some nineteenth century maps spell it as "Tecarte." The meaning is obscure. Stein (137) says it is named for a gourd that grew in the area called *tecats.* Langdon (in Gudde 387) thinks it might be from Kumeyaay *tuukatt* "to cut with an ax" referring to a place where a tree was cut. McCain (28) advances the theory, told to her by a Kumeyaay Indian, that this was an Indian mispronunciation of Secate, "grass valley" presumably derived from Spanish *zacatón.* There was a **Rancho Tecate Land Grant** given in 1834 to Juan Bandini who was driven out by Indians; most of it was in today's Mexico. Tecate, the American settlement at the border, has had a post office since 1912. Also in the area are **Tecate Peak, Creek,** and **Little Tecate Peak.** From 1911 to 1917 American troops were stationed here at a place called **Camp Tecate.** The soldiers came from Fort Rosecrans (Hinds 123). **Tecate Divide** is a long north-south ridge between La Posta and Boulevard, far from the border. Its high point is at elevation 4,140 feet; Interstate 8 surmounts it. The generic, divide, is unusual. (Cowan 101; Durham 75-76; Gudde 387; Salley 211)

Tecolote Valley, Creek. They lead down to Mission Bay. From Mexican Spanish "owl" from Aztec *tecolotl.* On the 1845 Fitch map. (Durham 76, Gudde 387)

Tekemak. See **Mesa Grande.**

Telegraph Canyon. Runs from 2nd St. in Chula Vista towards San Miguel Mountain. This was a stage route to Yuma, and a telegraph line to the east dating from the 1870s. Official opening was August 19, 1870. (Durham 76; Gudde 388; Stein 138)

Temecula Canyon. Northern San Diego County. Apparently based on a Luiseño word *temeko,* meaning unknown. This is the canyon through which the Santa Margarita River flows; the Temecula River is in Riverside County. (Durham 68, 76; Gudde 389)

Temescal. (Mexican Span. "sweathouse") **Temescal Creek, Canyon** are five miles north of Ramona. They open into Santa Ysabel Creek. There is another **Temescal Creek** south of Julian that flows into the San Diego River. (Durham 76; Gudde 389; Stein 138)

Tenaja. Also spelled **Tinaja.** (Span." a large earthen jar" but in the southwest it is a pool or tank cut into rock by running water). West of the deserts in San Diego County there is only one such place name, **Potrero del Tenaja** ("Pothole Meadow"?), located at the Riverside County line northwest of Fallbrook; a Tenaja Forest Station is just over the line. There was a small community in this area—a Tenaja School dates from 1914. (Durham 24; Gudde 390 San Diego County School Records Inventory)

Tent City. Also called **Coronado Tent City.** A popular tent community extending south of the Hotel Del Coronado. Open from June 1 to September 30, the first Tent City dates from 1900 and the last one was in 1916, although some remnants of its past glory survived until 1931. Offered golf, tennis, band concerts, and, of course, sea bathing. It was still on the 1942 Point Loma 7.5' Quadrangle. (J. Davidson, "Tent City Renowned Beach Resort," *SDET,* July 28, 1939; Durham 76)

Teralta. See **City Heights.**

Terrace. A stop on the National City & Otay Railroad between Olivewood and Sweetwater Junction. (Christian Brown Interview 2)

Terrenitos. See **Los Terrenitos.**

The. For names with this article see the specific names. For example **Willows, The.**

Thing Valley. Seven miles northeast of Buckman Springs. Originally called **Hollister Valley** for Oscar Hollister who had a ranch here. He's mentioned in the *SDU,* April 30, 1875, and in the 1870 U.S. Census. In 1874 Damon Thing and his sons Joseph and Edward bought land here. According to Stein the family got their unusual name because they asked a judge to change their name from its original Hogg. "Give us anything," they requested. So he gave them Thing. (Durham 76; Gudde 392; Stein 139-140)

Thomas, Camp. Briefly a Marine Corps base on North Island March-July 1911. Established because of fear of the Mexican Revolution. Origin of the name unknown. (Hinds 43)

Three Sisters. Waterfall on Boulder Creek two miles below Boulder Creek Road. This is 13 miles north of Descanso. The falls are about two miles below the road and about half a mile below Devil's Punchbowl, also on Boulder Creek. In high water the falls divides into three strands, hence the name. (Schad 162-163)

Thum Park. See **Cactus Park.**

Thunder Valley. Six miles northeast of Buckman Springs. Perhaps named for some dramatic incident. (Durham 77)

Tia Juana. See **Tijuana.**

Tierra del Fuego. In Mission Bay near today's Vacation Isle. This was apparently a peninsula extending into the bay. Someone gave it this fanciful name from the South American feature, perhaps because in shape it resembled Tierra del Fuego in miniature. On the La Jolla 1953 7.5' Quadrangle. (Durham 79)

Tierra del Sol. (Span. "sun land") This is the high point on the San Diego and Arizona Railroad at elevation 3,660 feet. It is south of Live Oak Springs near the Mexican border. It has been called **Mills Crossing Station,** probably because a road crossed the railroad line at this point. Named for Lewis N. Mills who was a rancher and school trustee in the Campo district in 1916 (SDHS Biographical Files). From 1917 to 1956 it had a post office named **Hipass,** certainly a variant of High Pass. That year, for unknown reasons, the name was changed to Tierra del Sol. The post office closed in 1964. There was also a **Tierra del Sol Navy Communications Facility** at La Posta. (Durham 77; Gudde 393; Salley 95; Stein 59, 140)

Tierrasanta S.D. Eastern Neighborhood. (Span. "holy land") Formerly part of Camp Elliott. Christiana Oil Company developed it in 1970 and later. It was planned for 11,000 dwellings with 25,000 residents. (*SDU,* September 6, 1970)

Tijuana. The name is recorded as early as 1829 as **Tiajuan** and as **Tijuan** in 1833. It is a Kumeyaay word whose meaning is unknown. In the nineteenth century Spanish speakers modified it into the more comfortable Tia Juana "Aunt Jane" by a process called "folk etymology." (For another example of this process, but in English, see **Kitchen Creek**). Until fairly recently most American mapmakers spelled the name as Tiajuana or Tia Juana. In 1968 the U.S. Board on Geographic Names gave its formal approval to the spelling "Tijuana." The translation "Aunt Jane" has given birth in the U.S. to wild stories that the place was named for a middle-aged Mexican cook, etc. The **Tijuana River** rises in the U.S. as Cottonwood Creek but re-enters the U.S. as the Tijuana River. There was a longtime American settlement at the border called **Tia Juana**. In this name it had a post office from 1876 to 1881 and then again from 1887 to 1904. The place had a wild reputation, and it's even said that Wyatt Earp promoted bear and bull fights here (Menzel 91-92). The site of **Tijuana River Valley S.D. Southern Neighborhood.** (Durham 77; Gudde 393; Salley 214)

Tims Canyon. Enters San Pasqual Valley from the north. Named for Louis J. Timm (sic), recorded as a settler here in 1919. (Durham 77; Peet 195; Stein 140)

Tin Can Flat. On Nate Harrison Grade two miles west of Boucher Hill on Palomar Mountain. This was a popular picnic spot and revelers left their garbage behind. (Stein 140; Durham 77)

Titus. Station on the San Diego & Arizona Railroad between Jacumba and Dubbers. Named for Harry L. Titus, vice president and general manager of the railroad (d. 1917). (Durham 77; Hanft, inside front cover)

Torrey Pines State Reserve. On the coast between La Jolla and Del Mar. Here Dr. C. C. Parry of the 1850 U.S. Border Commission discovered Torrey pines, naming them *Pinus Torreyana* in honor of Dr. John Torrey (1796-1873) of New

York, one of his teachers. On early coastal maps the place was called **Punta de los Arboles** (Span. "point of the trees") because it was the only conspicuously wooded point on the coast. For the same reason in the American era it was called **Pine Hill** on coastal maps. (Gudde 398; Schaelchlin 20-22; Stein 141; *U.S. Coast Pilot,* 43)

Tourmaline Queen Mountain. One mile north of Pala. Named for the **Tourmaline Queen Mine**, 800 feet from the mountain's summit. In 1903 John Giddens, Frank A. Salmons, Pedro Feiletch, and Bernardo Heriot (Hiriart) discovered this mine. (They also discovered the Pala Chief Mine.) It was once very productive, with many gemstones consigned to New York's Tiffany and Company (Weber 97, 115). In 1903 F.D. Schuyler and D.G. Harrington discovered the **Tourmaline King Mine**. It is just northwest of Tourmaline Queen Mountain's summit; it had a thousand feet of underground workings. Both mines are on the 1997 Pechanga 7.5' Quadrangle. The use of *king* and *queen* for mine names was common, see the Gold King and Gold Queen Mines. (Durham 77; Stein 141-142; Weber 86, 97)

Trouble, Camp. U.S. Navy base that trained flyers. Established on January 15, 1912 on North Island and closed on May 3, 1912. A very unusual name for a military base. (Hinds 43)

Troy Canyon, Flat. Three miles northeast of Buckman Springs. Named for Jorma (?) Troy, 55-year old laborer listed in the 1880 U.S. Census in the Campo district, 136. (Durham 77)

Trujillo Creek. Five miles long, flows into the San Luis Rey River at Pala. According to Stein (142), the stream was named for an Indian, Gregory Trujillo, who had a nearby sheep camp. Called **Salmons Creek** on some maps for the well-known gem miner Frank Salmons. (Durham 78)

Tule. This is the common name for the aquatic plant also known as cattail or bulrush. The word Tule is Mexican Spanish from the Aztec *tollin* (Gudde 402). **Tule Springs** is near Sand Creek east of El Capitan Reservoir. **Tule Creek** is just north of Manzanita. **Tule Lake** is five miles northwest of Jacumba. **Los Tules** is a settlement east of Warner Springs off Highway 79. (Durham 44, 78; Stein 75, 143)

Twin. An obvious name for a doubled feature. **Twin Flats** is two miles southeast of Rodriguez Mountain. **Twin Lakes** is about ten miles northwest of Warner Springs in Cooper Canyon. **Twin Peaks** is two miles north of Poway. For **Twin Oaks** see **Oak**. (Durham 78; Stein 143)

- U -

Un Gallo Flat. See **Emery.**

University City S.D. Northern Neighborhood. The university is the University of California at San Diego in La Jolla. This area has been carefully planned; the master plan dates from 1959. This district is also known as the **Golden Triangle.** (*SDU,* December 12, 1959)

University Heights S.D. Western Neighborhood. North of University Ave. and west of Park Blvd. extending to the Mission Valley rim. In the boom years of the late 1880s the University of Southern California at Los Angeles was supposed to establish a branch at this location to be called the San Diego College of Arts and Sciences. The collapse of the boom in 1888 killed the project. Remnants of the plan survive in the names of this neighborhood and University Ave. (Kooperman 280)

- V -

Vaileta, Vailleta Point. Four miles northwest of Encinitas. The post office of Vaileta was established in 1887 and discontinued in 1888. The name comes from the postmaster Albert H. Vail. Vailleta (sic) Point is just north of Batequitos Lagoon. Presumably, it was also named for Mr. Vail. (Durham 25; Salley 221)

Valencia Park S.D. Southeastern Neighborhood. Ultimately, the name comes from Valencia Spain. There were unsuccessful subdivisions in this area in the 1880s, but most of it was developed in the 1920s. (Security Title 47)

Vallado. See **Pelican Point.**

Valle de las Viejas. See **Viejas.**

Valle de los Amigos. (Span. "Valley of the Friends") Northeast from Ramona. It got this name because there was a Quaker ("Friends") meeting house here as early as in the 1880s. An early name for this area was **Rincón Refugio** (Span. "Refugio's Corner"), possibly for Refugio Ortega, wife of Edward Stokes, claimant for the Rancho Santa Maria. Also see **Goose Valley.** (Durham 79; LeMenager, *Ramona,* 10)

Valle de los Pinos. See **Pine Valley.**

Valle Santa Isabel. See **Soledad Canyon.**

Valley Center. Located in Bear Valley eight miles northeast of Escondido. Its first post office in 1874 was called **Valley.** Valley Center became the official name only in 1887. Obviously got its name because it was in the center of Bear Valley. (Durham 80; Gudde 409; see McHenry; Salley 221; Stein 144-145)

Van Dam Peak. Two miles west of Poway. An honorific name for Edward Van Dam, county superintendent of roads from 1933 to 1961. The U.S. Board on Geographic Names officially named the mountain in 1984 after rejecting the name Mount Van Dam. The board prefers to have the proper name precede the generic; this puts the specific name in alphabetical order. (Durham 80)

Verde Ravine. (Span. "green") Canyon six miles northeast of Buckman Springs. (Durham 80)

Verruga Settlement, Canyon. (Span. "wart") Three miles northwest of Ranchita. According to Jasper a Mexican lived here with "a wart under his chin the size of a quail egg" (*Trail-Breakers* 368). In the 1920s the Verruga Marble Company quarried here. Verruga post office was open here from 1917 to 1926. (Durham 60-61; Gudde 63; Salley 223; Stein 25)

Victoria. A district in Alpine north of Interstate 8 completely enclosed by a semi-circular Victoria Drive. Named for a granite roadside boulder resembling a weighty contemplative Queen Victoria.

Viejas. (Span. "old women") Five miles east of Alpine. Various theories exist about how this place name came into being, but none appear to have much authority. Bawden (n.p.) suggests that the name may have come from the rounded contours of the surrounding mountains, resembling old women; this is an appealing theory. The name appears on the 1845 Rancho Cuyamaca *diseño*, and it was the name of the **Valle de las Viejas Land Grant** issued to Ramón Osuna in 1846. The U.S. Land Commission rejected his claim. There was a post office here from 1873 to 1893. **Viejas Mountain** dominates **Viejas Valley** on the west. In 1923 San Diego businessman Baron Long established a ranch here in his name. He sold it to the U.S. Government in 1931 for the **Viejas Indian Reservation.** To this valley in 1934 moved a group of Kumeyaay Indians displaced from the Capitan Grande Indian Reservation by the construction of El Capitan Dam. Others moved to the Barona Reservation. The Viejas Reservation has 1,609 acres of land. (Cowan 107; Durham 80; Gudde 412; Salley 224; Stein 146)

Viejas Stage Stop. See **Alpine.**

Vineyard. Seventeen miles northeast of Escondido in Boden Canyon on the western edge of the Cleveland National Forest. On the forest map it is shown as Vineyard Ranch. The place was once called **Maxcy's Vineyard** for Asher C. Maxcy (sometimes spelled Maxey) who came to San Diego in 1850 and had 1,500 acres of grapes here. Probably the grapes were made into wine to sell to the local population. He is on the 1870 U.S. Census rolls with $50,000 in property—he was a rich man. The place had a post office from 1884 to 1922. (J. Davidson, "San Diego County Gazeteer," *SDET,* January 25, 1943; Durham 80; Salley 224)

Virginia. Eight miles southwest of Poway in San Clemente Valley. On Rueger's 1903 *Automobile and Miner's Road Map of Southern California.* Had a post office from 1890 to 1900. Named for the first postmaster, Virginia A. Tower. According to the *San Diego City-County Directory 1895,* it had seven adult male residents, some, no doubt, with families. (Durham 59; Salley 225)

Vista. (Span. "view") The name comes from the Buena Vista Ranch. See **Buena Vista.** Eight miles east of Oceanside on the Escondido spur of the Santa Fe Railroad and Highway 79. Had a post office 1882-1886 and then after 1888. Stein says that the railroad stations named Vista and Buena were created in 1890 after the arrival of the railroad, but note that a Vista post office existed as early as 1882 and a Buena post office in 1883. There is a **South Vista,** half a mile south of Vista. Gudde has noted that the name Vista is especially popular in San Diego County, with most of the Vistas dating from the American period (See Chula Vista and Linda Vista). (Durham 72; Gudde 413; Salley 202, 225; Stein 146-147)

Volcan Mountain. (Span. "volcano") Northwest of Julian. This is a long massive ridge, which in no way resembles the classic conical volcano. The Spanish origins of this name are obscure. The name is listed on the San Diego County Assessor's Office Tax List for 1850 under the name of Guillermo Sandoval who had a ranch nearby. Often misspelled by English speakers as Balcon, Vaulcan, etc. (J. Davidson, "Volcan Mountain Named for Volcano," *SDET,* September 23, 1938; Durham 80; Stein 147)

Von Meter Creek. Five miles northwest of Valley Center. Named for early settlers Abraham J. Von Meter and Isaac L. Von Meter. They were registered to vote in San Diego County in 1869. (McHenry 69-70)

- W -

Wahita Spring. See **Jollita Spring.**

Walker Canyon, Creek. Three miles north of Jacumba. Captain George P. Walker homesteaded near Boulevard about 1865. (Durham 81; McCain 56, 87, 98; Stein 148)

Ward Canyon. Three miles northwest of Warner Springs. Named for S.L. Ward who homesteaded here in the 1880s. (Black, II, 137, Durham 81)

Ware Mine. See **Mountain Lily Mine.**

Wares. Station on the National City & Otay Railroad south of Chula Vista. More correctly Ware's because it was named for Levi J. Ware who homesteaded in the South Bay District in 1884. (Christian Brown Interview; *SDU,* December 23, 1884)

Warlock Mine. Located not far above and west of Banner on the Banner Mine Road. In older English a warlock was someone who broke his faith, a sorcerer, a wizard, or even the Devil himself. George McKean claimed the mine in October 1870. A modest producer, it yielded $25,000 to $50,000 in gold. In the last half of the twentieth century an unsuccessful attempt was made to revive the mine. It had the longest tunnel (adit) in the district—1,600 feet. The 2002 Pines Fire destroyed all the buildings at the mine site. In the 1960s it was a remote and inaccessible, but official, bomb shelter. It is on the Julian 7.5' Quadrangle. (Fetzer, *Good Camp,* 56-57; Schad 167-168)

Warner. John Trumbull (Juan José) Warner (1807-1895) was an important figure in the northeastern districts of the county. Coming to California as early as 1831, he recognized that money could be made selling to hungry immigrants on the southern trail and so he established a store at what became known as **Warner's Ranch** well before the American conquest. In the south he played the role as host and supplier that Sutter and his fort played in the north. The place had a post office as early as 1859; after 1887 it was known as **Warner** and after 1907 it was **Warner Springs.** Warner also received two land grants. See **San José.** For more about Warner see Lindsay 356-359. The hot springs north of his house and store were technically on his property, but until 1903 when the Cupeño people were compelled to move to Pala they were considered Indian land. The springs were called **Cupa** in the Cupeño language, hence the name of the people. In Kumeyaay the springs were called **Jacupin,** spelled Haakupin in Couro and Hutcheson (19), "literally 'warm water'." Spanish speakers called Warner Springs **Agua Caliente**. **Warner Pass** was the name sometimes given to Teofulio or San Felipe Summit. (see Lindsay 340). (Durham 81; Gudde 417; Salley 227)

Warren Canyon. Eight miles southeast of Escondido near Woodson Mountain. Named for Edward Boyle Warren, an English immigrant who ran a store here. (Durham 81; Stein 150)

Wash Hollow Creek. Three miles east of Ramona. It flows into Hatfield Creek. The name seems to indicate some kind of potholes or water-worn hollows. (Durham 81)

Washington Mine. Also known as the George Washington Mine. Just east of Julian; Washington St. once led directly to it. On Washington's birthday, February 22, 1870, Henry C. Bickers, J.T. Gower, and Reverend J. Bruen Wells discovered the mine, hence the name. It was the first gold discovery in hard rock quartz at Julian, and began the mining boom in the district. The mine had about 500 feet of workings and produced between $25,000 and $50,000 in gold. Now collapsed, the mine is the property of the Julian Historical Society. It is on the 1997 Julian 7.5' Quadrangle. (Fetzer *Good Camp,* 13, 18)

Washtub Falls. One mile west of Mesa Grande. Another distinctive name for a water feature. (Durham 81)

Weaver Mountain. South of the Pala Indian Reservation. U.S. Weaver homesteaded in the Rainbow area about 1919. (Durham 81; Stein 150)

Webster S.D. Mid-City Neighborhood. North of Highway 94 and south of City Heights East. Named for developer E. Bartlett Webster, president of the South Park and East Side Railway, founded in March 1906. The line was supposed to go to El Cajon, but never made it. His father Erastus was the developer of South Park Addition. (Smythe 442)

Weed. Three miles southeast of Del Mar and five miles southwest of San Dieguito. Had a post office from 1880 to 1886. Named for William Seaman Weed, the first postmaster. (Durham 20; Ewing 37-38; Salley 228)

Westgate Park. Padre baseball field at the intersection of Interstate 8 and Highway 163, close to Friars Road. Named for the Westgate-California Tuna Packing Corporation. Opening in April 1958, it had 8,268 seats; built by C. Arnholt Smith. The Padres left it to play their first game at San Diego Stadium in 1969. (SDHS Subject File "Baseball")

Whale Mountain. Six miles northeast of Ramona, elevation 3,043 feet. Not far away is Ballena Valley, the Spanish name for whale. In Anza-Borrego Desert Park there is also a Whale Peak. (Durham 81, Stein 151)

Whaler's Bight. An inlet at the entrance to San Diego Bay on North Island opposite Ballast Point. Bight is another name for a bay (See **Spanish Bight**). About 1870 development forced whalers at La Playa to cross over to North Island to ply their trade at this location. (J. Davidson, "Whaler's Bight," *SDET,* June 14, 1935)

Whelan Lake. Three miles northeast of Oceanside. Named for an Irish immigrant settler, his name sometimes spelled Whalan, who leased land nearby. Sometimes called **Pico's Lake** for early owners of the Santa Margarita Rancho. (Durham 82; Stein 151)

Whispering Pines. One mile east of Julian. Edith Austin Ayers, a businesswoman from Spring Valley established this mountain subdivision in 1929. From the first it was successful; it is conveniently close to Julian, and has adequate water.

White Queen Mine. A gem mine located on the west slope of Heriot Mountain about two miles northeast of Pala. The name may refer to white quartz crystals. Frederick Sickler discovered pink Kunzite crystals (named for gemologist George F. Kunz) here in 1901. The mine's highest production was late, in the 1960s and 1970s, and it is best known for its quartz and beryls. (Foord 164-165)

Whitney, Mount. Four miles west of Escondido. Named for Willard J. Whitney, an early rancher and something of a recluse. It was originally called **High Mountain.** (J. Davidson, "Mt. Whitney named for S.D. Rancher," *SDET,* July 15, 1938; Durham 50; Gudde 422; Ryan 5, 170; Stein 85)

Wild Man Canyon. Six miles southwest of Jamul near Sweetwater Reservoir. Probably named for a recluse who took shelter here, a circumstance not unknown in San Diego's mild climate. (Durham 82)

Wild Pigeon Flat. Four miles east of Descanso. Probably named for conspicuous band-tail pigeons that feed on local acorns. (Durham 82)

Wildcat. Bobcats, or wildcats, are very common in the county. **Wildcat Canyon** is two miles northeast of Lakeside, leading to Barona Indian Reservation. **Wildcat Spring** is six miles north of Descanso. (Durham 82)

Wildwood Glen. Originally a resort west of Descanso Junction near the Sweetwater River. The first owner was Bea Griscombe. The name is now applied to the district. (Friends, *When,* 140)

Will Valley. Three miles northwest of Lake Henshaw. An early settler, Jeff Cook (See **Jeff Valley**) had three sons, Hiram, George, and Will. The third one had a valley named for him. (Durham 82; Stein 152)

William H. Heise County Park. Four miles west of Julian near Pine Hillls. Heise, an inventor and landowner, sold land for the park to the county at a reduced price. It opened in 1970. (*SDU,* June 14, 1970)

Willows, The. Three miles east of Alpine along old Highway 80. Frederick B. Walker established a popular resort in this area in 1896 which he called The Willows. Other people also had resorts in this area. It was sometimes called **Alpine Berry Fields.** The construction of Interstate 8 played havoc with the district, and today only the names West and East Willows Roads survive. (La Force 228-241)

Winacka Camp. West of Pine Hills. A girl scout camp opened in 1976 after Camp Tapawingo closed in Cuyamaca Rancho State Park. According to one of its founders, the word expresses "a simple feeling of joy."

Windansea Beach. In La Jolla near the point. The name of a La Jolla hotel built in 1909. Windansea was the name of both a surfing team in 1962 and a sport shop. An unusual but catchy name. How about Sunanmoon? Hillanstream? Landanwater? (Cleary and Stern 200-201; Schaelchlin 149; *SDU-T,* January 11, 2004)

Windmill. Windmills were common features in pre-electrical San Diego County. They were especially useful to pump water to fill watering troughs for livestock. **Windmill Canyon** is on Point Loma where Canon St. is today. About 1890 there was a windmill over a well towards the head of the canyon. (J. Davidson, "Pt. Loma," *SDET,* May 31, 1935). Near Oceanside are **Windmill Canyon** and **Lake. Windmill Flat** is five miles north of El Cajon Mountain. (Durham 82; Stein 152)

Winter Gardens. Two miles southwest of Lakeside. This was a subdivision dating from 1920 located in both Lakeside and El Cajon. (Durham 82; Lakeside iv)

Winterwarm. About three miles southeast of Fallbrook A nice name with pleasant associations, especially for northerners. It has a harmonious sound because of the repetition of the w's. (Durham 82)

Wire Mountain. North of San Luis Rey River and northeast of Oceanside. Lots of conjecture about this name. Stein thought it was named for a Marine Corps radio school, but it is on the 1901 Oceanside 15' Quadrangle, 40 years before marines were here. It may have gotten its name from barbed wire or electrical wire, possibly from power lines. It may also have been named for a member of the Wire (also spelled Wiro) family of Olivenhain. See, for example, William Wire who is in the 1903 *San Diego City-County Directory,* 565. (Durham 82; Stein 152).

Witch Creek, Mountain. Five miles west of Santa Ysabel. Had its own post office 1893-1938. There were so many English immigrants in this area that it was sometimes called **New London.** In the case of this place name we have a rare and plausible eyewitness account of a name's origin. Reverend Thomas J. Wood, English immigrant resident and brother of James Wood, long-time postmaster here, told John Davidson, "The Indians who lived there called it a name that sounded to us like 'Sissero' or 'Sissera.' I believe they were mispronouncing the Spanish word 'hechicero' or 'hechicera' which means wizard or witch, enchanter or bewitcher. We translated their word as witch, however, and that is the origin of the present name Witch Creek." (J. Davidson, "Witch Creek Given Name by Indians," *SDET,* date illegible; Durham 83; Gudde 426; Salley 234; Stein 152)

Wohlford, Lake. Five miles northwest of Escondido. The name honors Alvin Webster Wohlford, an officer of the Escondido Mutual Water Company. It got this name in 1924. It had been called **Bear Valley Reservoir** and **Lake Escondido** before this date. (Durham 39; Gudde 426; Stein 69)

Wolahi, Camp. Near Cuyamaca Rancho State Park and Cuyamaca Reservoir. In 1931 developer Ed Fletcher donated seven acres in his wife's name, Mary, to the Campfire Girls for a camp. In gratitude they referred to her as "Our Lady of the WOods, LAkes, and HIlls, hence the acronym Wolahi.

Wolf Canyon. Opens from the north into Otay Valley west of Otay Mountain. This might be taken as evidence for the presence of wolves in this area, but experience shows that some people cannot distinguish coyotes from wolves. It might have been one or the other that gave this place its name—both were present in early nineteenth century California. (Durham 83)

Wolfskill Plains. See **Rincon del Diablo**.

Wonderland. A good name for an amusement park. Located on eight acres between Voltaire and Abbot Streets and the ocean in Ocean Beach, it opened in 1913. It had a dance pavilion, restaurant, zoo, roller coaster, etc. The Hatfield floods of 1916 damaged the park and it never recovered. (Held 26-32)

Woods Valley. Four miles south of Rodriguez Mountains. Named for the pioneer Woods family of Valley Center. The first family member to settle here was Goolsby Woods who came here with his family in the late 1870s. (Durham 83; McHenry 79-80)

Wooded Area S.D. Western Neighborhood. This is the official name for the top of Point Loma. It had more than 4,800 residents in 1999. An unexpected name.

Woodson Mountain. Between Poway and Ramona. An old name for the peak was **Cobbleback Mountain,** no doubt for the giant boulders strewn over it. Named for Dr. Marshall Clay Woodson, who settled on the east side of the mountain about 1895 (*SDU,* July 7, 1895). He was a dentist who had served in the Confederate army. (Durham 83; Gudde 427; LeMenager, *Ramona,* 86; Stein 153)

Wright, Camp. At first near Oak Grove and then moved close to Warner Springs. Major Edwin A. Rigg established the post on October 18, 1861. Named for Brigadier General George Wright (1801-1865), commander of both the Pacific Department and the California Department from 1861 to 1865. The camp was established to apprehend southern sympathizers on the southern immigrant trail. Troops from here seized the Dan Showalter Party near Mesa Grande, the only Civil War skirmish of any significance in the state. Closed in 1866. (J. Davidson, "Oak Grove Site of Wright Camps," *SDET,* August 19, 1938; Durham 52; Hinds 50-51; Stein 91)

Wruck Canyon. Six miles east of Imperial Beach. Named for William F. Wruck (d. 1939), German native who became a National City rancher. (Durham 83; *San Diego City-County Directory 1923,* 1361)

Wynola, Wynola Valley. Three miles west of Julian. Had its own post office from 1889 to 1913. According to James A. Jasper, the government rejected Spencer Valley as a name for a post office (there was already a Spenceville in Nevada County) and W.A. Sickler proposed Wynola, saying that it was an Indian name meaning lake. Sickler almost had it right. This is probably a transfer name from Lake Winola (sic) in Wyoming County, Pennsylvania. (Jasper, *Trail-Breakers*, 187; Salley 235; Stein 153-154)

- Y -

Yuima. See **Pauma.**

Ysidora. Three miles northeast of Los Angeles Junction on the 1882 California Southern Railroad line to Fallbrook. Named for Ysidora María Ygnacia Pico, younger sister of Andrés and Pío Pico. She married John Forster in 1837. She appears as the compassionate "Miss Peaks" (that is, Pico) in James Ohio Pattie's famous memoirs of his San Diego incarceration. A very early name for an Indian village here that preceded the railroad was **Pueblito,** Spanish "little town." (J. Davidson, "Ysidora Named for Pico Sister," *SDET,* March 4, 1938; Durham 84; Gudde 432)

- Z -

Zorro Ranch. See **Fairbanks Ranch.**

Zuñiga. Although two features with this name are quite close, apparently they were named for two men from different eras. **Zuñiga Point** is located opposite Ballast Point at the entrance to San Diego Harbor. Captain George Vancouver named it in 1793 for Lieutenant José de Zuñiga, officer at the San Diego Presidio, 1781 to 1792. According to Engelhardt (*San Diego Mission* 176) who cites George Davidson in *U.S. Coast Pilot,* in 1602 Sebastián Vizcaíno named **Zuñiga Shoal,** south of Zuñiga Point off North Island, for Gaspar de Zuñiga, Viceroy of Mexico 1595-1603. Zuñiga Shoal, but not Zuñiga Point, is on the 1782 Pantoja map of San Diego Bay. On John Hall's 1839 *Sketch of Puerto de San Diego* Zuñiga Shoal is called **Bossun Shoal,** a variant of bos'n, from boatswain. In 1936 the U.S. Board on Geographic Names rejected changing the spelling of both place names as "Zuninga." (Durham 84, Gudde 434, Stein 155)

Bibliography

Abbot, Clinton G. "Bears in S.D. County," *Journal of Mammalogy,* 16, 149-151. 1935.

Adema, Thomas Joseph. *OurHills and Valleys: A History of the Helix and Spring Valley Regions* (San Diego: SDHS, 1993)

Alter, Ruth. *Painted Rocks* (San Diego: San Dieguito River Valley Regional Open Space Park Joint Powers Authority, 1955)

Alvarez, Ila. "Document no. 35: A Map Maker's Story," in San Diego Corral of the Westerners, *Brand Book* V, 122-134, 1978.

Anonymous. "Bonnie Brae," *Golden Era,* 1021-1021, August, 1891.

———. *History of San Diego County* (San Francisco: W.W. Elliott and Co., 1883)

———. "Julius A. Rice: Educator," *Naional City Star-News,* Agust 8, 1957.

———. "Leucadia Developed in 1880s. Is Named after Greek Island," *San Dieguito Citizen,* July 30, 1959.

———. "Many Readers Recall Gregory Springs," *Southern California Rancher,* 19, April 1956.

———. "Moreno—The Beautiful Town," *Golden Era,* 759, December, 1887.

———. *San Diego: Our Italy.* (San Diego: San Diego Chamber of Commerce, 1895)

Bancroft, H.H. *History of California.* 7 vols. (San Francisco: History Company, 1886-1890)

Bawden, Hubert H. *Place Names of San Diego County.* Federal Writers Project Field Notes, W.P.A. At SDHS.

Berlo, Robert C. *Population History Maps of California Place Names 1770 to 1998: San Diego Area* (Livermore, CA: The Author, 1997-1998)

Biographical Files. At SDHS.

Black, Samuel T. *San Diego County, California.* 2 vols. (Chicago: S.J. Clarke, 1913)

Blossom, Edson D. *The History of Blossom Valley* (Houston: The Author, 2003)

Brandais, Jack. *Weekend Driver San Diego* (San Diego: Sunbelt Publications, 2004)

Breder, Marie. "Nostalgia Lane," *La Jolla Journal,* June 4, 1964

Bright, William. *1500 California Place Names* (Berkeley, University of California Press, 1998)

Brown, Adam K. ed. and trans. *Gaspar de Portolá* (Lerida, Spain: Instituto de Estudios Ilerdenses, 1983)

Brown, Christian. "Hey-Day of the N.C. & O," *San Diego Historical Society Quarterly* IV, 23-25 (April 1958)

———. Interview at the SDHS, April 5, 1957.

Bugbee, Susan and Kathleen Flanigan. *San Diego's Historic Gaslamp Quarter: Then and Now* (San Diego: Tecolote Publications, 2003)

Bumann, Richard. *Colony Olivenhain* (Solana Beach, CA: The Author, 1981)

Carlin, Katherine and Ray Brandes. *Coronado: The Enchanted Isle* (Coronado, CA: Coronado Historical Society, 1987)

Carrico, Richard L. "A Brief Glimpse of the Kumeyaay Past: An Interview with Tom Lucas, Kwaaymii of Laguna Ranch," *Journal of San Diego History,* XXIX, no. 2, 115-139. (Spring 1983)

———. "Sociopolitical Aspects of the 1775 Revolt at Mission San Diego de Alcala," *Journal of San Diego History,* XLIII, no. 3, 143-157. (Summer 1997)

———. *Strangers in a Stolen Land* (Newcastle, CA: Sierra Oaks Publishing. Co., 1987)

Carroll, William. *San Marcos: A Brief History* (San Marcos, CA: Coda Publications, 1975)

Case, Thomas E. *The Story of San Diego de Alcalá* (Bi-lingual) (Alcalá, Spain: Universidad de Alcalá, 1998)

Christman, Florence. *The Romance of Balboa Park* (San Diego: Neyenesch Printers, 1973)

Cleary, Bill and David H. Stern. *Surfing Guide to Southern California* (Santa Barbara, The Authors, 1998)

Covington, Donald Patrick *Burlingame, 1912-1929. A Tract of Character: A Community History & Self-Guided Architectural Tour* (S.D., The Author, 1997)

Cowan, Robert G. *Ranchos of California* (Fresno, CA: Academy Library Guild, 1956)

Crosby, Rufina Porter. *Reminiscences* (unpublished manuscript at SDHS)

Crouch, Herbert. *Memoirs.* (unpublished manuscript at SDHS)

Davidson, George. "San Diego Bay," *U.S. Coast Pilot,* 17.

Davidson, John. *Place Name File* (Approx. 5,000 cards) At SDHS

———. *Place Name Scrapbooks.* Clippings, mostly from the *SDET.* At SDHS.

Davis, Edward H. *Diegueño Indian Words: Place Names.* Notebook with pencil entries. No pagination. Edward H. Davis Collection, Box 5, File 32, SDHS.

De Frate, Julia Flinn. *This Was Yesterday: Recollecting San Diego's Back County 1870-1930* (San Diego: The Author, 1951)

Durham, David L. *Place Names of San Diego County* (Clovis, CA: Word Dancer Press, 2000)

Engelhardt, Zephyrin. *San Diego Mission* (San Francisco: James H. Barry Co., 1920)

———. *San Luis Rey Mission* (San Francisco: James H. Barry Co., 1921)

Ewing, Nancy Hanks. *Del Mar: Looking Back.* (Del Mar, CA: Del Mar Historical Foundation, 1988)

Fetherling, Douglas. *The Gold Crusades.* (Toronto, Canada: University of Toronto Press, 1997)

Fetzer, Leland. *A Good Camp: Gold Mines of Julian and the Cuyamacas* (San Diego: Sunbelt Publications, 2002)

———. *A Year in the Cuyamacas* (San Diego: Tecolote Publications, 1998)

Fletcher, Ed. *Memoirs.* (San Diego: The Author, 1952)

Foord, Eugene E. and David London, Anthony R. Kampf, James E. Shigley, Lawrence W. Snee. "Gem-Bearing Pegmatites of San Diego County, California," in *Geology of the Elsinore Fault Zone, San Diego Region* (San Diego: Sunbelt Publications, 2003)

Freeman, Larry. "Living is Rustic, Regal in North County Castle," *SDU, March 3, 1963*

Friends of the Descanso Library. *Descanso, Place of Rest* (San Diego: Tecolote Publications, 1988)

————. *When Descanso Was Young* (San Diego: Tecolote Publications, 1994)

Gaona, Elena. "Upgrading to Business Class," *SDU-T,* June 20, 2004

Gleason, Duncan. *The Islands and Ports of California* (New York: Devin-Adair, 1958)

Gudde, Erwin G. *California Place Names.* ed. By William Bright (Berkeley: University of California Press, 1998)

Guinn, James. *A History of California and an Extended History of Its Southern Coast Counties* 2 vols. (Los Angeles: Historic Record Co., 1907)

Gunn, Chester. Interview November 27, 1923. At SDHS

Gunn, Douglas. *Picturesque San Diego* (Chicago: Knight and Leonard, 1887)

Gunn, Guard. "Border Ranchos of a Century Ago," *Southern California Rancher.* No pages. September, 1946.

Gunther, Jane Davies. *Riverside County, California Place Names: Their Origins and Their Stories.* (Riverside, CA: Rubidoux Printing, 1984)

Guy, Hubert. *Grossmont Isn't Just a Shopping Center* (La Mesa, CA: The Author, 1996)

Hall, George P. "Lemon Grove," *Silver Gate,* 3-5, September 1899

Hanft, Robert M. *San Diego & Arizona: The Impossible Railroad* (Glendale, CA: Trans-Anglo Books, 1984)

Hanna, Phil Townsend. *Dictionary of California Land Names* (Los Angeles: Automobile Club of Southern California, 1951)

Harlow, Neal. *Maps of the Pueblo Lands of San Diego, 1602-1874* (Los Angeles: Dawson's Book Shop, 1987)

Harrison, Donald H. *Louis Rose: San Diego's First Jewish Settler and Entrepreneur* (San Diego: Sunbelt Publications, 2005)

Hartley, Mac. *Encinitas: History and Heritage.* (Virginia Beach, VA.: Donning Co., 1999)

Hayes, Benjamin Ignatius. *Pioneer Notes* (New York: Arno Press, 1976)

Head W.S. *The California Chaparral: An Elfin Forest* (Happy Camp, CA: Naturegraph, 1972)

Hearn, Lorrie, "Southeast R.I.P.," *SDU-T,* June 21, 1992

Heilbron, Carl H. *History of San Diego County* (San Diego: San Diego. Press Club, 1936)

Heizer, Robert F. *Handbook of North American Indians: California.* (Washington D.C.: Smithsonian Institution, 1978)

Held, Ruth Varney. *Beach Town: Early Days in Ocean Beach* (San Diego: The Author, 1975)

Hill, Joseph J. *History of Warner's Ranch and Its Environs* (Los Angeles: Privately printed, 1927)

Hinds, James. W. *San Diego's Military Sites,* 1986 (unpublished manuscript at SDHS)

Hoover, Mildred, Hero Eugene Rensch and Ethel Grace Rensch. *Historic Spots in California* (Stanford, Stanford University Press, 1966)

Hunzicker, Lena B. *San Diego County Place Names* (Letters G-Z only. Bound Typescript at SDHS)

Innis, Jack. *San Diego Legends* (San Diego: Sunbelt Publications, 2004)

Jackson, Helen Hunt. *A Century of Dishonor* (Boston: Roberts Bros., 1886)

Jasper, James A. *Julian and Round-About* 1928 (unpublished manuscript at SDHS)

————. *Trail-Breakers and History-Makers* ca. 1930 (unpublished manuscript at SDHS)

Kooperman, Evelyn L. *San Diego Trivia* (San Diego: Silver Gate Publications, 1989)

————. *San Diego Trivia II* (San Diego: Silver Gate Publications, 1993)

Kroeber, Alfred L. "California Place Names of Indian Origin" *University of California Publications in American Archaeology and Ethnology* XII, no. 2, 31-69 (1916)

La Force, Beatrice. *Alpine, Southern California: History of a Mountain Settlement* (Lakeside, CA: Sunlight Press, 1971)

La Mesa Historical Society. *La Mesa Through the Years* (La Mesa, CA: La Mesa Historical Society, 2001)

Lakeside Historical Society. *Legends of Lakeside* (Lakeside, CA: Logan's Printing Co., 1985)

Land, Pearl " Death of Pioneer Recalls Past," *San Dieguito Citizen,* November 18, 1971

Lansley, Alf. "How Cockatoo Grove Got Its Name," *Stories, Tales, Folklore of Our Communities,* 19-20 (Chula Vista, CA: Chula Vista Historical Society, 1983)

Lay, El Donna. *Valley of Opportunity: The History of El Cajon* (El Cajon, CA: El Donna Lay and Associates, 1987)

LeMenager, Charles R. *Julian City and Cuyamaca Country* (Ramona, CA: Eagle Peak Pub. Co., 1992)

———. *Off the Main Road: San Vicente and Barona* (Ramona, CA: Eagle Peak Pub. Co., 1990)

———, *Ramona and Round About* (Ramona, CA: Eagle Peak Pub. Co., 1989)

Lindsay, Diana. *Anza-Borrego A to Z* (San Diego: Sunbelt Publications, 2001)

Loop, Arnot M. "The Fight of the Paso Del Mar," 13-16, *Silver Gate,* January 1900

Luckman, Charles. *Twice in a Lifetime: From Soaps to Skyscrapers* (New York: W.W. Norton, 1988

MacMullen, Jerry. "San Diego Names That Might Have Been," *SDU,* December 18, 1965

———. "Who Can Solve the Mystery of Gammon Shoal?" *SDU,* June 9, 1974

MacPhail, Elizabeth C. *The Story of New San Diego and Its Founder Alonzo E. Horton* (San Diego: San Diego Historical Society, 1989)

———. *When the Red Lights Went Out in San Diego* (San Diego: San Diego Historical Society, 1974)

Marinacci, Barbara. *California's Spanish Place Names* (San Rafael, CA: Presidio Press, 1980)

McCain, Ella. *Memories of the Early Settlements: Dulzura, Potrero and Campo* (San Diego: The Author, 1955)

McGrew, Alan B. *Hidden Valley Heritage: Escondido's First 100 Years* (Escondido, CA: Blue-Ribbon Centennial History Committee, 1988)

McGrew, Clarence Alan. *City of San Diego and San Diego County* (Chicago: American Historical Society, 1922)

McHenry, Petei. *The History of Valley Center, California: The Homestead Years 1860-1900* (Escondido, GP Marketing, 1998)

McKinstry, George. *Diary,* at SDHS

Menzel, Spencer Lewis. *The Development of the Sweetwater Area (*M.A. Thesis, University of Southern California, Department. of History, 1942)

Merriam, Richard. "Geology and Mineral Resources of Santa Ysabel Quadrangle," Bulletin 177 (San Francisco: California Division of Mines, 1958)

Meyer, Ruth S., ed. *Historic Buildings of the Ramona Area* (Ramona, CA: Ramona Pioneer Historical Soc., 1987)

Miller, D.D. "Harritt Dam Nearly Done," *SDET,* August 16, 1962

Miller, George M. *Spanish and Mexican Land Grants in California* (Laguna Niguel, CA: National Archives, n.d.)

Mining and Scientific Press. Index. WPA, 1935-1939. (Sacramento, CA: California State Library, 1986)

Murray, Vickie. "Pottery Canyon Demolition a Puzzle with Many Pieces," *La Jolla Light,* July 9, 1998

Northrop, John A. *A Short History of Carmel Valley and McGonigle Canyon* (San Diego: The Author, 1989)

Peet, Mary Rockwood. *San Pasqual: A Crack in the Hills* (Ramona, CA: Ballena Press, 1973)

Phillips, Irene. *Around the Bay in Thirty Minutes* (National City, CA: South Bay Press, 1960)

————. *National City Story* (National City, CA: South Bay Press, 1960)

————. *San Diego Land and Town Company* (National City, CA: South Bay Press, 1959)

Poggi, Joseph. Interview March 26, 1959 at SDHS

Porter, Rufus K. *Papers* at SDHS

Price, James N. "The Railroad Stations of San Diego County: Then and Now," *Journal of San Diego History,* XXXIV, 122-174 (Spring 1988)

Pryde, Philip R. *San Diego. An Introduction to the Region* (Boston, Pearson Custom Publishing, 2004)

Pourade, Richard F. *The Explorers* (San Diego: Union-Tribune Publishing Co., 1960)

————. *The Glory Years* (San Diego: Union-Tribune Publishing Co., 1964)

————. *Gold In The Sun* (San Diego: Union-Tribune Publishing Co., 1965)

————. *The Rising Tide* (San Diego: Union-Tribune Publishing Co., 1967)

————. *The Silver Dons* (San Diego: Union Tribune Publishing Co., 1963)

————. *Time of the Bells* (San Diego: Union-Tribune Publishing Co., 1961)

Quinn, Charles Russell. *Mesa Grande Country* (Downey, CA: Privately Printed, 1962)

Reading, James E. *History of San Diego Highway Development* (San Diego: San Diego Highway Development Association, 1958)

Redman, Mary Jo, ed. *Echoes of Pine Valley* (Pine Valley, CA: Friends of the Library, 2001)

Rensch, Hero Eugene. "Cullamác, Alias Del Capitan Grande," *San Diego Historical Society Quarterly,* II, 2, 29-32 (July 1956)

———. "Fages' Crossing of the Cuyamacas," *California Historical Society Quarterly,* XXXIV, 3, 193-208 (1955)

———. *Indian Place Names of Rancho Cuyamaca* (unpublished manuscript, n.d., at SDHS)

———, and Ethel Grace Rensch. *Historic Spots in California. The Southern Counties* (Stanford, Stanford University Press, 1932)

Ridgely, Roberta. "Anna Held and the Green Dragon," *San Diego Magazine,* June 1969, 42-47

Roberts, Elizabeth Judson. *Indian Stories of the Southwest* (San Francisco: Harr Wagner, 1917)

Robinson, Alfred. *Life in California* (Santa Barbara CA: Peregrine Smith, 1970)

Rush, Philip S. *Some Old Ranchos and Adobes* (S.D., Neyenesch Printers, 1965)

Ryan, Frances Beven. *Early Days in Escondido* (Escondido, CA: The Author, 1970)

Salley, Harold E. *History of California Post Offices 1849-1976: Includes Branches and Stations, Navy Numbered Branches, Highway and Railway Post Offices* (La Mesa, CA: Postal History Associates, 1977)

San Diego City-County Directory. 1887-1943. At SDHS

San Diego County. *Assessment Rolls 1850, 1873-1874.* At SDHS

San Diego County. *Great Register of Voters 1873, 1888, 1890, 1891.* At SDHS

San Diego County School Records. At SDHS

San Diego Neighborhoods website: http://www.sandiego.gov/neighborhoods-map/

Sanchez, Nellie Van de Grift. *Spanish and Indian Place Names of California: Their Meaning and Their Romance* (San Francisco: A.M. Robertson, 1922)

Schad, Jerry. *Afoot and Afield in San Diego County* (Berkeley: Wilderness Press, 1998)

Schaelchlin, Patricia A. *La Jolla* (La Jolla: Friends of the La Jolla Library, 1988)

Schmid, Dorothy Clark. *Pioneering in Dulzura* (San Diego: Robert R. Knapp, 1963)

Security Title Insurance Co. *Subdivision Handbook* (San Diego: Security Title Insurance Co., 1956)

Showley, Roger. "Southeast San Diego Is Filled With Histories," *SDU,* January 10, 1993

Smythe, William Ellsworth. *History of San Diego, 1542-1908* (San Diego: History Co., 1907)

Sparkman, Philip Stedman. "The Culture of the Luiseño Indians," *University California Publications in American Archaeology and Ethnology,* VIII, no. 4, 187-234 (1908)

Stein, Lou. *San Diego County Place Names* (San Diego: Tofua Press, 1973)

Stewart, George R. *Names on the Land* (Boston: Houghton Mifflin Co., 1958)

Stone, Joe, "Baseball's Al Spalding," *SDU,* April 25, 1976

Subject Files. At SDHS

Sully, Langdon and Taryn Bigelow. *Oceanside: Crest of the Wave* (Oceanside, CA: Windsor Publications, 1988)

Tavares, Claire. Interview at SDHS. November 29, 1999.

Turley, Olga, W. *Lyons Valley* (San Diego: The Author, 1988)

U.S. Board on Geographical Names website: http://geonames.usgs.gov/bgn.html

U.S. Bureau of Land Management website: http://glorecords.BLM.Gov.

U.S. Census Decennial Reports, esp. 1860, 1870, 1880.

U.S. Coast Pilot. Pacific Coast. (Washington, G.P.O., 1909)

Unitt, Philip. *Birds of San Diego County* (San Diego: San Diego Society of Natural History, 1984)

Vezina, Meredith. "In 1880s, Water Fizzled," *SDU-T,* November 28, 1992

Weber, F. Harold. *Geology and Mineral Resources of San Diego County, California County Report 3* (Sacramento, CA: California Division of Mines and Geology, 1963)

Webster, Karna. *Chula Vista Heritage 1911-1986* (Chula Vista, CA: City of Chula Vista, 1987)

Weisberg, Lori and Rober M. Showley. "Community Takes Pride in its Eclectic Mix," *SDU-T,* August 27, 1997

Wermuth, Paul C. *Bayard Taylor* (New York: Twayne, 1973)

Wolfe, Tom. "The Pump House Gang Meets the Black Panthers—or Silver Threads Among the Gold in Surf City," and "The Pump House Gang Faces Life," in *New York,* the *World Journal Tribune's Sunday* Magazine. February 13 and 20, 1966

Wolin, Rita Larkin. *La Mesa—A Brief History* (La Mesa, CA: La Mesa Historical Society, 1976)

Wood, Catherine M. *Palomar from Teepee to Telescope* (San Diego: Frye and Smith, 1937)

Woodward, Ashbel. *Life of General Nathaniel Lyon* (Hartford, CT: Case, Lockwood & Co., 1862)

Woodward, Arthur. "Notes on the Indians of San Diego County: From the Manuscripts of Judge Benjamin Hayes," *The Masterkey,* VIII, 140-150 (Sept. 1934)

Wray, Christopher. *Historic Place Names: Eastern San Diego County and Imperial County, 1997* (unpublished manuscript at SDHS)

Maps

American Automobile Association. *AAA San Diego County Map, 1976, 1996.* At SDHS

Beasley, T.D. *Map of Part of San Diego County showing area drained by the San Diego and Sweetwater Rivers.* Drawn by T.D. Beasley, 1889. At SDHS

Blackburn's Map of San Diego County, 1931. At SDHS

Blake, W.P. *Geological Map of the Country Between San Diego and the Colorado River.* Drawn by W.P. Blake, 1855. In Parke, J.G. and A.H. Campbell, *Report of Explorations for Railroad Routes...West of the Coast Ranges...near the 32nd Parallel of North Latitude.* Vol. VI, Plate VIII. Property of the Author

Dalyrimple, Alexander. *Plan of Port of San Diego, 1789.* Printed by Alexander Dalyrimple. At SDHS

Fitch, Henry D. *Map of Pueblo Lands of San Diego, 1845.* At SDHS

Gray, A.B. *Sketch of the Port of San Diego, by A.B. Gray, 1850.* At SDHS

Hall, John. *Sketch of Puerto de San Diego, 1839, by Captain John Hall.* At SDHS

Hensley, George B. *Map of the City of San Diego, 1873, drawn by George B. Hensley.* At SDHS

Hubon, Irving A. *Official Map of San Diego and Imperial Counties, California, 1908, drawn by Irving A. Hubon.* At SDHS

Pantoja y Arriaga, Juan. *Plano del Puerto de San Diego, 1782.* At SDHS

Partition of Rancho Mission of San Diego, 1885. At SDHS

Rueger's Automobile and Miner's Map of Southern California, 1903. At SDHS

Stokes, Rodney. *Map of San Diego County Completed by T.A. Bedford and George Cromwell, 1910.* Published by Rodney Stokes Company. At SDHS

U.S. Coast and Geodetic Survey. *San Diego Bay Map, 1859.* At SDHS

Wheeler, M.G. *Official Map of the Western Portion of San Diego County, 1872.* Published by M.G. Wheeler Company. At SDHS

Newspapers

La Jolla Light

National City Star-News

Oceanside Enterprise

San Diego Evening Tribune (SDET)

San Diego Herald

San Diego Union (SDU)

San Diego Union-Tribune (SDU-T)

SUNBELT PUBLICATIONS
"Adventures in the Natural History and Cultural Heritage of the Californias"
Series Editor—Lowell Lindsay

Southern California Series:

Geology Terms in English and Spanish	Henry Aurand
Gateway to Alta California	Harry W. Crosby
Portrait of Paloma: A Novel	Harry W. Crosby
Follow the Sun: A Novel	J. and G. Gastil
Fire, Chaparral, and Survival in Southern California	Richard W. Halsey
California's El Camino Real and Its Historic Bells	Max Kurillo
Mission Memoirs: Reflections on California's Past	Terry Ruscin
Jackpot Trail: Indian Gaming in Southern California	David Valley
Will Thrall and the San Gabriels	Ronald Woolsey
The Sugar Bear Story: A Chumash Tale	Yee, Ygnacio-De Soto

California Desert Series:

Fossil Treasures of the Anza-Borrego Desert	Jefferson, Lindsay
Anza-Borrego A To Z: People, Places, and Things	Diana Lindsay
Marshal South and the Ghost Mountain Chronicles	Diana Lindsay
The Anza-Borrego Desert Region (Wilderness Press)	L. and D. Lindsay
Palm Springs Oasis: A Photographic Essay	Greg Lawson
Palm Springs Legends	Greg Niemann
Desert Lore of Southern California	Choral Pepper
Peaks, Palms, and Picnics: Journeys in Coachella Valley	Linda McMillan Pyle
Geology of Anza-Borrego: Edge of Creation	Remeika, Lindsay
California Desert Miracle: Parks and Wilderness	Frank Wheat

Baja California/Mexico Series:

The Other Side: Journeys in Baja California	Judy Goldstein Botello
Cave Paintings of Baja California	Harry W. Crosby
Backroad Baja: The Central Region	P. and T. Higginbotham
The Kelemen Journals	P. and E. Kelemen
Journey with a Baja Burro	Graham Mackintosh
Houses of Los Cabos (Amaroma)	M. Martinez, ed.
Houses by the Sea (Amaroma)	M. Martinez, ed.
Baja Legends: Historic Characters, Events, Locations	Greg Niemann
Loreto, Baja California: First Capital (Tio Press)	Ann O'Neil
Baja Outpost: The Guestbook from Patchen's Cabin	M. and A. Patchen
Sea of Cortez Review	Jennifer Redmond
Spanish Lingo for the Savvy Gringo	Elisabeth Reid
Tequila, Lemon, and Salt	Daniel Reveles
Mexican Slang Plus Graffiti	Linton Robinson

San Diego Series:

Sunbelt Publications, incorporated in 1988 with roots in publishing since 1973, produces and distributes natural science and outdoor guidebooks, regional histories and reference books, multi-language pictorials, and stories that celebrate the land and its people.

Our publishing program focuses on the Californias, which are today three states in two nations sharing one Pacific shore. Sunbelt books help to discover and conserve the natural and historical heritage of unique regions on the frontiers of adventure and learning. Our books guide readers into distinctive communities and special places, both natural and man-made.

We carry hundreds of books on San Diego and southern California!

Visit us online at:

www.sunbeltbooks.com